ORGANIZING
FOR THE
FUTURE

Jay R. Galbraith
Edward E. Lawler III
and Associates

ORGANIZING
FOR THE
FUTURE

The New Logic
for Managing
Complex
Organizations

Jossey-Bass Publishers · San Francisco

Substantial discounts on bulk quantities of Jossey-Bass books are available to corporations, professional associations, and other organizations. For details and discount information, contact the special sales department at Jossey-Bass Inc., Publishers. (415) 433-1740; Fax (415) 433-0499.

For sales outside the United States, contact Maxwell Macmillan International Publishing Group, 866 Third Avenue, New York, New York 10022.

Manufactured in the United States of America

 The paper used in this book is acid-free and meets the State of California requirements for recycled paper (50 percent recycled waste, including 10 percent postconsumer waste), which are the strictest guidelines for recycled paper currently in use in the United States.

10% POST CONSUMER WASTE

Library of Congress Cataloging-in-Publication Data

Galbraith, Jay R.
    Organizing for the future : the new logic for managing complex organizations / Jay R. Galbraith, Edward E. Lawler III and associates.
        p.   cm. — (The Jossey-Bass management series)
    Includes bibliographical references and index.
    ISBN 1-55542-528-3
    1. Industrial management. I. Lawler, Edward E. II. Title.
III. Series.
HD31.G2473   1993
658 — dc20   92-39634
                                                       CIP

FIRST EDITION
HB Printing   10 9 8 7 6 5 4 3 2   *Code 9329*

The Jossey-Bass

Management Series

CONTENTS

PREFACE

Organizing for the Future: The New Logic For Managing Complex Organizations focuses on how organizations must change in order to be effective in the future. We argue that an increasingly competitive and dynamic environment will demand that organizations adopt new management practices and new organizational structures. We describe new approaches to organizing and explain how and where they can operate effectively.

The research work of the Center for Effective Organizations (CEO) played a critical role in the development of this book. As an organization, CEO is committed to doing research that is relevant to the practice of management and based on sound research methods. Our initial impetus for writing this book was the realization that we had been doing research on organizations and organizational change for more than a decade and that it was time to look at what we had learned and how our knowlege about organizations had evolved. We wanted to create a book that was both a summary and an integration of our past research, as well as a practical, forward-looking volume on how organizations need to change in order to be competitive. We feel that we have accomplished these objectives.

The book is more future-oriented than we originally intended. As the authors of the different chapters began to write and as we discussed our individual chapters, we all came to the same conclusion: new forms of organization and new approaches to management are vital to the effectiveness of organizations. Therefore, in many of the chapters, we focus on what is likely to be effective in the future. Admittedly, some of what we have written is speculative, but it is grounded in more than a decade of theoretical and empirical research work done by the Center for Effective Organizations. We have also drawn on the research work of others who study organizational effectiveness.

Audience

Organizing for the Future presents a balanced discussion of practice, research, and theory. It brings together practical issues and academic research, to focus on future directions in organizational design. It should be useful to anyone working in the area of organizational design and organizational change, to consultants and practicing managers who are interested in major organizational design issues, and particularly to human resource (HR) management professionals, given the book's extensive focus on HR systems and the role of staff (management) groups. The book also contains information relevant for researchers and those studying organizations. It draws together a considerable amount of theory and research and shows how they can be applied to solving the design issues that many complex organizations face today. It should help all who are charged with the task of organizational design and organizational change to put their issues into context, and it should provide them with useful ideas for solving particular problems.

Overview of the Contents

The book begins with an introduction that focuses on why we believe organizations need to be organized differently and perform differently if they are to be effective in the future. It stresses the need for higher performance, as well as the increasing complexity of the environment in which organizations must operate.

Part One is concerned with the nature and structure of organizations. It begins with Chapter One, which deals with how corporate entities can add value in today's environment. The author, Jay R. Galbraith, points out the important ways in which corporations can add value to their business units, but he is cautious in the claims he makes. The new business environment can make it more difficult for the corporate entity to add value to business units, according to Galbraith, and new ways of doing so may have to be found, particularly for relatively independent business units.

Chapter Two, also by Galbraith, focuses on business units and how they can be organized. It introduces the emphasis, which runs throughout the book, on lateral organizations and the movement away from functionally driven, hierarchical approaches to organizing. The chapter shows how businesses can be integrated other than through hierarchical structures.

In Chapter Three, Edward E. Lawler III and Jay Galbraith consider the new role of staff groups in corporations. Because of the changing nature of corporations, staff groups need not only to be positioned differently but also to be managed differently. In many respects, Lawler and Galbraith advocate that staff groups return to their traditional role of advising line employees on how to carry out business, and that they abandon their more recently developed tendency to control and coordinate.

Part Two of the book (Chapters Four through Eight) focuses on internal organizational effectiveness. These chapters integrate much of the work that has been done by CEO.

Chapter Four, by Susan Albers Mohrman and Allan M. Mohrman, Jr., begins the discussion of internal effectiveness by considering how organizations can operate as learning systems. The authors point out that organizational design is the critical determinant of whether an organization can develop a learning orientation. They place strong emphasis on organizations' experimenting and learning from their efforts and call for a data-based, self-design–oriented approach that stresses continuous improvement.

Chapter Five, by Susan Albers Mohrman, discusses ways to integrate organizations in the absence of hierarchy. Mohrman points out that the most critical issues in an organization are often lateral integration and quality of the work force.

Chapter Six, by Gerald E. Ledford, Jr., focuses on a particular management style: employee involvement. Ledford begins by summarizing the work that has been done at CEO, and goes on to discuss future trends. He predicts increasing use of employee involvement in management practice because it produces many of the performance characteristics that organizations need in order to be effective.

Chapter Seven, by Lawler, takes the argument regarding employee involvement one step further. Lawler outlines the major design features that an organization needs in order to be effective as a high-involvement work system. He examines issues ranging from pay systems to communications structures, and argues that these elements must be aligned with the idea of distributing information, power, knowledge, and rewards throughout the organization.

Chapter Eight, by Susan G. Cohen, focuses on a particular feature of organizations: teams. They are critical to most of the organizational designs mentioned in the earlier chapters. Cohen adds to the work of the earlier chapters by providing a useful classification of teams and by considering what makes teams effective.

Part Three is concerned with the management and development of human resources. It contains two chapters.

Chapter Nine, by Allan Mohrman and Edward Lawler, examines how the human resource management function should operate in order to provide a competitive advantage. Building on the earlier discussion of staff organizations, Mohrman and Lawler stress the importance of the human resource department's being a strategic partner of the line organization.

Chapter Ten, by Morgan W. McCall, Jr., considers a specific issue in human resources: the development of managers. The author summarizes and integrates decades of research on how to develop managers and discusses the role managers play in effective organizations.

The concluding chapter, by Galbraith and Lawler, offers a general discussion of the new logic of organizing. The authors firmly maintain that many of the old principles of organizing are no longer valid and that we are developing a new logic about what makes for organizational effectiveness. This new logic calls for changes in communication structures, as well as in organizational designs.

Acknowledgments

This book is a reflection both of the collaborative work that goes on at the Center for Effective Organizations and of the support that CEO receives from others, of which we are very appreciative. CEO is part of the Graduate School of Business at the University of Southern California (USC) and for over a decade has received enthusiastic support from other parts of the school.

A critical aspect of CEO's ability to operate as an organization derives from the help that we receive from our corporate sponsors. Over fifty corporations have given us support, and almost as many have cooperated with us in carrying out the research mentioned in this book.

Our research model is very much one of forming partnerships with organizations to explore mutually interesting research issues. This approach has helped us keep in touch with the realities of the work environment and has given us access to many organizations. Time after time, we have found that a collaborative model leads to strong commitment on the part of organizations to see that research is done right, as well as to research that is well grounded in the reality of organizational life.

CEO has also received support from many faculty members in the business school at USC. Warren Bennis, David Bowen, Thomas Cummings, Michael Driver, Larry Greiner, Steven Kerr, Barry Leskin, Ian Mitroff, Barry Nathan, James O'Toole, Mary Ann Von Glinow, and others have influenced the direction of CEO and contributed to our research.

Finally, the operations staff of CEO has played a major role in the production of this book, as well as in our development as an organization. Adriana Gutierrez, Alice Mark, Karen Mayo, and Annette Yakushi all deserve special mention for their contributions.

Los Angeles, California   Jay R. Galbraith
February 1993   Edward E. Lawler III

THE AUTHORS

Susan G. Cohen is a research scientist at the Center for Effective Organizations, Graduate School of Business, University of Southern California. She received her B.A. degree (1972) from the State University of New York, Buffalo, in psychology, her M.A. degree (1977) from Whitworth College in applied behavioral science, and her M. Phil. (1984) and Ph.D. (1988) degrees from Yale University in organizational behavior. She has done research in and consulted on a variety of approaches to improving organizational effectiveness, including group empowerment and effectiveness, employee involvement, organizational development and change, participative management, and strategies for executive education and management development. She is particularly interested in team effectiveness in the white-collar and service industries. She has published papers on employee involvement and empowerment, human resource strategies, and teams in professional journals and in books. She is the author of several chapters dealing with customer service and top management teams in *Groups That Work (and Those That Don't)* (1990, J. R. Hackman, ed.).

Jay R. Galbraith is professor of management and organization and senior research scientist at the Center for Effective Organizations. Before joining the faculty at the University of Southern California, he directed his own management consulting firm. He has also been on the faculty of the Wharton School at the University of Pennsylvania and the Sloan School of Management at the Massachusetts Institute of Technology. He received his Ch.E. degree (1962) from the University of Cincinnati in chemical engineering, and his M.B.A. (1964) and D.B.A. (1966) degrees from Indiana University. His principal areas of research are organizational design, change, and development. Another interest is strategy and organization at the corporate, business-unit, and international levels of analysis. He has had considerable consulting experience in the United States, Europe, and South America, and has written numerous articles for professional journals, handbooks, and research collections. He is coauthor of *Strategy Implementation: The Role of Structure and Process* (1986, with R. Kazanjian).

Edward E. Lawler III is professor of management and organization in the business school at the University of Southern California and founding director of the Center for Effective Organizations. He received his B.A. degree (1960) from Brown University in psychology and his Ph.D. degree (1964) from the University of California, Berkeley, also in psychology. He has consulted with more than one hundred organizations and with four national governments on employee involvement, organizational change, and compensation and has been honored as a top contributor to the fields of organizational development, organizational behavior, and compensation. He is the author of more than two hundred articles and twenty-two books, and his works have been translated into seven languages. His books include *High-Involvement Management* (1986), *Strategic Pay* (1990), and *The Ultimate Advantage* (1992). He is coauthor of *Employee Involvement and Total Quality Management: Practices and Results in Fortune 1000 Companies* (1992, with S. A. Mohrman and G. E. Ledford, Jr.).

Gerald E. Ledford, Jr., is senior research scientist at the Center for Effective Organizations. He received his B.A. degree (1973) from George Washington University in psychology and his M.A. (1979) and Ph.D. (1984) degrees from the University of Michigan, also in psychology. He has conducted research, published, and consulted on a wide variety of approaches to improving organizational effectiveness and employee well-being, including employee involvement, innovative reward systems, organizational design, job design, and union-management cooperation. He has also done extensive work on skill-based pay systems, consulting with over two dozen major corporations, and has conducted studies of such systems in seven companies. He has published forty articles and book chapters and is coauthor of four books, including *Employee Involvement and Total Quality Management: Practices and Results in Fortune 1000 Companies* (1992, with E. E. Lawler III and S. A. Mohrman) and *Large-Scale Organizational Change* (1989, with A. M. Mohrman, Jr., S. A. Mohrman, T. G. Cummings, E. E. Lawler III, and Associates). He is an active member of the American Psychological Association, the Academy of Management, and the American Compensation Association.

Morgan W. McCall, Jr., is professor of clinical management and organization in the School of Business Administration at the University of Southern California (USC). He also works with the USC Office of Executive Education in the design and delivery of executive programs, is involved in the development of the USC Leadership Institute, and teaches in the International Business Education and Research (IBEAR) program. Prior to joining USC, he was director of research and senior behavioral scientist at the Center for Creative Leadership in Greensboro, North Carolina. McCall received his B.S. degree (1970) from Yale University in administrative science and his Ph.D. degree (1974) from the New York State School of Industrial and Labor Relations at Cornell. He is a fellow of the American Psychological Association, the American Psychological Society, and the Society for Industrial and Organizational

Psychology. He has served on numerous editorial boards, including the *Academy of Management Review, Academy of Management Executive, Human Resource Development Quarterly,* and *Executive Development Journal.* The primary focus of his research and writing is executive leadership, especially executive selection, development, and derailment. He is principal author of *The Lessons of Experience* (1988, with M. M. Lombardo and A. M. Morrison) and coauthor of *Whatever It Takes: The Realities of Managerial Decision Making* (1990, with R. K. Kaplan), *Leadership: Where Else Can We Go?* (1978, with M. M. Lombardo), and *Key Events in Executives' Lives* (1987, with E. H. Lindsey and V. Homes). He led the team that created *Looking Glass, Inc.,* a simulation of managerial work widely used in corporate management development and university programs. He has authored articles published in scholarly books and journals as well as in *Psychology Today, Across the Board, The Physician Executive,* the *Journal of Business Strategy,* and the *New York Times.*

Allan M. Mohrman, Jr., is associate director of research and a research scientist at the Center for Effective Organizations. He was formerly on the faculty of the College of Administrative Sciences at Ohio State University. He earned his Ph.D. degree (1979) at the Graduate School of Management, Northwestern University, in organizational behavior. His major current interests are the design of effective organizational systems for human resource management, high-involvement management approaches, information technologies in organizations, management of teamwork, and the ways these elements relate to one another and to the larger organizational context. He is currently involved in a number of action research projects directly investigating these issues in organizations. Mohrman is also interested in organizational design, organizational change, and social action models for understanding organizational behavior. He is coauthor of *Designing Performance Appraisal Systems* (1989, with S. M. Resnick-West and E. E. Lawler III), *Large-Scale Organizational Change* (1989, with S. A. Mohrman, G. E. Ledford, Jr., T. G. Cummings, E. E. Lawler III, and Associates), and *Doing*

Research That Is Useful for Theory and Practice (1985, with E. E. Lawler III, S. A. Mohrman, G. E. Ledford, Jr., T. G. Cummings, and Associates).

Susan Albers Mohrman is a senior research scientist at the Center for Effective Organizations. She received her A.B. degree (1967) from Stanford University in psychology, her M.Ed. degree (1970) from the University of Cincinnati in education, and her Ph.D. degree (1978) from Northwestern University in organizational behavior. She has served on the faculty of the organizational behavior department in the business school of the University of Southern California. Her research focuses on innovations in human resource management, organizational change, and organizational design processes. She has consulted with a variety of organizations introducing employee involvement programs and labor-management cooperative projects, as well as with organizations that are redesigning structures and systems. Her publications deal with employee participation, quality of work life, self-designing processes in organizations, high-technology management, and the production of research useful to organizations and include *Self-Designing Organizations: Learning How to Create High Performance* (1989, with T. G. Cummings) and *Managing Large-Scale Organizational Change* (1989, with A. M. Mohrman, Jr., G. E. Ledford, Jr., T. G. Cummings, E. E. Lawler III, and Associates). She is active in the Organization Development and Change Division of the Academy of Management and serves on the review and editorial boards of several journals.

ORGANIZING
FOR THE
FUTURE

Introduction

Challenges to the Established Order

Jay R. Galbraith

Edward E. Lawler III

Some have called this the "age of unreason" (Handy, 1990); others have talked about the changing nature of the work force. We have all witnessed rapid change in national boundaries and identities. We are in an era when accelerating rates of change are common in almost every sector of people's lives. Organizations must adapt to this fact if they are to survive (Hannan and Freeman, 1989). Nevertheless, most organizational designs and management practices were not created with the current rate of change in mind. They were created to work well in a more stable, predictable world.

Organizational design and management are changing. The discipline and the practitioners are maturing and becoming more sophisticated. It is less and less common to hear quips like "People are important, not organizations" and "Good people will make any organization work." Of course, having good people is important, but it is no longer sufficient. Only so much can be accomplished with raw talent and sleepless nights. Good people alone will not dramatically reduce a company's time to market. This takes teamwork, team building, team incentives,

1

and shared information. In short, it takes organization, and companies have to be good at organizing if they are to excel.

Historically, organizational design usually meant organizational structure. Today it means an alignment of structure, management processes, information systems, reward systems, people, and other features of the organization with the business strategy (Galbraith, 1987). The "fit" model of organization is well known and widely used (Waterman, 1982; Nadler, Gerstein, and Shaw, 1992).

Organizational design decisions increasingly must be seen as complex trade-offs and contingency decisions, rather than as adoptions of fashion. Twenty years ago, companies rushed into matrix organization, irrespective of whether it fit the business or their people's skills. Matrix was the trend. Today the slogan "Small is beautiful" is fashionable again (Gilder, 1989; Mills, 1991). Fragmenting markets, the decline of mass media, and the need for quick action all seem to favor small firms. Economies of scale are reported to be dead (Adams and Brock, 1986). This is the age of the entrepreneur, it is said. Still, niche firms like Jaguar and Saab could not stay independent and maintain the investment in research and development (R&D) necessary to stay competitive in the auto industry. The last automotive entrepreneur was John DeLorean. Some say economies of scale still live. Who is right?

The organizational design challenge arises, we believe, because both views are correct. Key contingencies must be assessed in determining which approach to organizational design fits a particular industry or company. Tough trade-off decisions are required in order to get scale and simultaneously reduce cycle time. Sometimes it takes the invention of new organizational forms, such as network organizations, which permit a company to be large when it is advantageous to be large and small when it is good to be small (Miles and Snow, 1986). In these cases, organizational design shows a maturity befitting the nature of the complex problems it faces.

There is a growing belief, which we share, that organization will be the basis for gaining competitive advantage in the foreseeable future. Throughout the 1980s, companies pursued competitive advantage or competitive catch-up by launching initiatives in productivity, total quality, and customer service. Usually vice presidents were put in charge of such initiatives. Despite making some progress, companies have been disappointed with the results most of the time. Progress has led to *survival,* rather than to any advantage; productivity, quality, and customer service are competitive *necessities,* not competitive advantages, because most companies have launched initiatives and made some progress. A company gets a competitive advantage only if it is early in adopting the next strategic initiative or if it is much better than others at executing it.

The latest strategic battleground is time-based competition (Stalk and Hout, 1990). The early 1990s have seen time-based competition replace customer service as the chief executive officer's "hot button." Reducing cycle time and reducing time to market are inherently organizational issues. Simultaneous engineering requires the elimination of cross-functional barriers to cooperation. It calls for delegation to project teams and, some suggest, the long-run decline of the functions themselves. A key to time-based competition is lateral organization (Galbraith, 1973).

Ultimately, there may be no long-term sustainable advantage except the ability to organize and manage. The most effective organizations adopt the newest strategic issue early, perfect it, institutionalize it, and move on to the next. As it becomes more difficult to attain competitive advantage through unique strategies (What bank is not targeting the upscale individual and the midmarket company?), it becomes important to adopt and execute the common strategy better. This action requires organizational learning and flexibility — in short, the development of organizational capabilities (Senge, 1990; Lawler, 1992; Stalk, Evans, and Shulman, 1992). Core competencies, which are the important technological underpinnings for products and services, are important. The key to long-term competitive advantage, however, is more likely to be found in organizational effectiveness (Hamel and Prahalad, 1990, Prahalad and Doz, 1987; Bartlett and Ghoshal, 1989). Organizations not only must adopt new initiatives but also have to continue performing well in areas that have been the focus of past initiatives (for example, as speed becomes more important, quality cannot be forgotten). The winners will do well on both speed and quality, and they will control costs. This combination of performance imperatives is what makes effective organizational management so necessary and such a potentially powerful source of competitive advantage.

Organizational Drivers

A number of factors in the business environment increasingly drive the choice of organizational forms. Perhaps the most important factor is the competition that exists because of the key strategic initiatives of cost, speed, and quality. The other factors are technology, buyer power, worldwide skill shortages, unsustainable trade imbalances, information technology, the changing nature of organizational control, and the rate and nature of societal change.

Strategic Initiatives

The forces of global competition have caused companies to substantially improve on cost, quality, and responsiveness to customers. These improvement efforts have led to the establishment of strategic initiatives for cost-effectiveness, total quality, customer service, and time-based competition.

Cost. As more and more competitors come into markets, there is every reason to believe that cost pressures will continue to escalate. Indeed, there seems to be an unlimited number of countries with potentially lower labor costs than those of the industrialized countries. The fall of Communism has produced a staggering number of new competitors with low labor costs and a desire to enter world markets. As a result, the decades ahead promise constant pressure on costs, particularly in organizations competing in global manufacturing. When any organization seeks to gain competitive advantage through cost-effectiveness, the implications for all parts of the organization are profound.

Each cost must be analyzed and examined from a cost-benefit perspective, and decisions must be made about whether it is justified. The new activity-based costing systems are an important tool designed to segment overhead costs into their elements (Cooper and Kaplan, 1991). These overhead elements can then become targets for cost reduction.

The corporate office is coming under pressure for productivity improvement from another source. As a percentage of capital, office equipment has risen from 3 percent to 18 percent, yet office productivity has not improved. Robotics and other technology have radically altered factories, but personal computers, electronic mail, and fax machines have had very little effect on productivity in the office. Attempts to re-engineer business processes represent the current movement aimed at reducing white-collar costs (Hammer, 1990).

Speed. Speed in getting to market, speed in responding to customers' demands, and speed in correcting organizational problems are all potential sources of competitive advantage (Stalk and Hout, 1990). The emphasis on speed has very direct implications for the design of organizations. Organizations have to be structured so as to bring about quick organizational responses and support the kind of flexibility needed to produce them. This may call for behavior very different from what has often been characteristic of both line and staff groups. The staff groups have often focused on protecting the organization from making large mistakes (and perhaps even very small ones). In a fast-changing global business, however, overanalysis and slowness in decision making can be as damaging or costly as incorrect decisions. If an organization is quick, adaptive, and flexible, it can often overcome mistakes with midcourse corrections and adjustments (Mohrman and Cummings, 1989). If it simply does not act, however, it is in no position to learn from its mistakes and correct them; ultimately, it may simply fall so far behind that it is no longer in the game.

Quality. The future shows no sign of any reduction in emphasis on product and service quality. Indeed, this emphasis is likely to increase. More and more organizations are seeking competitive advantage by offering higher-quality products and services and focusing on customer satisfaction. This trend has strong implications for all the functions of organizations.

The implications for the line parts of an organization have been discussed as part of the extensive literature on total quality management. Staff roles are also critical in helping an organization achieve competitive advantage through high-quality performance. Staff need to support the line organization, because how well staff perform their activities shows up in the ultimate quality of the product and services that an organization offers (Bowen and Lawler, 1992). In many respects, a staff unit is a service organization to the line. It is subject to demands from the line for higher-quality service and better customer relations. Therefore, it is reasonable to expect that as the line operations of organizations develop and perfect their own concepts of how to deliver high quality, they will in turn demand high-quality service from their staff organizations. Line managers are likely to expect staff organizations to treat them as customers.

Technology

Technology is not just an isolated force; it is also the engine that drives global competition. The expenditures on commercial research and development (R&D) that are typical of all developed countries are critical here. The start of the new era of global competition, in the late 1970s, marked the beginning of increased commercial R&D expenditures on the part of industrialized nations. The real increase in R&D expenditures is striking and important because it raises everyone's fixed costs. By the 1980s, even U.S. firms could not get enough volume from their domestic markets alone to cover their fixed costs. They needed and will continue to need global volume to cover the increasing R&D investment. The shortening of product life cycles exacerbates the situation by reducing the number of years over which fixed costs can be written off. Greater volume from more countries must be attained in fewer years. The result is that more companies need global volume in order to survive.

Buyer Power

One effect of global competition has been to shift power to the buyer. In most industries, a buyer's market exists simply because there are more competitors and a surplus of supply. The buyer is learning how to use this new power. Companies with the auto industry as their customer find that they cannot *sell to* the auto makers; the auto companies *buy from* them. Ford spends $40 billion per year and does not want simply parts. Ford wants technology, information exchange, electronic hookups, and systems integration. Ford wants a relationship. As a result, organizing by customer segment is a powerful trend and will continue to be one. The customer will continue to penetrate farther and lower into the organization. Increasingly, it will be the customer's demand, not the boss's command, that drives organizational activity.

Skill Shortages

Countries differ in the kinds of skills their work forces posses and in the cost of employing individuals with particular skills (Johnston, 1991; Porter, 1990). This reality, as well as the continued development of information technology and information "highways," will lead to location-free organization structures and work environments. With skills in short supply, work will be taken to wherever the skills exist or wherever the costs are lowest. Electrical engineering work already moves to Israel, software moves to India, and micromachinery moves to Switzerland. These dispersed activities can be integrated through telecommunications as we move from personal computers to interpersonal computing.

It has been suggested that demographics and technology will combine to shift power from the boardroom to the workplace, and that this shift will truly empower workers who have skills (Lawler, 1992). Organizations will have to create jobs and structures that attract knowledge workers and allow them to grow and develop. If they fail, organizations will risk losing their core competencies, because these usually reside in the individuals who make up the employee population. This fact clearly gives employees more power than they have when they can easily be replaced because of limited skills.

Trade Imbalances

Another driver of organizational forms will be the existing and unsustainable trade imbalances. According to economic theory, trade imbalances are corrected by exchange-rate changes: the dollar drops against the yen, imports into the United States stop, exports to Japan begin, and the imbalance is corrected. Some experts suggest, however, that exchange rates cannot fall far enough to correct imbalances with Japan (Johnson, 1989). Japanese institutional arrangements, such as banking groups (*keiretsu*), prevent markets from clearing. As a result, Western organizations will begin to look more like Japanese organizations, in order to compete with them. The longer the imbalances exist, the stronger the pressure to create Western *keiretsu* and ignore antitrust laws.

Information Technology

The new information technology will permit some new forms of organization to evolve. These new forms may very well generate a new paradigm for organizing. Hierarchy has been the "natural" form of organizational structure. Attempts to design less hierarchical organizations have succeeded in reducing some of the debilitating side effects of rigid hierarchies, but decision processes are still hierarchical (Lawler, 1992). The reason is that hierarchy is the most efficient social form for coordinating the interdependent behavior of thousands of people (Galbraith, 1977). The information-processing task of managing all the interfaces in a nonhierarchical organization is overwhelming. Hierarchies reduce the number of interfaces by creating fewer at each level, but now thousands can communicate quickly through computer conferencing, and this will continue to be true. "Groupware" and "organizationware" can aid in the formation of a consensus for action (Morton, 1991).

Information technology may tip the balance in favor of markets in the trade-off between using markets or using hierarchies to coordinate economic decisions (Williamson, 1975). More and more markets, such as those in stocks, cattle, and used cars, are going electronic. Location-free organizations, facilitated by telecommunications, may make us cottage industries again, coordinated by market forces rather than by superiors wielding authority.

Changing Nature of Organizational Control

Every organization needs to control the behavior and performance of its members. Traditional organizations rely on formal bureaucratic controls and on supervision by a hierarchy of authority. Bureaucratic control is increasingly being replaced by customer control, peer control, and automated formal controls. This change reduces the need for control-oriented managerial units, as well as the need for layers of management. In this respect, it is a direct response to cost pressures. In effect, it simultaneously eliminates high-paid jobs and transfers work to lower-paid employees (Lawler, 1992). Organizations are creating customer teams, linking up with customer information systems, and granting bonuses based on surveys of customer satisfaction. As we have said, customers are penetrating more frequently and more deeply into organizations. More employees are working in direct contact with customers. Teams are working directly for customers, and the rest of the organization supports this effort. Customer-driven organizations are substituting the customer's demand for the boss's command.

The development of self-managing work teams and employee involvement turns an organization away from formal bureaucratic control (Lawler, 1986, 1992). More control activities are performed by team members themselves. The use of reward systems, such as gain sharing, creates greater alignment of team goals and organizational goals. Peer-group enforcement of team goals and norms substitutes for formal hierarchical controls.

A similar form of control arises in distributed organizations. Mutual dependence is created through distributing company missions to various units in the organization. Control is achieved through reciprocity in delivering and receiving services among interdependent units. Therefore, there is less need for formal control from headquarters. The automation of formal control systems further reduces the need for control systems and for control-oriented management (Zuboff, 1988).

   In summary, the changing nature of organizational control is eliminating the need for hierarchical, control-oriented management. In some cases, the control function has been transferred to customers and peers; in others, computerization of the information flow has automated the formal control system. In all cases, the control staff is redundant.

Conclusion

In this chapter, we have argued that substantial forces are challenging current methods of working and organizing. Competition and rivalry have intensified due to increasing fixed costs incurred in research and development. In order to compete more effectively, companies are launching strategic cost, speed, and quality initiatives and introducing new information technology. In addition to these internally generated changes, external forces such as skill shortages, trade imbalances, and buyer power are also influencing change. Business as usual no longer suffices. In the next chapters, we discuss how organizations will change to compete, survive, and win in the future.

References

Adams, W., and Brock, J. W. *The Bigness Complex.* New York: Pantheon, 1986.

Bartlett, C. A., and Ghoshal, S. *Managing Across Borders: The Transnational Solution.* Boston: Harvard Business School Press, 1989.

Bowen, D., and Lawler, E. E., III. "Total Quality-Oriented Human Resource Management." *Organizational Dynamics,* 1992, *20*(4), 29–41.

Cooper, R., and Kaplan, R. "Profit Priorities from Activities-Based Costing." *Harvard Business Review,* 1991, *69*(3), 130–137.

Galbraith, J. R. *Designing Complex Organizations.* Reading, Mass.: Addison-Wesley, 1973.

Galbraith, J. R. *Organization Design.* Reading, Mass.: Addison-Wesley, 1977.

Galbraith, J. R. "Organization Design." In J. Lorsch (ed.), *Handbook of Organization Behavior.* Englewood Cliffs, N.J.: Prentice-Hall, 1987.

Gilder, G. *Microcosm.* New York: Simon & Schuster, 1989.

Hamel, G., and Prahalad, C. K. "Strategic Intent." *Harvard Business Review,* 1990, *67*(3), 63–76.

Hammer, M. "Reengineering Work: Don't Automate, Obliterate." *Harvard Business Review,* 1990, *68*(4), 104–113.

Handy, C. *The Age of Unreason.* Boston: Harvard Business School Press, 1990.

Hannan, M. T., and Freeman, J. *Organizational Ecology.* Cambridge, Mass.: Harvard University Press, 1989.

Johnson, C. "Sectoral and Regional Growth in the Pacific." Paper presented at the PECC Economic Outlook Conference, University of San Diego, Mar. 25, 1989.

Johnston, W. B. "Global Workforce 2000: The New World Labor Market." *Harvard Business Review,* 1991, *69*(2), 115–127.

Lawler, E. E., III. *High-Involvement Management: Participative Strategies for Improving Organizational Performance.* San Francisco: Jossey-Bass, 1986.

Lawler, E. E., III. *The Ultimate Advantage: Creating the High-Involvement Organization.* San Francisco: Jossey-Bass, 1992.

Miles, R. E., and Snow, C. "Organizations: New Concepts for New Forms." *California Management Review,* 1986, *28,* 62–73.

Mills, D. Q. *Rebirth of the Corporation.* New York: Wiley, 1991.

Mohrman, S. A., and Cummings, T. G. *Self-Designing Organizations: Learning How to Create High Performance.* Reading, Mass.: Addison-Wesley, 1989.

Morton, M.S.S. *The Corporation of the 1990s.* New York: Oxford University Press, 1991.

Nadler, D. A., Gerstein, M. S., and Shaw, R. B. *Organizational Architecture: Designs for Changing Organizations.* San Francisco: Jossey-Bass, 1992.

Porter, M. E. *The Competitive Advantage of Nations.* New York: Free Press, 1990.

Prahalad, C. K., and Doz, Y. L. *The Multinational Mission.* New York: Free Press, 1987.

Senge, P. M. *The Fifth Discipline: The Art and Practice of the Learning Organization.* New York: Doubleday, 1990.

Stalk, G., Evans, P., and Shulman, L. E. "Competing on Capabilities: The New Rules of Corporate Strategy." *Harvard Business Review,* 1992, *70*(1), 57–69.

Stalk, G., and Hout, T. M. *Competing Against Time.* New York: Free Press, 1990.

Waterman, R. "The Seven Elements of Strategic Fit." *The Journal of Business Strategy,* Winter 1982, pp. 69–73.

Williamson, O. E. *Markets and Hierarchies.* New York: Free Press, 1975.

Zuboff, S. *In the Age of the Smart Machine.* New York: Basic Books, 1988.

PART ONE

New Organizational Forms

The modern organization is made up of a complex set of units and the relationships among them. The focus in Part One is on the nature of these units and how they should be managed, designed, and focused. We begin by looking at the total corporate structure, with a focus on the role of the top levels of a corporation. A critical issue at this point in history is the type of value that can be added by the top levels of an organization. As pointed out in several chapters, this issue is particularly critical in corporations that are engaged in multiple businesses. Particularly where independent businesses are part of the same corporation, it may be that only a very limited role is appropriate for the top levels. From a design perspective, the challenge is to find the right set of businesses and to define the right relationship between the business units and the corproate organization of which they are a part. Staff groups, both at the corporate level and at the business-unit level, are a second focus of Part One. Concepts are changing rapidly about what their role is, how they should be structured, and how they should relate to the business and corporate units that they support. New questions are raised about how much value they can add and how they can help a business be effective. It is particularly important that they operate in the most efficient way, and that they operate in new ways, so that they can deliver services effectively.

Chapter One

The Value-Adding Corporation: Matching Structure with Strategy

Jay R. Galbraith

The concept of the American corporation has been evolving for some time. By the early 1980s, a consensus had developed around the different types of corporations and how they should be organized. As the decade closed, however, that consensus had all but unraveled. In its place arose a variety of proposals for rethinking the nature of the corporation (Jensen, 1989).

Most of these proposals have been presented as replacements for the current corporate forms. This chapter presents a different view. It argues that these new forms will exist along with the older ones. The 1990s are seen as a period of increasing variety in the forms of institutions through which economic activity will be conducted. This variety represents differing types and amounts of value that the corporation adds to its business units.

The chapter begins by describing the original consensus. Next, changes in business strategy that are leading to changes in corporate organizational structure are presented. The various corporate forms resulting from these changes are then placed in the framework of strategy and organization.

15

Strategy and Structure

The relationship between strategy and structure was first articulated by Chandler (1962), in his historical study of American enterprises. Until that time, managers had debated the pros and cons of functional versus product organizations. Chandler showed that firms in a single business used a functional organization. When the company diversified into several businesses, the multidivisional profit-center organization was created. Chandler's work established the concept that different strategies lead to different organizations. Both the functional and the product organization were appropriate for their respective strategies.

The conglomerates appeared in the 1970s. Instead of using internally generated business opportunities, as General Electric and Procter & Gamble did, companies like Textron, Teledyne, ITT, and Litton used acquisition to diversify into new business areas. They bought and sold companies. They came to administer portfolios of unrelated businesses through holding companies. Other types of organizations were suggested, but a consensus developed around the following three classical models:

Strategy	Growth	Structure
Single business	Internal	Functional
Related diversification	Internal	Divisional
Unrelated diversification	Acquisition	Holding company

The next step was the expansion of structure to the concept of organization. Organization was considered to consist of compensation policy, career paths, and control processes, in addition to structure. These dimensions also fit with the strategy and the structure (Galbraith, 1987). For example, relationships were discovered to exist between strategy and careers (Pitts, 1976) and between strategy and compensation (Kerr, 1985). Organization became an aligned set of policies that fit with one another and with the portfolio strategy (Galbraith and Kazanjian, 1986).

A relatively complete display of organizational structure and strategy is shown here:

Strategy	Structure	Centralization	Staff	Staff Role
Single	Functional	High	Small	Policy
Related	Divisional	Moderate	Large	Policy/review
Unrelated	Holding company	Low	Small	Service

In addition to organizational structure, the degree of centralization, the size of the corporate staff, and the staff's role are listed as policy headings. The degree of centralization varies from high to low when we move from the functional model to the model of the holding company. Control in the functional structure is exercised through the line organization; in the multidivisional organization, control is exercised partly through the corporate staff. Indeed, the size and role of the corporate staff are distinguishing features between the divisionalized organizations and those that use the holding company. The staffs of divisionalized companies are large (1,700 at Hewlett-Packard, 3,500 at Procter & Gamble) and active. They review divisional plans and guarantee the competence of their functions in the divisions. They set company policy for their functions. They strive for a single policy for all divisions. Indeed, they add value by using their expertise, longer time horizons, and total company view to formulate functional policy in one place for all divisions, thereby reducing duplications across divisions. By contrast, the corporate staff in the holding company numbers a few hundred, is mostly financial, and offers services to the divisions.

Control processes also vary directly with portfolio strategies, as shown here:

Strategy	Control Data	Type of Control
Single	Cost	Operational
Related	Profit	Strategic
Unrelated	Investment	Financial

The control system of the functional organization is a cost-center process, while the divisionalized organization is managed through a profit-center process. The more autonomous divisions of the holding company are managed as investment centers.

The corporation exerts different types of control over the

units that report directly to it. The functional organization exerts three types of control over its cost centers: operational, strategic, and financial. A cost center is subject to such operational controls as schedules, forecasts, and day-to-day activities. Operational control is delegated to divisions in the multidivisional company. The corporation maintains strategic control over the divisional profit centers. Strategic control entails the designation of products, markets, technologies, and charters to be pursued by the divisions. It restricts the domain of its divisions so that they can neither compete with one another nor duplicate activities. These strategic decisions are delegated to the divisions in a holding company. Whereas the functional organization exerts all three types of control, the holding company exercises only financial control. It specifies return on investment, asset levels, return on assets, inventory turnover ratios, and so forth. As a result, the holding company requires only a small corporate staff.

Human resource policies also vary with portfolio strategy, as follows:

Strategy	Compensation	Variable	Bases	Measures	Career
Single	Company	Low	Company	Subjective	Company
Related	Company	Medium	Division/company	Subjective/objective	Company
Unrelated	Industry	High	Division	Objective	Division

Compensation policies vary, from company-based salary structures for single-business and divisionalized companies to industry-based compensation for the divisions of a holding company. Managers in different divisions of a related business company receive the same salary for the same level of job. Managers in a holding company receive salaries defined by the industry in which the division competes, rather than a company-defined salary. Managers working in the divisions of a holding company receive much higher amounts of variable compensation than managers do in divisionalized companies. Divisional managers of a holding company may receive 50 percent of their take-home pay in the form of bonuses. Managers of a divisionalized company may only receive 10 to 30 percent of salary as bonuses. If managers in functional and divisionalized companies do receive bonuses, these are usually based on company profits, rather than on divisional profitability. The division's general manager may receive some mixture of divisional and company-based bonuses. The divisional manager of a holding company receives a bonus that is based only on the performance of his or her division.

The performance measures on which salaries and promotions are granted increase in objectivity as strategy changes from a single business to an unrelated portfolio of businesses. The manager of a division in a holding company is measured strictly on meeting financial goals. The manager of a cost center in a single business is measured on budgetary performance but may also be judged on other characteristics of performance (such as cooperation), as well as on personal goals.

Line managers can expect different careers in different types of organizations. Managers in single-business companies and related diversified companies tend to move throughout the entire organization. Managers in a holding company stay within their own divisions. As a result, management development is centralized in single-business and related diversified organizations. It is decentralized to the divisions in a holding company. The holding company may use external firms to recruit division managers.

The key to success with each of these models is the alignment of all the policies with the strategy. Table 1.1 shows all the policies and contrasts them for the two diversified models. Since the businesses are related in the divisional model, they can share resources, people, technologies, and ideas; hence, the divisions are not completely autonomous. A large corporate office moves resources and people across divisions. The respective staffs ensure that there is enough commonality of policy so that interdivisional transfers take place effectively. Since there is resource sharing and lack of autonomy, it is difficult to get objective measures of divisional performance. These companies use subjective and multidimensional performance measures. They do not use much variable compensation. When they do use variable pay, they use a combination of corporate and divisional

Table 1.1. Policies Contrasted for Two Diversified Models.

Strategy	Related	Unrelated
Structure	Divisional	Holding company
Centralization	Moderate	Low
Staff	Large	Small
Staff role	Policy/review	Service
Control	Profit center	Investment center
Control type	Strategic/financial	Financial
Compensation	Company	Industry
Percentage variable	10–30%	50% or more
Measures	Subjective/objective	Objective
Careers	Company	Division

profitability as the performance measure. These policies form a self-reinforcing system. They fit together. Indeed, the high-performing companies, both divisionalized and holding companies, are those that have aligned policies and strategy (Nathanson and Cassano, 1982).

Misalignment leads to ineffective performance. If related companies paid large bonuses based on objective measures of divisional performance, the motivation of divisional managers would increase, but their behavior would be dysfunctional. They would be motivated to be independent, look out for their own divisions, and be reluctant to share resources and adopt common policies. Similarly, if a holding company adopted a compensation policy designed for a related business strategy, it would not be using all the motivational leverage it could use for autonomous, measurable businesses. The task of the organizational designer is to determine the company's diversification strategy and then align structure, processes, and practices to fit with it.

A great deal of empirical attention has been focused on comparing the economic performance of related and unrelated diversified companies. Early studies found that related diversifiers outperformed unrelated conglomerates (Rumelt, 1974). Peters and Waterman (1982) popularized that idea with the lesson that "excellent" companies "stick to their knitting." The idea that businesses must be related is the conventional wisdom both on and off Wall Street today. There is very little research support for the conventional wisdom, however. A review of twenty-three studies shows no consistent evidence that related business diversifiers outperform unrelated ones (Grant, Jammine, and Thomas, 1988), and the majority of recent studies find no difference in performance whatsoever. One reason has been suggested by Grant, Jammine, and Thomas, who have found a curvilinear relationship between diversity and performance. That relationship is shown in Figure 1.1. They suggest that an optimal level of diversity is achieved through operating in three or four different industries. Another study, using different measures of diversity, also found an optimum level, but in two business areas (Nathanson and Cassano, 1982). Still another study focused only on conglomerates and found that high-performing conglomerates limited their diversity to three or four general business areas (Dundas and Richardson, 1982). Thus there appears to be some support for the idea that unrelated diversification, administered through a holding company, can be a viable corporate form. It can even be successful when business diversity is limited to three or four industries.

Figure 1.1. Diversity and Performance.

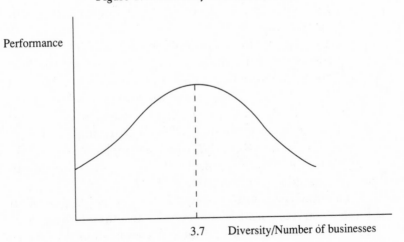

Source: Adapted from Grant, Jammine, and Thomas, 1988, p. 788. Used with permission.

I believe that the conglomerate is a viable form of organization if the issue of management development can be resolved — that is, successful strategies of unrelated diversification have been implemented by exceptional individuals. For example, very wide diversity companies were successfully managed by Harold Geneen at ITT, Henry Singleton at Teledyne, and Lords Hanson and White at Hanson Trust.

The difficulties usually begin when these exceptional people retire. Their replacements often appear to be unable to manage the same breadth of diversity. It seems that industry has been unable to "grow" general managers who have the deal-making skills and the business intuition that spans a variety of industries. The successful conglomerate appears to depend on unique individuals; it has not become an institutionalized form. The successful corporation that has become an institution, such as Procter & Gamble or IBM, has devised a succession process intended to perpetuate the institution beyond its founders. Not so with the conglomerate: indeed, Henry Singleton is planning to liquidate Teledyne, rather than groom a successor, and similar proposals have come from Lord Hanson at Hanson Trust. Perhaps if diversity is limited to three or four business areas, however, succession can be accomplished, and the institution can be perpetuated.

Overall, the death of the conglomerate has been greatly exaggerated. There will always be conglomerates, although in lesser numbers. There will be sons and daughters of Hanson Trust and Carlo De Benedetti. There will also be neoconglomerates that limit themselves to three or four business areas, and there will be leveraged-buyout (LBO) partnerships (such as Kohlberg, Kravis, and Roberts), which are replacing the widely diversified conglomerates (Jensen, 1989). All these forms will come to exist side by side in the 1990s.

In summary, a consensus was formed in the 1980s around the three classic corporate strategies and structures: single business/functional organization, related diversification/divisionalized structure, and unrelated diversification/holding company. The concept of organization was expanded from structure to include compensation practices, career paths, control systems, and staff policies. The key concept in the design of organizations became alignment, or fit, between organizational policies themselves and strategies (Galbraith, 1987). When all these policies were aligned, the company was a high performer (Nathanson and Cassano, 1982).

As already suggested, however, the consensus has begun to unravel. My own position is that the conglomerate will continue to exist, as will the single-business type of company and the divisionalized company. Alongside them, however, will exist the LBO partnership, the neoconglomerate or mixed form, and the front-end/back-end model.

New Forms of Corporate Organization

In this section, the new organizations are described, along with the business forces that are creating them and a framework for ordering the forms of corporate strategy and organization along a continuum. The new forms are illustrated in Table 1.2. They are displayed, with the classical models, along a continuum representing portfolio strategies of increasing diversity, from a single business to a multibusiness, multi-industry LBO partnership. The continuum also represents the decreasing amounts of value added to the businesses from the corporation. To add different amounts of value, different forms of corporate organization are used.

Table 1.2. Corporate Strategy and Organization.

Strategy	Single	Dual	Related	Mixed	Unrelated	Unrelated
Organization	Functional	Front/back	Divisional	Cluster	Holding	LBO
Diversity	Low				High	Very high
Value-added	High					Low

Emerging Front-End/Back-End Model

The front-end/back-end (or *front/back*) model is a hybrid form, which combines features of the single business form and the divisional profit-center model. There is some decentralization around profit-measurable units, yet there is still a great deal of strategic and operational control exercised from the corporation. The distinguishing feature of the model is the division of activities between the front end (or ends), organized by customer and/or geography, and a back end organized by product and technology. The structure is shown in Figure 1.2.

Figure 1.2. Front-End/Back-End Structure.

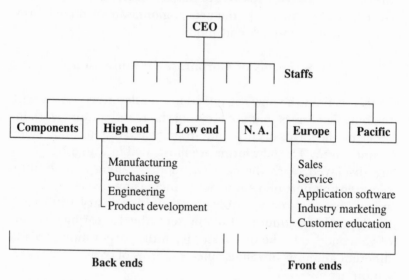

This form of organization is largely driven by the customer. The strategic forces are as follows:

- Buyer power
- Cross-selling
- Systems integration
- Sourcing
- Value-added to service and software

As a company grows, it diversifies into several related product lines. If these product lines go to common customers who buy them in a coordinated fashion, there is a good chance that the company will adopt the front/back model. In many industries, customers prefer sourcing arrangements whereby they certify fewer suppliers and work with them more closely over longer periods. The supplier organizations in turn organize the front end around these customers. In industries that are buying complete systems rather than stand-alone products, there is a need for customer-specific expertise and programs. When customers have and use buying power, desire systems integration, and prefer to source from a few suppliers, those suppliers feel pressure to organize around the customers. In addition to the strategic forces already listed, the firm may see an advantage in offering a full product line, cross-selling products, and/or bundling them (Porter, 1985). In all these cases, there is a need for cross-product strategies and coordination.

Companies facing these five strategic forces try to align as many functions as possible around the customer or customer segment. Manufacturing usually cannot have a factory for each customer segment, however. Multiple customers buy the same product. To get scale in manufacturing, product development, and component purchasing, a back end of the business is created around products and specialties (like graphics). Hence, the firm operates with a product-oriented back end and a customer-driven front end.

The computer industry is typical of companies organized into front/back structures. Digital Equipment evolved to that structure from functional organization. In the early 1980s, both IBM and Xerox changed from divisional product profit centers to a front/back structure. In all cases, the adoption of the structure was driven by the customer, who did not want to see competing, uncoordinated product proposals coming from autonomous product divisions. Even as IBM and Xerox split apart in the 1990s, it is the product-oriented back end that is creating more autonomous units. All sales to IBM customers still go through a common front end. All these companies organized so as to present a single face to the customer.

Other industries are reflecting these strategic changes. Packaged-goods producers are presenting a single face to the customer, reflecting the increased buying power of such retail trade leaders as Wal-Mart. In addition, some retailers decentralize buying and promotion decisions to the store level. Manufacturers are creating customer teams involving multiple functions, geographical sales, and marketing units to complement the divisional sales forces.

In many industries, the strength of the front end is increasing. The sales function has always been customer- and geography-oriented, but now more value-added is moving to service, customer education, information, and application software. These services are provided by the front end. Indeed, Digital and IBM are selling consulting services and application software, providing systems integration, and even operating the customer's facilities.

The front/back organization is a hybrid. It experiences the need for decentralization because it manages product and market diversity. It adopts quasi profit centers around the front and/or the back, but the profit centers are less autonomous than in a related diversified/divisionalized organization. The back is usually the sole supplier to the front, which is the sole customer. Although these internal monopolies are being challenged, the product lines and customer segments are operated as single businesses. Products are compromised in their stand-alone applications, so that the product line as a whole is more attractive. Products may have to be announced together and made available simultaneously. The result is considerable strategic and operational control, which is exercised by the corporation. Nevertheless, for businesses selling stand-alone products and services to fragmented buyers who do not desire sourcing and systems-integration arrangements, diversification still leads to the divisional profit-center model. As described in the following section, however, that classic model is subject to strategic change forces of its own, which are reshaping its structure and processes.

From Related to Value-Added

The following strategic forces are being experienced by related diversified firms and are changing the relationship between corporate offices and business units:

- Level of competition
- Shift from manufacturing to service
- Vertical disaggregation
- Ownership of less than 100 percent
- Acquisitions and divestiture

In all cases, there is more decentralization to businesses and more differentiation of policy across businesses. The result is that the divisionalized firms are adopting some of the features of the holding company.

Many industries are experiencing a heightened level of competition because of new entrants, industry shakeouts, and slower market growth. In these industries, the cross-functional coordination requirements within a business unit are exceeding the cross-divisional coordination requirements for managing a shared capability. There is often the choice of being competitive within an industry and being common across the corporation. Today, many companies are choosing to be more competitive and less common.

Another view is that the costs of cross-business-unit cooperation are too high to be competitive. Porter (1985) has identified three costs of sharing capabilities. First is the cost of administering the coordination processes. Corporate staff units are often part of the administrative process and are viewed as places where cost and overhead can be reduced. Corporate staffs are viewed as luxuries that globally competitive companies can no longer afford. The second cost is the cost of compromise. To share a resource, a business unit must suboptimize and adopt a component, a policy, or a strategy that may compromise its competitiveness within its industry. In a less competitive time, these costs were tolerable. In industries subject to extreme international competition, compromise means demise. As a result, more decisional autonomy is being given to the business units. The third cost is the cost of inflexibility. A business cannot rapidly change components if those components are used by other business units; a collective or corporate decision must be reached. In industries competing on cycle time and time to market, inflexibility can be an intolerable cost. As time-based competition increases, more business-unit autonomy will be required. All three costs of cooperating are being reduced by more decentralization and differentiation.

The same organizational change results from the trend of owning less than 100 percent of a division. The partnering process is creating joint ventures and minority investments with other companies. Other firms are spinning off divisions, selling equity to divisional management, and acting as venture capitalists. In each case, the partners will object to the costs of compromise and inflexibility. As a result, the relationship between the business and the corporation is one of more decentralization to the business unit and differentiation from the corporation.

As companies move from manufacturing to service businesses, a similar organizational change results. Some companies stop manufacturing products but retain the product-service activity as a business unit. Still others spin off the service activity and expand it into a stand-alone business. In each case, compensation policies, labor agreements, and financial measures for a manufacturing business do not fit the service business. Service-oriented policies must be adopted that make the business unit more differentiated, less consistent, and therefore less like the manufacturing business units.

Finally, many vertically integrated companies are breaking up into smaller business units. Oil companies are breaking into an upstream business of exploration and production, a downstream business of refining and marketing, and a petrochemicals business. These units are related, since they are in the same industry and use the same feedstocks, but they are also different. Upstream oil is capital-intensive and global; downstream oil is marketing-oriented and local. Therefore, decision making is decentralized to the business units, and business policies are differentiated.

The related diversified companies are also growing by acquisition and selling off businesses that no longer fit. Procter & Gamble finds it more efficient to buy brands from Richardson-Vicks and Revlon than to create new ones. The acquisition process itself brings in more diversity of policy and practice. Pieces of companies are sold off because they do not fit any longer. For its beverage business to receive a good sale price, Procter & Gamble had to allow it to differentiate itself, because to be effective in its industry it needed to be different from other Procter & Gamble divisions. A market for business units is developing, so that the business for sale is not always seen as a "lemon." The relationship between the corporate office and a recently acquired business, or one to be sold, is usually more decentralized.

All of these forces have an impact on related diversified companies. Organizations are changing by decentralizing and differentiating businesses. Staffs are being moved out of the corporate level to the group, sector, or business-unit levels. The staffs that remain are more service-oriented and less active. In short, the divisionalized organizations are becoming more like holding companies; and, oddly enough, the holding companies are becoming more like related divisionalized organizations.

From Unrelated to Value-Added

The conglomerates have been subject to strategic forces that are causing them to reduce the number of business areas in which they participate and to add value to those businesses that they retain. These forces are as follows:

- Performance (actual and perceived)
- Breakup values greater than market value
- Value-added

As stated earlier, the conglomerates have become unpopular, both with academia and with Wall Street. In some cases, actual performance has declined. When the champion of unrelated diversification leaves, the successor usually experiences a decline in performance, such as at ITT and United Technologies. In general, successors have had difficulty managing conglomerates.

Whether performance declines are real or perceived, the "sell" recommendations from Wall Street push price earnings ratios to the point where the breakup value may exceed the market value of a company. At this point, the company breaks itself apart, or a takeover bid does so. In both cases, business areas and diversity are reduced. In general, companies are decreasing business diversity and increasing geographical diversity. The corporation must also add value to its businesses. Financial diversification by itself is not a value. Diversity is not valuable to shareholders who can diversify their own portfolios, nor is it valuable to a business unit that must pay increased overhead. Rockwell must show why Allen-Bradley, purchased in the late 1980s, is more valuable as part of Rockwell than as a stand-alone business with a board of directors. To add value, the corporation must exercise some strategic control, in addition to financial control, over its business units. The corporation must be more active and must employ some people at the corporate office, or in the businesses that are coordinated across businesses, to share resources, information, and/or people, so as to add value. The stronger corporate office makes the modified holding company more like the divisionalized structure. Such a corporation pursues a mixed strategy, whereby differentiation and decentralization are attributes of a holding company, and value-added and coordination are attributes of a divisionalized model.

In summary, both of the classical forms of diversified corporation will continue to exist, but the three strategic forces just mentioned are creating some hybrids. The divisionalized firms are decentralizing and differentiating their business units. The conglomerates are reducing diversity, adding value to their business units, and exercising more strategic control over them. The result is the range of corporate forms shown in Table 1.2. The two key decisions for the corporate strategy involve the diversity of the business units that make up the portfolio and the types and amounts of value to be added to those business units. These two decisions are not independent. The more diversity in the portfolio, the more difficult it is to add value other than financial value. Similarly, the organization that is to implement the strategy will vary with the types and amounts of value-added. The next section describes the value-adding organization and the alignment of its various organizational policies.

Organizing the Value-Adding Corporation

This discussion of the value-adding corporation will concentrate on the portion of the continuum in Table 1.2 that runs from the related to the unrelated strategies. The strategy between the two classical ones is termed *mixed;* that is, elements of both unrelated and related diversification strategies are being followed in these companies. In fact, there is continuous variation in the types and amounts of value-added. The organization to be chosen will likewise vary with the types and amounts of value-added.

The structure that fits these mixed strategies is identified as a cluster in Table 1.2. This means that business units are clustered into a group- or sector-type organization. The clustering brings together businesses that are more related to each other than to other businesses in the portfolio. Four related issues arise as a result of the formation of clusters of business units:

1. What is the criterion for forming clusters?
2. What is the cluster strategy?
3. What is the size and role of the cluster organization?
4. What activities are left to the corporation?

Clustering Criterion

This discussion of the criterion for forming clusters requires an elaboration of what is meant by the term *related diversification.* Most research studies sort companies into related and unrelated categories, on the basis of standard industry classification (SIC) codes. Businesses in the same or similar industries are related, and the others are unrelated. Some judgment is usually applied in the categorization (Rumelt, 1974). The use of SIC codes has not been altogether satisfactory. For example, Procter & Gamble can be seen to be very diverse because it produces products in the soap, paper, food, pharmaceutical, and toiletries industries; but every product is a low-price, repeat-purchase, consumable product sold to homemakers through mass merchandisers.

Therefore, from a marketing and distribution perspective, the products are very related. As another example, 3M produces a wide variety of products for a wide variety of markets, and therefore it appears to be very diverse, but over 90 percent of these products are developed by chemical engineers using coating and bonding technologies. From the standpoint of technology, the products are all related. Thus businesses can be related by products (Hewlett-Packard), by markets (Procter & Gamble), and by technology (3M).

The ways in which businesses may be related are endless. A group of businesses may be related because they are mature, are capital-intensive, are start-ups, are commoditylike, and so on. It is not farfetched to conclude that there simply are no unrelated businesses, nor is it difficult to find some dimension on which a set of businesses is related. The real question is whether any advantage can be achieved through incurring the costs of managing such relatedness.

In summary, there are multiple criteria for grouping businesses into clusters. Difficulty arises because criteria may conflict. A pharmaceutical company may invent a compound that demonstrates therapeutic value. The company may manufacture related products, with one product sold as a prescription drug and the other sold as an over-the-counter (OTC) drug. The products are related, but the markets are not; the product-market combinations represent two different businesses. Companies that are good at prescription drugs (Upjohn, Merck) are typically not good at OTC drugs. Prescription pharmaceuticals is an R&D business; OTC drugs is a marketing business. The two require *different* management skills, while *common* management skills are the critical determinant of whether the businesses are related.

The question now becomes one of which criterion or combination of criteria will lead to the greatest commonality of management skills. There is some evidence to suggest that common markets, followed by common product industry, create the relatedness with the most commonality (Galbraith and Kazanjian, 1986). Therefore, it is hypothesized that companies will place all profit centers serving the consumer market into one cluster. Those profit centers serving commercial end users form another cluster. Profit centers serving government and defense, producing components for original equipment manufacturers, and extracting and refining raw materials will form other clusters. Each cluster consists of a set of profit centers more related to one another than to others in the company's portfolio. Each cluster consists of a set of profit centers that share a business logic in their management.

Procter & Gamble (P&G), which serves only one market, anchors the left-hand (related) side of the continuum in Figure 1.3. Almost all of P&G's profit centers serve the consumer market. They share common customers, distribution channels, and information infrastructure and are united by a common business logic based on brand management. Since the entire company serves one market, profit centers are clustered by product industry, such as soap, food, paper, and OTC pharmaceuticals. These profit centers share common manufacturing plants, suppliers, technologies, and R&D labs. Profit centers are clustered, first by market and then by product. In this way, the greatest number of tangible resources can be shared (Porter, 1985).

A little farther to the right in Figure 1.3 is Hewlett-Packard (H-P), which serves four major markets. The first is industry-standard computer products, which are sold through distributors. The second is electronic products, sold through a direct sales force to commercial customers. Electronic products are further broken down into clusters serving submarkets for analytical chemistry, medical instruments, and electronic measurement instruments. A final breakdown of electronic measurement instruments is based on product differences. The third market is components for original equipment manufacturer (OEM) customers that are placed in a semiconductor cluster. The fourth

Figure 1.3. The Diversity Continuum.

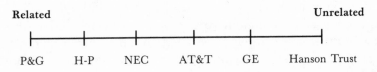

Related					Unrelated
P&G	H-P	NEC	AT&T	GE	Hanson Trust

market is computer-systems products, utilizing H-P's proprietary architecture, which are sold as systems (versus stand-alone products) to end users. The result is seven clusters of profit centers. The market diversity yields little sharing of marketing and distribution resources beyond a common H-P brand. There is considerable sharing of manufacturing and product development resources. All products consist of circuit designs and software, placed on semiconductor chips and printed circuit boards that are contained in plastic boxes. Resources and know-how can be shared in several areas, including printed circuit board fabrication and assembly, semiconducter technology and suppliers, R&D labs, and design. H-P shows some market diversity and product relatedness.

The Nippon Electric Corporation (NEC) follows a strategy of yet more market diversity while managing product and technology relatedness. Like H-P, NEC produces semiconductor components for OEMs and acts as an OEM itself while producing computers, telecommunications equipment, and other industrial electronics products for commercial markets. Also like H-P, NEC manages the relatedness of manufacturing, purchasing, technologies, R&D, and product development across profit centers (Prahalad and Hamel, 1990). The structure of NEC is also based on clusters of profit centers around markets. One cluster each has been created for the consumer market and OEM components. The industrial market is further divided by submarkets and products for computers, telecommunications, and other industrial electronics. Unlike H-P, however, NEC produces products for the consumer electronics market.

AT&T is still more diverse. Like NEC, it manufactures semiconductor components, telecommunications equipment, computers, and consumer electronics. In addition, it is a telephone company to which NEC sells products. It also has profit centers in financial services. The telephone and financial services form their own clusters.

The last diversified corporation shown in Figure 1.3 that is not a classical conglomerate is General Electric (GE). GE is the most diverse company discussed until now. Its profit centers range from raw materials markets (petroleum) to consumer products (major appliances). Its profit centers span about twenty of the twenty-six double-digit SIC codes. Some of the profit centers are clustered into such market categories as defense, consumer, and medical. Others are clustered by such product industries as chemicals, lighting, jet engines, power products, factory automation, communications, financial services, and information services. GE and AT&T are companies that fall into the mixed-strategy category. They span multiple products and markets, and their businesses are manufacturing and services, yet they are not holding companies, because they attempt to add value to their business units. They clearly represent an intermediate form.

Hanson Trust anchors the right-hand side of the scale in Figure 1.3. It buys and sells companies in any industry in which it finds undervalued assets or underperforming management. It attempts to add no value other than financial skills and resources. It is a classic conglomerate.

In summary, clustering by market and then by product appears to combine profit centers so that they have maximum likelihood of sharing resources and know-how. They are also likely to share management skills. The result should be greater relatedness between profit centers within clusters than between clusters.

Cluster Strategy and Organization

The clusters themselves vary in strategy and organization. They are actually corporations within corporations. The clusters can vary across the entire continuum shown in Table 2.1.

General Electric can serve as an example. Its clusters are called strategic business units (SBUs). They have been reduced in number, from forty-three in 1980 to about thirteen today. Some SBUs are single-business functional organizations, like the units for jet engines and major appliances. At least one is a front/back organization. The unit for medical systems presents a common front to its customers while producing x-ray equipment, CAT scanners, and magnetic-resonance products in its back ends. The aerospace and defense cluster has about twelve profit centers, collected into a related divisionalized model. The profit centers share manufacturing, procurement, information systems, and a Washington office, as well as the normal financial and human resource functions. GE Capital is a collection of financial service businesses that create a minineoconglomerate.

At Westinghouse, whatever businesses do not fit into clusters are themselves grouped into a miniature holding company. Such businesses as Seven-Up Bottling, Longines-Wittnauer watches, and Thermo King (manufacturer of refrigerated trucks and railway cars) form a cluster. Thus clusters may run the gamut from single-business, functional organizations to mini-holding companies of several unrelated businesses. The size and role of the cluster organization matches its corporate organizational equivalent. The organization of the cluster also matches its corporate equivalent.

Corporate Value-Added

The previous section described the placement of businesses requiring cross-divisional coordination into clusters. The idea was to maximize relatedness within a cluster and decentralize coordination from the corporate to the cluster level. The question that remains is, "What is left for the corporation to do?" Typical sources of value-added supplied by the corporation include the following:

- Capital resources
- Management talent
- Technology
- Leverage (buying, selling, partnering)
- Government relations
- Brand
- Banking
- Proprietary expertise

At a minimum, the corporation provides access to capital resources. Borrowing capacity is greater and borrowing costs are lower for the corporation than for its individual business units. For example, Hanson's acquisition of Beazer will greatly reduce Beazer's interest expense when its debt is refinanced at Hanson's cost of borrowing. Holding companies like Hanson Trust do not try to add value other than financing and financial expertise to their business units.

The neoconglomerate attempts to add at least two more sources of value. Westinghouse and Daimler-Benz centrally manage their key technologies and top management talent. Daimler has identified microelectronics, advanced materials, and robotics as central to all its businesses. Strategic investments and projects in these areas are centrally managed. It is as if Daimler, to create proprietary technology, has formed its own research consortium among its diverse businesses.

Westinghouse centrally manages the development, assignment, and compensation of its top 250 managers. It is its own executive recruiter and knows in detail the background, profile, and performance of its management team. The business units have access to a talent pool that would be unavailable to them as separate businesses.

These sources of value can be used in combination, to great effect. For example, Rockwell's graphics business, as a manufacturer of printing equipment for newspapers, was experiencing a strategic shift from electromechanical to digital electronic technology and from chemical imaging to color electronic imaging. As the manager of the business approached his upcoming retirement, he and the corporation agreed on a succession plan. A manager from the automotive group became the number two man at graphics for two years. The new manager was familiar with large projects and digital systems. He, in turn, brought in a chief engineer from the space shuttle program. The new engineer led the conversion to digital printing technology. The project was supported by several research efforts, conducted jointly with the corporate R&D labs and the electronics group. The new processes have been well received by the market and have achieved a worldwide market share of 50 percent. The graphics business profited from being part of the Rockwell organization by having access to management talent and digital technology.

General Electric is an example of a corporation that also tries to leverage its size in buying and selling. The central negotiation of contracts, to get buying volume and leverage, is well known. The more related the businesses, the greater the number of items on which buying volume can lead to lower costs. GE also tries to cross-sell across business units. When General Motors (GM) announced its Saturn project, GE approached GM with a package deal. GE could provide lighting for the plant and cars, plastics for construction and for the cars, the usual electrical equipment for the plant, cogenerating power equipment, a service agreement to run the cogeneration plant, factory automation equipment, project financing, and telecommunications equipment. GM could negotiate one contract and receive one bill; GE would coordinate the rest. Some companies like this "one-stop shopping."

Another corporation is coordinating its partnering activities. This effort began when the corporation became aware of a possible alliance between one of its businesses and Northern Telecom. It became aware of this possibility because a second business unit was promoting the relationship: Northern Telecom was a good customer and a partner in two alliances with the second business unit. Corporate management asked how many deals the company had with Northern. A search revealed thirteen arrangements, at various stages of development, with a number of business units. Suddenly, the transaction revealed a relationship between the companies. The next question was, "Why have a relationship with Northern? Why not AT&T or Ericson from Sweden?" At this point, the company wanted to get "out front" and choose its partners and relationships. Intelligence on partners and partnering skills is being centrally coordinated.

All these sources of leverage can be used together. As companies become suppliers, customers, partners, and competitors, the corporation can add value by leveraging its contacts, providing intelligence, and creating new opportunities. It is common now for chief executives of corporations to discuss ways of improving the "balance of trade" among their companies. Central coordination of buying, selling, and partnering can create new opportunities for the business units, opportunities that would be unavailable to them on their own. Similarly, a business unit may have to be a loss leader on a transaction. It may lose business because it is part of a larger, out-of-favor corporation. There is a chance for negative as well as positive value-added.

The positive and negative aspects of value-added also apply to government relations and to brand. Some companies are effective at establishing relationships with governments. Business units within a corporation can achieve an advantage if they wish to enter a country in which the corporation is viewed with favor. A well-known brand franchise can give a business an advantage if it shares the brand, such as Sony, GE, or Kodak. If a corporation is not viewed favorably in a country, or if a brand gets a bad reputation then a business unit will be tarred with the same brush. A centrally coordinated approach to brand and to government relations can add positive or negative value.

Corporations can also add value through their credit subsidiaries. Some companies have built virtual banks out of former credit subsidiaries. In a period of tight capital, GE Capital and IBM Credit can provide loans to customers, suppliers, and partners of business units. This credit availability adds value to business units.

Finally, the corporation can make its proprietary expertise available to business units. For related units, sharing best practices across business units in many functional areas is central to the role of the corporate functional staff. Know-how can still be shared in less related businesses. Usually, more general expertise is involved (total quality skills, just-in-time skill, and so on).

The list is endless; new forms of value are always being added. As environmental issues arise, many corporations are creating their own "green" departments. Many are also creating their own universities. Some sources of value are temporary, and others are sustainable, but the search for value to be added to businesses has replaced control as the primary purpose of corporate headquarters.

In summary, corporations are seeking many sources of value. If the businesses are not too diverse, multiple sources of value can be found. If the businesses are very diverse, little beyond finance can be shared. The amount of value-added will determine the size and role of the corporate unit and its equivalent at the cluster level. High value-adding corporations will be more centralized, have larger staffs, use less variable compensation, and transfer people across businesses. Figure 1.4 summarizes the strategy and organizational continuum. As a corporation adds less value or shifts value-adding activities to clusters of similar businesses, the staff organization gets smaller, compensation for clusters gets more variable and measurable, and employees' careers are more within the clusters. The range of strategies is increased. Alignment between strategy and organization is still required for effective performance, however.

Figure 1.4. Strategy and Organizational Continuum.

	├───────────────────────────┤		
Strategy	Related	Mixed	Unrelated
Diversity	Low		High
Value-added	High		Low
Structure	Divisional	Cluster	Holding company
Centralization	High		Low
Staff Size	Large		Small
Variable compensation	Low		High
Careers	Company	Cluster	Division

Conclusion

This chapter has presented a framework for aligning corporate strategy and organization. Corporate strategy consists of two components. The first component is the amount of diversity in the portfolio of businesses that the corporation operates. Diversity is measured by the number of business areas in which the business units compete. Some judgment is also applied, to increase diversity if different markets are served or if the businesses vary from manufacturing to services. The second component is the type and amount of value that the corporation adds to its businesses.

To some degree, these two components complement each other. More diversity means less chance for value-added, although there is some choice of value-added for any level of diversity. For example, General Electric has a set of businesses similar to but somewhat more diverse than those of Westinghouse, yet GE tries to add more value to its business units.

To add value to its businesses, the corporation needs an organization designed to accomplish its purpose. Figure 1.4 shows the framework for choosing organizational policies that align with the value-adding strategy. If the strategy can be placed in a relative position along the continuum, then the organizational policies can be estimated.

Recent business trends have been pushing companies away from pure functional, divisionalized, and holding-company models. These models are still being implemented, but a range of other models is also being used. Each type is appropriate for a different level of diversification. Because of the increased rate of change in the business environment and increased performance demands, there is every reason to believe that organizations will use a wide variety of regularly changing approaches. Gaining competitive advantage through organization requires the regular invention and adoption of new approaches.

References

Chandler, A. D., Jr. *Strategy and Structure: Chapters in the History of the American Industrial Enterprise.* Cambridge, Mass.: MIT Press, 1962.

Dundas, K.N.M., and Richardson, P. R. "Implementing the Unrelated Product Strategy." *Strategic Management Journal,* 1982, *3,* 287–301.

Galbraith, J. R. "Organization Design." In J. Lorsch (ed.), *Handbook of Organization Behavior,* Englewood Cliffs, N.J.: Prentice-Hall, 1987.

Galbraith, J. R., and Kazanjian, R. *Strategy Implementation: The Role of Structure and Process.* (2nd ed.) St. Paul, Minn.: West Publishing, 1986.

Grant, R. M., Jammine, A. and Thomas, H. "Diversity, Diversification and Profitability Among British Manufacturing Companies, 1972–1984." *Academy of Management Journal,* 1988, *31*(4), 771–801.

Jensen, M. "The Eclipse of the Public Corporation." *Harvard Business Review,* 1989, *67,* 61–74.

Kerr, J. "Diversification Strategies and Managerial Rewards: An Empirical Study." *Academy of Management Journal,* Mar. 1985, pp. 155–179.

Nathanson, D., and Cassano, J. "Organization Diversity and Performance." *Wharton Magazine,* Summer 1982, pp. 18–26.

Peters, T., and Waterman, R., Jr. *In Search of Excellence.* New York: HarperCollins, 1982.

Pitts, R. "Diversification Strategies and Organizational Policies of Large Diversified Firms." *Journal of Economics and Business,* 1976, *28,* 181–188.

Porter, M. E. *Competitive Advantage: Creating and Sustaining Superior Performance.* New York: Free Press, 1985.

Prahalad, C. K., and Hamel, G. "The Core Competence of the Corporation." *Harvard Business Review,* 1990, *68*(3), 79–93.

Rumelt, R. *Strategy, Structure and Economic Performance.* Boston: Harvard Business School Press, 1974.

Chapter Two

The Business Unit
of the Future

Jay R. Galbraith

The business unit is a basic building block of a corporation's structure. Collections of businesses make up the corporation's portfolio. It is the basic profit-and-loss center. As such, it is a strategy center to which the corporation's limited resources are allocated. This organizational building block has been evolving for some time, and in the future it is likely to take a number of different forms. This chapter describes those forms and the business forces that are driving their evolution. First, however, some background on the business-unit concept is given.

Profit-Center Building Block

The study and design of organizations has always been based on standard building blocks, or units. Until a few years ago, these units were fairly clear. Individuals were the most basic unit of analysis. They joined teams or work groups, as shown in Figure 2.1. Work groups were clustered together to form such functions as sales, marketing, distribution, manufacturing, and engineering. There were usually several levels within a function.

Figure 2.1. Organizational Building Blocks.

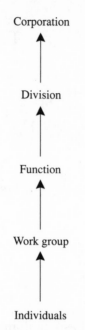

Corporation

Division

Function

Work group

Individuals

Salespeople collected in branches, which formed districts, which were clustered into regions, which formed the national sales force.

Through the process of vertical integration, these functions were linked to form a division (Chandler, 1962). The functions that were cost centers were vertically integrated into a division that was a profit center. The divisions, which varied in type and amount of vertical integration, were the basic business unit.

As companies diversified, the corporation evolved from a single-business functional organization to a multibusiness multidivisional structure. Procter & Gamble had the classic structure. Divisions were product lines, like bar soaps, packaged soaps, dentifrice, food, paper, and beverages. Each division consisted of purchasing, product development, manufacturing, advertising, sales, finance, and personnel.

Originally, size was the key to manageability. As a division reached the level of a few hundred million dollars in sales, it was split in two, to retain the advantages of a small business with access to the resources of a large corporation. At Procter

& Gamble, the soap division was split into bar soap and packaged soap (detergents). As size increased at corporations, however, the divisional structure soon got out of hand. At General Electric (GE), the department became the basic profit center. By 1970, there were over 250 departments collected into some fifty or sixty divisions, which formed about ten groups that reported to the office of the chairman, which consisted of three people. All units were profit centers.

In 1970, GE implemented the strategic business unit (SBU) structure. Size was no longer the determinant of the basic building block. Instead, the strategic business unit was to be a logical business or economic entity. A business unit had a unique set of products, customers, and competitors. It was to be fully functional and profit-measurable. It was neither a captive supplier nor a captive customer; it operated freely between input and output markets. Forty three SBUs of various sizes resulted and were implemented in 1970. The standard organization for a single business was the functional structure (Rumelt, 1974).

Today, the classic building blocks are becoming questionable. New competitive initiatives, such as total quality and competing in time, along with the new information technology, are leading to some fundamental changes in the functional organization. Indeed, the functions as power bases are in decline and are likely to continue declining. Six basic models of a business unit seem to be in existence:

- Functional unit
- Lateral unit
- Superfunctions unit
- Front-end/back-end model
- Network organization
- Functional specialist

Types of Business Units

The Functional Unit

The fully functional profit center is still very much in existence. Increasingly, however, it exists in modified form. The cost-reduction pressures of the early 1980s actually brought about a resurgence of the functional form, especially in companies where wages and salaries were a major cost component. The reason is that the functional organization allows work to be performed with the fewest number of people because it pools specialists and time-shares them. The early 1980s were a period of consolidation and head-count reduction. Companies downsized the functional organization, which was the historical structure of choice. Nevertheless, as total quality, then customer service, and now time-based competition replaced productivity as management's top concern, the defects of the functional organization began to appear. Functional careers, performance measures, information systems, and rewards created barriers to interfunctional coordination. Large functions force cross-functional decisions to be made too far from the points of action. Quality, customer service, and cycle-time reduction all reveal numerous cross-functional issues for rapid resolution and day-to-day coordination.

Some incremental changes to the functional structure, like the reduction of hierarchical levels and the use of fewer functional specialties, have helped make it more responsive. Most companies have been eliminating levels of hierarchy, to bring points of decision making closer to sources of information. This trend, facilitated by information technology, will continue. The trend to reduce specialization will also continue. BMW, for example, used to have functions for manufacturing operations, industrial engineering, process engineering, and maintenance. Today, the more routine engineering and maintenance activities have been moved into the operation's line organization and decentralized to the points of action. Fewer levels, as well as more self-contained generalist units, facilitate faster decision making and/or reduce barriers to cross-functional coordination.

The Lateral Unit

The lateral organization consists of the horizontal cross-functional processes that cross hierarchical lines. Figure 2.2 depicts, schematically, the effects of the lateral processes on the functional organization. Information, careers, and performance incentives were originally vertical, functional, and hierarchical. Today and in the future, the organization will be flatter, more lateral, and less hierarchical. It will consist of cross-functional teams dedicated to products, projects, or customers.

The lateral processes can be informal, voluntary, and spontaneous, or they can be formal and explicit, but even the informal can and will be designed and influenced by organizational designers. For example, functions working on a product or a project are increasingly co-located. The aircraft industry co-locates design engineering, process engineering, industrial engineering, purchasing, quality, assembly, and production-control functions around major sections of the aircraft (wing, tail, forward fuselage, cabin). Careers are increasingly multifunctional, and managers are more generalist. Reward systems are less functional and more flexible. All these policies are intended to reduce barriers to cross-functional communication and coordination, necessitated by quality demands or cycle-time reduction.

Figure 2.2. Hierarchical to Lateral Organization.

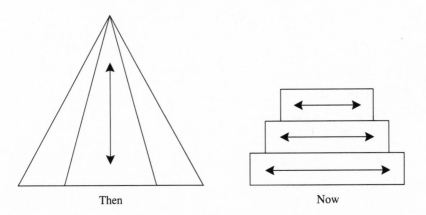

Then   Now

Structure modifications can also facilitate spontaneous, voluntary cooperation. Usually, each function is organized according to its own logic, in order to be efficient. A pet-food business has the sales function organized by geography and national accounts. Marketing is organized by brands (dog and cat). Manufacturing is organized by products (canned meat plants and dry packaged plants), engineering is organized by products and manufacturing processes, and purchasing is organized by commodity (meat, fish, grain, and so on). A customer-service or quality issue will affect all brands, all plants, and all commodities. It is impossible for a person in one function to find a counterpart in another function, short of the top team, who speaks the same language and has a matching responsibility. It is impossible to get teams around products, brands, and customers. There is no clear "line of sight" across functions.

To decentralize and work laterally, more companies are creating matching, mirror-image structures across as many functions as possible. The structure shown in Figure 2.3 illustrates the design at an aircraft manufacturer. By major section of the aircraft, there is a clear "line of sight" across all functions. An engineer making a design change can ask a counterpart in purchasing about delivery implications on a continuous basis. Spontaneous informal contacts are facilitated by this mirror-image structure.

Figure 2.3. Mirror-Image Structure.

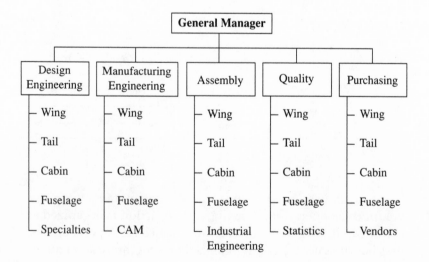

The mirror-image structure is not efficient, however. The quality function may find that there is not enough work on the wing alone to support a full-time specialist in nondestructive testing. The structure solution is like the one already described for BMW. Most of the function is placed in mirror-image groups of generalists (or groups with limited specialization). They work laterally with their mirror-image counterparts in the other functions. The rest of the function remains very specialized and is shared across mirror-image groups when expertise is needed.

In the future, there will be greater use of this generalist/specialist split in the functions. Greater numbers of people will be moving to the generalist category. The cross-functional coordination pressures of competing in time will tilt the trade-off toward the mirror-image alternative, and information technology will provide more efficient alternatives for delivering expertise. As companies accumulate expertise in data bases, this knowledge can be accessed by generalist groups anywhere in the corporation. When such expertise is combined with an interactive capability and artificial intelligence, the knowledge can be accessed by problem-solving groups everywhere. Finally, video capability will permit live demonstrations of difficult repairs and designs. "Video manuals" are already available to customer-service representatives in several company trials. Repair people can call up text, voice, and still or moving pictures to receive the needed expertise. The company-expert data base will increasingly replace the central staff expert. Expertise to update the data base will be bought outside or obtained from centers of expertise distributed around the company.

The real facilitator of spontaneous cross-functional contacts is the new information technology. Already, electronic mail (E-mail), conferencing on personal computers (PCs) and fax machines, and video conferencing can connect every person in a company with every other person. Fiberoptic networks and next-generation PCs will permit video calls from anyone to everyone. The technology removes some barriers by providing connection between people. Whether connection leads to communication and then to coordination depends on the organizational design.

For example, the newly emerging Volvo organization in
Sweden is an attempt to provide superior customer service
through a customer-driven organization. Figure 2.4 shows a
schematic of the communication flow between dealers and the
factories. Dealer organizations are being redesigned, and facilities
are being rebuilt, to support customer service. The functional,
dealer organizations are being replaced with self-managing teams
of mechanics who are dedicated to groups of frequent customers.
The customer always gets the same team, which is located in
a bay into which the customer drives directly. There is no
separate reception function; the reception function is rotated
among the group members. The purpose is to create a long-
term relationship between the customers and the mechanics.

Figure 2.4. Customer-Driven Organization.

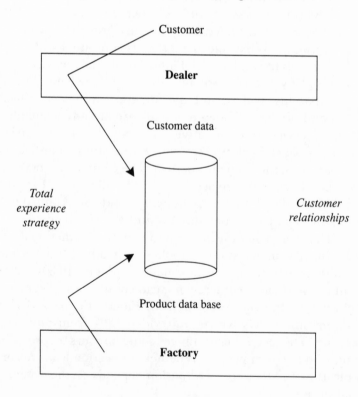

The dealers are also being assigned to specific factories. As flexible manufacturing is adopted, factories can produce all the models going to a dealer. This dedication facilitates a long-term relationship and communication links between dealers and factories. The greatest degree of dedication takes place at the new factory at Uddevalla. Self-managing work teams of ten people assemble a whole car, four at a time. To the extent that work loads can be balanced, a team or contiguous teams are dedicated to dealers. Relationships can be established between assemblers and mechanics. These groups are now directly connected by E-mail, phones, and PCs. In the future, video contacts will also be possible.

Each car will contain the photos and signatures of the assemblers. The nameplate on the car will contain their phone numbers and E-mail addresses. Mechanics and customers with questions about the car can access them directly. A data base is continuously updated with information about the car as it is designed and assembled, as well as throughout its lifetime. The total cost of the car can be accumulated. The groups can become responsible for total quality and total cost through warranty experiences.

Information about the customer and the car can be accumulated as well. Every time the customer makes a purchase or a repair, the history can be updated. The Volvo credit card can record gasoline and accessories purchases. The teams can have access to customer data and suggest the sale of parts or accessories. The customer can be contacted by the mechanics or the assemblers. The dedicated relationship and the data base facilitate communication and coordination across the self-managing teams and the customers. Informal gatherings of assemblers and mechanics, contests, and gain-sharing systems can all cement the cross-unit relationship and facilitate integration around total quality and customer service.

The role of management is significantly altered under this model. The customer becomes the "boss" who drives activity. The manager supports work teams in serving the customer, sees that teams are trained, facilitates communication, and so on.

This is often called the *internal network organization* or *upside-down structure*. It provides a good example of what is possible in the use of self-managing work teams, flexible manufacturing, and new information technology in the service of the customer. In the next ten years, there will be more of these lateral, cross-functional processes.

At higher levels of the hierarchy, there is increased use of formal teams. Managers are dedicated to product teams, in order to cut time to market, or to customer teams, in order to improve service. More people are spending more time in product, project, customer, quality, or vendor teams. It is a relatively easy transition to make mirror-image units (shown in Figure 2.3) into formal teams. The team can prepare a plan for quality and cost improvement, which would be the basis for gain sharing and team rewards. None of these organizational design issues are new (Galbraith, 1973); what is new is the facilitation provided by information technology, as already described. Teams will be increasingly location-free, giving companies the ability to connect the most appropriate people, no matter where they live and work. Again, technology provides the connection; communication and coordination come from team building, teamwork, and team incentives.

Decision making in teams is increasingly required as competition becomes time-based. Decision making is facilitated by the establishment of project or product managers, to whom considerable autonomy is delegated. Fewer operating decisions will be made by functional managers, and more will be made by project teams and project managers. The design issues of these roles are also well known (Galbraith, 1973). In summary, communication patterns, decision processes, careers, and reward systems will be increasingly horizontal. Functional organizations will still exist, to balance variable work loads, transfer best practices, serve as "homerooms," house true specialists, plan human resource policies, and acquire many of the capability-building human resource functions. The lateral organization will take on more day-to-day coordination and decision making.

The Superfunctions Unit

In recent years, a number of superfunctions or combinations of functions have appeared. In some cases, mirror-image structures and formal teams have evolved into structural changes of a more permanent nature. The new units are often collections of functions around management processes. There is usually a performance measure that acts as a superordinate goal for the unit and assists in cross-functional trade-off decisions. The purpose is to achieve better integration across a set of functions. Structural integration makes coordination easier and more permanent. Again, the coordination demands of total quality, customer service, and/or cycle-time reduction are the main driving forces.

An example is the product supply system at Procter & Gamble. It is a combination of the previously independent functions of purchasing, engineering, manufacturing, and distribution. Experts in logistics have long advocated such a function, called *materials management.* Initially, the corporate staff functions were brought under a single senior vice president. After policy integration, a product supply manager was created for each division (or, currently, *category*) manager. The four functions report to the product supply manager, rather than to the division manager. Working against a "total delivered cost" metric, the unit is reducing flow times, reducing inventories, and increasing on-time delivery and quality.

Hewlett-Packard (H-P) has started a similar change, called the product generation process. At the corporate staff level, it has combined R&D, manufacturing, and purchasing under a single vice president. With representatives from marketing and finance, H-P is busy integrating systems and information infrastructure. The corporate staff itself is experimenting with team incentives, before recommending changes for the divisions, and working to develop a metric of break-even time (BET) to measure product generation teams. The company has the goal of halving the break-even time on new products.

Other functions are being clustered around customers, to improve customer service. One company has formed a customer-service unit for each of its five largest customers. Each team consists of salespeople from different product lines, as well as people from distribution, manufacturing, information systems, and accounting. All are committed, for several years, to helping coordinate the ordering, delivery, and billing processes for these customers, so as to reduce everyone's inventory, improve the speed of product flow, reduce stockouts, speed payments, and eliminate the need for long-term forecasts. The units report to the vice president of sales.

In aerospace, Northrop has organized its advanced tactical fighter program around the twin processes of product definition and product delivery. Each is a multifunctional unit, even though product definition is engineering design–intensive and product delivery is manufacturing-intensive. Each process is judged to be relatively self-contained yet sequential. Tighter integration across functions is desired during each phase. The objectives are to design for manufacturing, in order to attain built-in quality, low-cost manufacturing, and faster time to market.

In all these examples, multiple functions are being grouped for integration at a level below that of the general manager with profit responsibility. The grouping is given a name for identity purposes and a metric to measure trade-off decisions. The unit is not just another level or a span-breaking role; very often, superfunction groupings are around products and customer segments. As such, they lend themselves to profit measurement below the level of the general manager. The creation of these quasi–profit centers, as well as more decentralization, will be the next steps in organizational evolution. The result is a bifurcated organization, described in the next section.

The Front-End/Back-End Model

The front-end/back-end (or *front/back*) model represents an organizational structure whose front end is organized around customer and/or geographical categories and whose back end is organized around products and technologies. (This structure and the forces shaping it were described in Chapter One.) The key to the success of this form of organization is the quality of the lateral integrating processes, such as new-product development. These lateral processes tie the front and the back together. A critical process is planning and budgeting, to manage joint profit-and-loss negotiations. A prior requirement is an information system that permits the assignment of costs, revenues, market share, and so on, to products and markets. The matrix in Figure 2.5 shows that there is a box for each product and market.

Figure 2.5. The Product-Market Matrix.

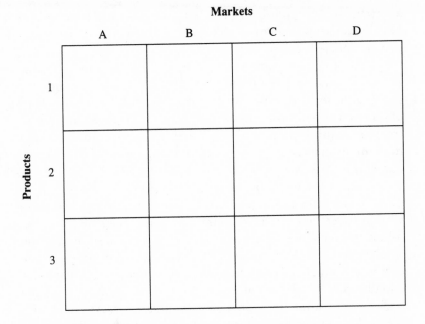

The planning process is a negotiation process whereby the front-end market manager (A) and the back-end product manager (1) jointly decide on revenues, market share, profits, and growth rates for their respective cell in the matrix. Meeting these targets becomes the joint responsibility of both the front-end manager and the back-end manager. The targets become the basis of performance measurement and rewards. At present, not many companies have the accounting systems and skill sets to manage this process, but it is critical to linking the front and the back on a profit-and-loss basis.

The time period underlying the matrix in Figure 2.5 is being compressed and becoming more event-driven. As competing in time becomes the strategic issue, companies are finding that their planning and budgeting processes are in need of redesign. Today, the product-market matrix is negotiated after several months of effort, and the next iteration takes place twelve months in the future. The budget lags badly behind reality. It either hinders or distorts actions or is ignored and useless. The trend is to keep budgets fresher by redoing portions of them as circumstances change, rather than waiting for a fixed period of calendar time to elapse. Decisions will become more event-driven and less calendar-driven.

In summary, functions are being collected into organizational units, to serve customers better on the front end and bring products to market in less time on the back end. Both of these customer and product units are profit-measurable and treated as quasi–profit-and-loss centers. The key to successful implementation is the creation and management of lateral processes that link the front and the back.

There is enormous potential for conflict in this organizational form. Inevitably, the issue arises of supplying customers with products not provided by the company's back end. As customers prefer sourcing arrangements and system solutions, the front end will seek to supply a complete line of products to the customer. The back end often cannot produce all the products equally well. The front end may want to buy products from the back end of competitors, on a private-label basis. Alternatively, the back end may want to sell, outside, the products that it does make well. Heavy investment in R&D creates the need for volume to cover fixed costs, but the customers for the product volume may be competitors to the front end. This conflict, if not managed well, can destroy the cooperation needed between the front and the back on new-product development.

A business development–type of function is emerging to mediate such conflicts. This function examines the best way to profit from a technology created by the back end and from a customer franchise created by the front end. Staffing this function is the crucial organizational design decision. Generalists are needed to balance products, technologies, and markets. Some people are permanent in the function, while others rotate on two-year assignments. These people are usually marketing types who work in customer marketing on the front end and in product marketing on the back end. These marketing "nomads" are part of the glue that holds front and back together.

The debate over selling only what the company makes and making only what it sells leads to issues of self-sufficiency. What will the company do itself, and what will it rely on others to do? In the future, more and more businesses will not be self-sufficient. These business units are adopting the network form of organization.

The Network Organization

In the past, companies preferred to have business units that were self-sufficient and fully functional. They believed that they would get better service from functions that they controlled and that were staffed with their own people. Today, companies are discovering that they cannot do everything well. They are also discovering that, in a buyer's market, they cannot afford *not* to do everything well. As a result, firms are performing only those functions that they do best and arranging for other functions to be supplied by other companies doing what they do best. The resulting collection of independent, mostly single-function companies is referred to as a *network organization* (Miles and Snow, 1986).

The network of separate functional companies is to be contrasted with the fully functional hierarchical firm. The fully functional firm is held together by common ownership of all functions and is coordinated through a hierarchy of authority. The network consists of functions that are separate companies, profit-measurable, and coordinated through mutual interests or by a focal company, which plays the role of network integrator. Network integrators create governed networks, as contrasted with loosely coupled, informal networks. The governed network is designed and maintained by the integrator. It is the model of interest in this chapter.

The network business unit is less than fully functional and plays the integrator role. It is most apparent among new, young companies like Nike, Reebok, and Apple. The older companies, like Procter & Gamble and IBM, are not vertically disaggregating their fully functional business units. Nevertheless, on new business development ventures, such as applications software, IBM is using the model by forming alliances and taking minority ownership positions in key software developers. As more companies shift their priorities from downsizing to growth and development, the model will be more frequently adopted.

There are two organizational design issues for the integrator: Which function or functions does it own and perform itself, and which one does it acquire from other firms? How does the integrator influence the decisions of separate companies so as to coordinate the business of the network?

First, the integrator usually performs the dominant functions in the value-added chain of the business. For example, in consumer products, the integrator performs the marketing function. Indeed, a Reebok or a Benetton is virtually a product management house. The product managers manage the product line positioning, new-product development, advertising, price and promotion, and the brand. In short, they do the strategic management for the network. For technology-driven industrial products, the integrator does the R&D and product engineering. If there is no dominant function, then the model may not be viable. The integrator also does the buying of key items for the network. Central buying allows the network to be large when it is good to be large (buying) and yet be small when it is good to be small (informal research teams). Benetton is the world's largest buyer of wool thread. It buys on behalf of the 250 independent textile companies that perform its weaving, cutting, knitting, and sewing functions. Similarly, it acquires the computers and textile machinery used by the independents. When buying and selling in a market, it is usually good to be big and to exercise market power for price benefits. In addition, the integrator manages the logistics function and designs the information system to support it. When the issue is competing in time, logistics and information must be managed on behalf of the network. Some firms, like Federal Express, may perform the delivery and warehouse functions; many use General Electric's telecom network to tie together retail sales, inventories, and manufacturing. In either case, management and policy setting for product flow throughout the network are performed by the integrator.

The integrator does the difficult and proprietary tasks. The designer of the product will often design the manufacturing process and the equipment simultaneously. Small, low-overhead manufacturing shops operate the equipment; they have no expertise in designing equipment. The integrator may use outside designers. If the process is proprietary, however, it may use its own designer. The integrator develops and defends the intellectual property of the network, which the other companies could not afford to do. Benetton developed an artificial intelligence program to minimize fabric waste while cutting clothes to sizes. The program runs on PCs that are leased to all its suppliers, yet these suppliers may never have heard of artificial intelligence, let alone developed a program based on it. Thus the integrator takes on functions where size is an advantage; manages work flow and information throughout the network; manages the brand, product design, and development; does what is difficult and proprietary; and assumes responsibility for the effectiveness of the network as a whole. The integrator does not squeeze pennies out of suppliers; instead, the integrator wants them to make money. The network as a whole competes with other networks. The integrator's interest is in building and maintaining a healthy collection of suppliers and distributors. Even though the integrator does not own the firms it behaves as if it does.

Second, how does the integrator influence the independent companies in the network? In general, the integrator builds a power base but works from the mutual interest of the collection. The integrator builds trust and relationships among the members, but there is still the conflict of dividing margins among the members. Even in single companies, conflicts over cross-selling and transfer prices weaken cooperation among functions.

In the network organization, all these issues must be negotiated, but they are negotiated in the context of the overall goal of network effectiveness.

The power base from which the integrator operates has several sources. Often the integrator is the largest unit in the network and has buying and selling power within the network. The integrator usually performs the dominant function or functions in the business. By performing the marketing function, Reebok dominates its network the way brand managers dominate at Procter & Gamble. The performance of design engineering allows Apple to dominate in the same way that Hewlett-Packard is dominated by its engineers. To the extent that the integrator can solve the difficult problems, value is delivered to the other companies. The faster information and payments move through the network, the lower everyone's working capital is. The more value the integrator can create, the more powerful a negotiator it is. The integrator also performs the banking function for the network. Through credit, leasing, factoring, and other financial service subsidiaries, the integrator holds the network together. The credit subsidiaries make money, but they also play roles in network maintenance. Why should a manufacturer invest in a machine that can only make sweaters for Benetton? To overcome reluctance, Benetton's leasing subsidiary buys the machine and leases it to the manufacturer. With deregulation occurring in financial markets, the credit function is increasingly performed by credit subsidiaries of companies. These subsidiaries are to be profitable, but they are also to help build and maintain a competitive network of firms around the integrator. The integrator, in some senses, has moved from being the owner of the network units to being the banker of the network. Finally, the integrator often creates and maintains the information network of the organizational network. From point-of-sale cash registers to warehouses to the various stages of manufacturing, the fashion houses connect all units electronically. They speed the flow of information from one point in the logistics chain to the others. Often, the integrator has its own network, which all units plug in to for transactions. When combined with financial services, the integrator runs the payment systems for the network, to minimize total working capital and speed cash flow.

The integrator plays the role of systems integrator for the network. Each unit is a separate company, doing what it does best. Some are low-cost, low-overhead units; others are professional units with cultures, salaries, policies, sabbaticals, and organizations specifically designed for professionals. Each unit is owned by its managers, which provides ownership motivation. The main cost of this form of organization is the constant communication and negotiation among units.

The Functional Specialist

The functional specialist concentrates on a single function, or on a few functions and networks with other firms to complete the business, but it does not perform the network integration just described. Instead, the specialist invests in expertise and scale in the function, participating in networks that are often less managed.

A number of specialists exist in the high-technology area. Biotechnology firms like Genentech and Cetus, and semiconductor firms like Chips and Technologies, are research "boutiques" and product design houses. SCI has concentrated on printed circuit board design and manufacturing. Beginning with the contract for printed circuit boards for the IBM personal computer, SCI has kept that volume and acquired the manufacturing from other firms, like Chips and Technologies, which concentrate only on product design.

The company, like the network integrator, benefits from having an organization specifically designed for the competitive advantage it possesses. SCI is designed to be absolutely low-cost. It locates in low-wage areas, has minimal overheads, emphasizes scale and automation, and is run by experienced manufacturing executives. The design houses have compensation and benefit packages designed explicitly for professionals. The high-technology units also benefit from patents, licenses, and intellectual property, which can be sold worldwide. They are also experimenting with pricing schemes that allow them to secure more profit without vertically integrating farther down the value-added chain to the customer. Cetus has invented a process that can be useful in creating new pharmaceuticals. It has formed a joint venture with Perkin-Elmer to manufacture an instrument that pharmaceutical houses can use to invent new compounds. The instrument is reasonably priced, to encourage widespread use, but Cetus wants 10 percent of the royalties from all drugs commercialized from the use of the instrument. In this way, Cetus can profit from its intellectual property without vertically integrating into other functions.

Many single-function businesses are start-ups and stand-alone companies. As corporations downsize, consolidate, and restructure, however, they are seeking outside revenue for some of the functions that are scale-intensive. The outside revenue converts the functions from cost centers to profit centers. At some point, usually when outside revenue exceeds inside, they become business units whose task is to earn a profit. Banks have always used their computer departments to do data processing for other financial institutions. Semiconductor firms try to keep their silicon fabrication units fully loaded by becoming foundries to custom chip designers. The competitive pressures of the 1990s are forcing firms to profit from what they do best. These computer departments and foundries will become full-fledged business units, rather than sources of a little outside income. They will be profit-measurable and responsible, not just captive internal suppliers or customers.

The functional subcontractor role has always existed. In aerospace, there were second- and third-tier subcontractors that supplied systems integrators like Boeing and McDonnell Douglas. Second-tier often meant second-rate; in the future, the functional specialists will be first-rate. They will make themselves an attractive "buy" alternative in the make-buy decision. They will concentrate on functions where expertise and scale are important. They will be low-cost and flexible to do business with. They will be independent businesses, not internal monopolies.

Competitive pressures are forcing all companies to search, internally and externally, for lowest-cost and best-value suppliers. The trends toward sourcing and network integration provide many of the advantages of vertical integration, without the ownership costs and risks. Ownership also results in the extension of an ill-fitting business culture to a functional specialist.

The number of small firms seeking scale-intensive partners is increasing. Developers now create giant automated warehouses in key commercial centers. Many small companies get access to these giants and are billed monthly for as much space as they have used that month. Functional specialists are also learning to use pricing schemes, like licenses, to profit from their expertise. Rather than just receiving a fee for service, distributor specialists now share in the benefits of providing superior service and inventory levels. They participate in the profits of the industry, without vertically integrating. The internal or external functional specialist is also a partial offset to the decline of functions within product or market business units. All these factors are causing companies to choose sourcing from functional specialists more often.

Conclusion

The business unit—the basic profit-center building block of corporation and industry structures—is evolving from a fully functional division to five different forms. The *lateral functional form* is flatter, more lateral, and more general. Team overlays and mirror-image departments are often combined to form a *super-functions unit,* which is given a name and a metric for combining a group of functions below the level of the general manager. When the metric becomes profit and the business unit experiences buyer power, systems integration demands, and opportunities for cross-selling, the *front-end/back-end model* may emerge. As a company buys more functional activities to get the best value, functions themselves become increasingly profit measurable. Then two types of business units that are less than fully functional may be used. The *network integrator model* is being played out by such firms as Nike, Reebok, the Limited, and Benetton, which perform the marketing function and provide strategic management for a network of independent firms. They design the information and logistics systems for the entire network's benefit as well as their own, and often they provide banking and financial services to other members. The *functional specialist* remains expert in its specialty, becoming a world-class professional and growing globally, rather than waiting to become a major player by integrating vertically. Many specialists are new firms such as biotechnology companies, but many older firms facing consolidation in Europe and elsewhere are choosing to keep functions in which they are superior and make them into business units.

This evolution is being driven by the strategic initiatives of total quality, total customer service, and time-based competition. Such initiatives expose the weaknesses of the functional organization, since they require many multifunctional responses and trade-offs. Increasingly, the new information will allow greater cross-functional communication and integration, permitting this evolution to continue. Finally, the trends toward systems integration, buyer power, sourcing, and deregulation of financial services will drive new forms of business units to appear.

Current business forces favor integration versus specialization in the trade-off choice. In addition, information technology and functional specialists present alternatives that permit integration and specialization. In all cases, however, there will be a major problem in moving from the current (and dominant) functional form to any of the newer forms. The newer forms are most likely to be found in start-up operations, creating new business both inside and outside current corporations.

References

Chandler, A. D., Jr. *Strategy and Structure: Chapters in the History of the American Industrial Enterprise.* Cambridge, Mass.: MIT Press, 1962.

Galbraith, J. R. *Designing Complex Organizations.* Reading, Mass.: Addison-Wesley, 1973.

Miles, R. E., and Snow, C. "Organizations: New Concepts for New Forms." *California Management Review,* 1986, *28,* 62–73.

Rumelt, R. *Strategy, Structure and Economic Performance.* Boston: Harvard Business School Press, 1974.

Chapter Three

New Roles for the Staff: Strategic Support and Services

Edward E. Lawler III
Jay R. Galbraith

The pressure for change that is being felt throughout organizations points to a number of new directions that the staff functions in organizations need to take. As organizations redefine and reinvent themselves in order to cope with global competition, staff organizations must also change. Indeed, they probably have to change more than the line part of most organizations. The reason for this is simple: staffs have been uniquely structured to operate in a particular type of business environment and to support particular organizational structures. As the earlier chapters have pointed out, the business environment has changed, and the structures have changed as well.

Factors Affecting Change

Major factors shaping the new staff roles include the following:

- The changing nature of organizational control
- The strategic initiatives (cost-effectiveness, quality, customer service, and time-based competition) resulting from global competition

- The universal availability of information and computing power

The continual development of these factors calls for converting control-oriented staff specialists who administer internal monopolies into businesspeople who competitively deliver strategic services that add value to the businesses. This chapter discusses each of the factors and then considers the shape of the staff of the future.

Changing Nature of Organizational Control

When bureaucratic control is replaced by customer control, peer control, and automated formal controls, the need for control oriented staff units is greatly reduced. For example, according to a worker in a factory where the accounting and manufacturing processes are computerized, "With this new technology it is easier for operators to take on a managerial role because we have more data. There are data every few seconds on everything that is going on. Plus, managers don't have to be standing guard over you to find out what's happening. They can come back in 10 days and, from the computer, they can see everything that happened. This eliminates the middleman" (Zuboff, 1988, p. 265). In some cases, the control function has been transferred to customers and peers; in others, computerization of the information flow has automated the formal control system.

Strategic Initiatives

The forces of global competition have caused companies to substantially improve their costs, quality, and customer responsiveness. These improvement efforts have led to the establishment of strategic initiatives throughout companies for cost-effectiveness, total quality, customer service, and time-based competition.

Cost-Competitiveness. When an organization seeks competitive advantage through cost-effectiveness, the implications for all parts of the organization are profound. Each cost must be analyzed and examined from a cost-benefit perspective, and decisions must be made about whether it is justified. As more and more competitors come into many markets, there is every reason to believe that cost pressures will continue to escalate. Indeed, there seems to be an unlimited number of countries with potentially lower labor costs than in the industrialized countries. As a result, the decades ahead promise constant pressure on costs, particularly in organizations competing in global manufacturing.

Since staff organizations typically produce no products and directly offer no services, they are inevitably an overhead function and subject to challenges about the value that they add to organizations and about the costs associated with operating them. The new activity-based costing systems are designed to segment overhead costs into their elements (Cooper and Kaplan, 1991). These overhead elements can then become targets for cost reduction. Staff costs will be more identifiable and negotiable.

Overall, staff units are and will continue to be under relentless pressure for cost improvement. Global cost competition, the rising proportion of costs attributed to overhead, and the increased visibility of overhead cost components are responsible.

Speed. The emphasis on speed has important implications for any staff organization. To bring about quick organizational responses and to support the kind of organizational flexibility that is needed to produce it the staff organization needs to be restructured. Often staff groups have focused on protecting the organization from making mistakes. In a fast-changing global business, however, overanalysis and slow decision making can be as damaging as making incorrect decisions. A quick, adaptive, and flexible organization can often overcome mistakes by making midcourse corrections and adjustments (Mohrman and Cummings, 1989). On the other hand, if an organization does not act at all, it cannot learn from its mistakes and, ultimately, may fall so far behind that it is no longer a competitor in the game (Stalk and Hout, 1990).

Quality of Products and Services. Although many staff organizations are insulated from direct contact with products and customers, their roles, nevertheless, are critical in helping an organization achieve competitive advantage through high-quality performance. They support the line organization, and as a result, how well they perform shows up in the ultimate quality of the products and services an organization offers. In many respects, staff units are a service organization to the line units and are subject to demands from the line for higher-quality service and better customer relations. Thus, as the line operations of organizations perfect and develop their own concepts of how to deliver high-quality products and services, it is reasonable that they will in turn expect and demand high-quality service from the staff (Bowen and Lawler, 1992).

Universal Information and Computing Power

Staff work is essentially the handling of information, and new information technologies can radically alter how and where that work gets performed. As we have noted, many control processes can be automated (performance, for example, can be monitored with statistical sampling and post hoc audits), and the distributed organization is facilitated by modern telecommunications. Organizational activities of all types are becoming more location-free. Experts of all types can be available anytime and anywhere. Manufacturing firms can locate many small, flexible plants close to the customer for just-in-time delivery, without having a staff overhead structure at each one. Services can be provided via telecom from "source" plants.

Many staff units are providers of expertise. The coming widespread availability of multimedia workstations, interactive compact discs, relational data bases, and fiberoptic transmission makes the automated delivery of expertise very practical. More and cheaper computing power and memory make even crude versions of expert systems a reality. If even some of the forecast promises for "artificial intelligence" and "artificial realities" are realized, staff expertise can be at least partially automated and made universally available. Automation probably means fewer staff members and will certainly alter the role of those who remain.

Role of the New Staff

The new staff organization actually represents a return to the old staff role. Early writers featured the staff as providing advice and service to the line organization, which was responsible for the conduct of the business (Fayol, 1949). It added value by being a supportive business partner. Business pressures are now causing a return to the classic staff role.

Strategic Support, Expertise, and Service

The factors mentioned in the first part of this chapter are pushing staff units out of a control position and into one of providing strategic support, expertise, and service at high levels of quality. Decisions need to be made quickly by responsible employees at the point of customer or product contact. Staff groups have to be in a strategic support role in which they provide information and expertise to actual decision makers.

Critical to the success of any employee involvement activity is empowering individuals close to the customer or product to make decisions and be responsible for the success of the business. For this to happen effectively, individuals have to be knowledgeable about the business, must have considerable information about the business, and, of course, must have the power to act. If these components are to fall into place, the staff organization must be a major supporter of employee involvement. In many cases, staff employees possess the expertise that individuals need to gain (or at least need access to) in order to be effective decision makers. In addition, staff employees often need to provide information, so that empowered employees will be able to make good business decisions.

Historically, staff organizations have been asked to develop decision rules, to control the actions of the line organization. With the complexities and rapid change that exist in the environment, it is impossible for even the best staff organization to anticipate all the possible scenarios and prepare appropriate decision rules; inevitably, situations will appear that cannot be programmed and that require an effective on-line decision to be made. This, too, argues strongly for putting the staff organization into the role of providing information and advice that will help the line organization make these decisions, rather than providing rules, regulations, and constrictions that dictate decision making by the line organization.

The automation of routine control and expertise dissemination frees up the staff units for exceptions requiring policy changes and longer-run strategic considerations. The staff units are being freed up just when they are needed in the strategy-making process. Far Eastern competitors try to win by changing the rules of the game (Hamel and Prahalad, 1989). A competitive advantage will not last very long. As a result, a lot more strategy-making activity is taking place.

Each staff area also has its own peculiar strategic challenges. The global, deregulated financial markets have given rise to the "value-adding CFO" (Willigan, 1990). As more value-added derives from the technology, design, and talent embodied in a product (rather than derived from its direct labor or material content), intellectual property becomes an asset. As a result, the legal department becomes a member of the management strategy team. One company plans its litigation strategy as it plans its business strategy. As core skills and skill shortages (Prahalad and Hamel,, 1990; Irwin and Michaels, 1989) determine competitiveness, the human resource function becomes a partner in strategizing.

The green movement and the rising interest in "political advantage" (Choate, 1990) create a need for expertise in external affairs. The strategic challenges to which staff units can contribute are abundant. These issues are too important to have staff units second-guessing and duplicating the line organization's activity.

Support for the shift of the staff role to one of advice and service also comes from the quality movement. Total quality emphasizes that everyone has a customer. For the staff, the customer is the line organization. The model of the staff organization as a service company supplying the line is evolving in a number of companies. In human resource management, for example, the line organization is now being asked to assess its satisfaction with the various services offered by the staff organization (Ellig, 1989). This process has the desirable effect of giving feedback to the staff organization while allowing the line organization to have influence over the behavior of the staff. Where problems with customer satisfaction occur, this process can also be used to trigger a quality analysis of the services offered by the staff. Problem-solving groups can be set up, and work processes can be analyzed and improved. This has the very desirable effect of putting pressure on the staff to improve its performance and creating greater accountability on the part of the staff functions.

Corporations must show how and why businesses are more valuable under their corporate umbrella than as stand-alone companies. To do so, corporations must add value to the businesses. With every activity coming under scrutiny from a cost-effectiveness perspective, corporate staffs are having to demonstrate how they add value. One way to add value to a business is to give it access to the unique expertise of the larger corporate entity. This expertise must be maintained and delivered at a reasonable cost and in a manner that shows an understanding of the business. The staff organization needs to build the expertise that uniquely adds value, place it in a data base, and devise user-friendly ways to deliver it.

In summary, staff units need to move away from a control orientation to one of strategic support and expert service. Decision-making activities must be moved to the point of customer and product contact in order to achieve speed, quality, customer service, and employee commitment. Staffs need to turn over control activities to self-managing groups controlled by customers and/or by line employees. Other controls can be automated. Staffs need to deliver expertise to help these decision makers realize customer satisfaction on a timely basis. Staff time needs to be redirected toward building the expertise to be delivered and toward strategy making. Staffs should have plenty of strategic challenges on which to work with top management. The resulting strategies need to be communicated to the line organization's decision makers.

Orchestrating Change

The staff role of strategic support and expert service assumes that customers demand these services. In many cases, there are decision makers who need and request functional expertise and information. In other cases, the staff and top management may perceive a need for change before decision makers make such requests. Indeed, one of the roles of the staff is to look farther ahead than day-to-day line activity permits. Staff people should have the opportunity to look out from the corporate "crow's nest" at the future. They then have the luxury of time to determine the significance of coming events for the company and what can be done about them. Sometimes temporary staff groups can be used to deal with them or slots for vice presidents of productivity, quality, energy, or environment can be created.

When successful, these groups see their role as providing expert service. Along with top management, they help create a sense of urgency for change. They survey best practices inside and outside the company. They build on successes already under way. They fund demonstration projects, link people with common interests, provide outside speakers and consultants, appear on management agendas, spread best practices, create training materials, support local efforts, and keep management informed of progress. They seek out opportunities to give credit and rewards. In general, they orchestrate a change process in concert with line management.

The successful orchestration of change is a real source of potential value-added. Businesses are more valuable under a corporate umbrella, rather than as stand-alone companies, when staff groups keep them one step ahead of the competition. Orchestration of change is often the greatest source of unrealized potential, and some of the blame lies with staff groups themselves. Staff people often become "gurus" of particular activities. They discover the "best" way to perform a function; top management's support become imposing the "best" way on all divisions. Staffs then monitor, to see that policy execution takes place. In this manner, the best intentions of a value-added service are subverted into a control orientation. Value-added must come from orchestration, not from imposition.

Partnering and Teaming

Another source of value-added is the identification of opportunities for cross–business unit partnering, sharing of information and resources, and coordination. From their corporate perspective, staff units often can perceive these opportunities. In the past, business units in U.S. companies have been reluctant to work with sister business units, but competitive pressures have made external and internal partnering more acceptable. Internal partnering is an advantage that Japanese companies have used effectively. Corporate management is working to create more cooperative climates and incentives in the value-adding corporation. Staff units can identify opportunities, create awareness, set up networks, introduce people, fund projects, and offer support when it is needed. These opportunities will arise more frequently as deregulation, globalization, and technology continue to change. Industry structures are changing, and partnerships of all kinds are possible and advantageous. Corporations cannot ignore these opportunities. Increasingly, they will become an important opportunity for staff groups to provide service.

In summary, the new role of the staff organization should be one of strategic support, expert service, and change orchestration. There is a decline in the need for traditional control activities and an increase in the need for strategy making, expertise building and dissemination, opportunity sensing, and change orchestration. From the perspective of cost and speed, companies cannot afford a checking, reviewing, and second-guessing superstructure, but companies cannot do without strategic support and expertise from people who know the business. In this way, the new staff role will represent a return to the original role for staff.

Staff Structure and Process

The new staff roles will be administered through a different structure and a different management process. Many staff units will be decentralized to the business units, as described in Chapter One. More of the staff work will be contracted out, and the remaining corporate staff will be much smaller. Exactly what gets decentralized, what gets contracted out, what services should be delivered to the business, and what those services cost will be governed by a contracting process between the business units and the staff units. Finally, there will be greater use of cross–staff-unit teams devoted to management processes.

Business units will take on more of the staff-level policy making in order to compete more effectively in their industries. Therefore, it is important that staffs know the businesses and the relationship of their specialties to the businesses (Schulz, 1990). If a staff organization is to become a service provider to its customers in the line organization, it is logical to locate the staff close to its customer.

Distributed Staff

Chapter One described the emergence of a value-adding, distributed corporate structure. Staff units are directly affected by this trend. For companies that operate under a divisionalized structure, the change is to a more decentralized one. To be competitive in its own industry, the business unit will have to differentiate itself from other business units in the corporation. Hence, it will be more decentralized and will show more policy differentiation than typically exists in the classic divisionalized structure. For a company that has operated as a conglomerate, the staff will remain decentralized, but new staffs may be added. These will be more strategically active in areas where there is potential value-added from the corporation. In both cases, staff units will be under pressure to show value-added to the business units.

The distributed corporation arises when corporate missions and activities are distributed to "lead divisions" or "centers of responsibility" throughout the company. Originally, all expert strategic and policy-making activities were located in the country of ownership and at corporate headquarters. In the future, an activity will increasingly take place at the most effective location in the world. Instead of purchasing at headquarters, the business unit with the most expertise will buy for everyone. In this way, staff activities will be distributed to the division or subsidiary best able to perform the activity. These distributed activities will still be funded and staffed by the corporation.

Locating the staff organization at the business level also

creates a possibility for strong business teams, which share much of the responsibility for managing the business. The business-team approach in turn creates the potential for staff employees to become intimately involved in understanding and contributing to the operations of the particular business. This should allow them to provide the kind of ongoing strategic direction and support that the particular business needs — in essence, to become true business partners. Decision making can be faster when expertise is located in the business and shares the same sense of urgency.

A possible evolution of the team model could be toward self-managing business management teams. If these teams followed the same model that has been used in production areas, they could involve considerable cross-training and substantially blur the lines between line and staff managers. There might still be a differentiation between line work and staff work, but individuals need not necessarily be classified as line managers or staff managers. According to their expertise and the particular activity to be accomplished, individuals could be simultaneously doing some staff work and some line work or, over time, could rotate from what is essentially line work to what is essentially staff work. This approach has the obvious advantage of allowing individuals to continue developing and understanding the business, and it locates staff services where they are often needed most — in the groups that actually control and run particular business units.

Contracting Out

Several factors are encouraging companies to contract out for staff expertise. Companies are realizing that while they cannot do everything well, they must in order to be competitive. Therefore, they do only what they do well and buy what others do well. This trend is significant for staff units because there is an external competitor for every staff activity. Consultants, data-processing firms, and a host of others can do what staff groups do. This raises the possibility of contracting out many or most staff activities. Legal, accounting, and payroll services are examples of staff activities that can be and are increasingly being contracted to outside vendors specializing in those activities. Because of this specialization, vendors may be able to do this work better and at a lower cost. Of course, contracting out does not necessarily mean that all internal expertise is eliminated; at least some may be needed in order to direct suppliers and evaluate their work.

The extensive use of benchmarking can provide measures for judging the "make" or "buy" decision for staffs. Companies may also want their staffs to compete for business and to dismantle internal monopolies. The possibility of competition can help convert staffs from controlling monopolies to more service-oriented providers of high-quality, timely expertise.

Once the staff group has been moved from focusing on functional control activities to providing primarily strategic guidance and information, its work load may vary considerably from time to time. One of the characteristics of strategic analysis and planning is that it may not represent a demand that is constant throughout the business cycles that an organization faces. At times, there is a need for additional help in analyzing new business areas, new products, new markets, and so on; at other times, there may be little need for this kind of analytical work. This suggests that the staff organization has to be not only lean but also flexible. There is an obvious and potentially effective way to make the staff organization very flexible. It is to rely heavily on temporary consulting help to carry out large analytical and strategic activities.

Consultants have several advantages over inside staff experts. Typically, consultants have experience across a number of companies and can bring a broader perspective to issues. They can also devote virtually their full time to an analysis, because they do not have to worry so much about internal organizational issues and career issues. Perhaps most important, they are easily hired and easily dismissed when the work is not going well or has been completed. They do not represent a fixed cost in the same way that an internal staff group does. The advantages that consultants have over internal staff groups argue strongly for the idea that they will be an increasingly popular way to get staff work done during the next decade.

The advantage of using consultants raises the issue of whether all staff work can actually be contracted out. In a few extreme cases, it may be true that most of it can. It is probably better, however, for the organization to maintain key experts in each functional area. In the absence of internal staff expertise, organizations may have trouble knowing how to utilize consulting help effectively and may have trouble recognizing what is good help. The model that makes the most sense is the one in which extensive use is made of external resources, to get particular projects done, but in which high-level experts are also permanently positioned in the organization. In human resources, for example, it makes sense to use compensation consulting firms to do much of the strategic design and analysis associated with compensation, but it still makes sense for an organization to have a few high-level compensation experts on its own staff. They are needed not only to keep the consulting activities honest but also to provide continuity and help with effective utilization of the outside resources. They can also offer a particular understanding of the organization, its culture, and its business. They can add value to many projects because they can bring a different and important perspective. They are also usually needed for implementation and ongoing support.

Lean Structure

A number of factors suggest a reduction in the number of people on corporate staffs. Cost pressures, which most organizations face, clearly encourage relatively lean staffing levels in all areas. In many businesses, labor remains a major cost, particularly when an organization operates in high-wage countries. This in itself argues that the staff organization should be lean, since it is one part of the organization that does not directly add value to the product or to services, and staff employees often command relatively high salaries.

The argument for a lean staff organization goes beyond salary costs, however. Staff organizations may create work that has to be done by individuals who actually are in the position of adding value to the organization's products or services. Each staff person, in a sense, should therefore be seen as representing a double cost: the cost of employing that person, and the cost associated with the work that he or she creates for others to do.

Many of the factors already discussed should reduce the need for staff employees. Automation of the control function, information processing, and routine expertise delivery will further reduce the numbers. To determine how many staff people will be needed and where they will be located, companies can employ a continuous contracting process.

Contracting Process

In many companies, the business units prepare five-year plans and annual operating budgets. The staff units review these plans and critique and approve activities in their functional areas. Staff units also need to prepare business plans and reach contracts with their organizations. These plans should cover the services that will be provided to the business units and state the costs. A staff business plan should be reviewed and critiqued by the business units, and differences should be negotiated. A contract for services is the end result.

The contracting process is a discussion clarifying what services will be provided at what quality levels and at what cost. The benchmarking process and new accounting systems can provide valuable data for this discussion. In addition, the discussion should address how best to provide the service. Is it best to deliver the service from the corporate level or from within the business unit? Should the service be purchased from outside? Is the service needed at all? In this manner, the size, the task, and the location of the staff are continuously examined. Companies often study the effectiveness of their corporate staffs every few years, using internal task forces or consulting firms. These studies usually arise because of the natural tendency for staffs to grow and add to their numbers. The contracting process is an ongoing discussion, meant to replace these intense periodic studies.

There are several benefits of the contracting process. First, the process forces a dialogue that is long overdue. Business units are rarely aware of all the services available from staff units, and staff units do not always receive feedback from their customers. The process sorts out and clarifies expectations. Second, the process makes the staff compete for business and earn the right to serve the line in a quality manner. Third, the process sets service levels and budgets for which the staffs can be accountable. Finally, the process implements the transition to the "new" staff organization. It introduces the staff to service of the line at cost-effective levels. It introduces benchmarking and competing with outside vendors. It forces the staff to justify its activities in the same way the business unit does.

As in any other change process, the first few times through the contracting process are likely to be contentious and time-consuming. Corporate management must participate and keep discussions at a responsible level. Business units may overreact and ask for unreasonable cutbacks. Outside vendors may overpromise in order to get the business. Some ground rules may have to be set up — for example, to use the data center for the next three years. This rule may make sense: if two business units go outside for a data center's services, the overhead for others goes up. During the transition, some internal monopolies may need protection. Eventually, the process will become institutionalized. It will become a process by which organizations constantly ask the value-added question about whether staff groups are appropriately sized and positioned in a competitive economic environment that demands fast responsiveness and low cost.

Use of Teams

Work teams are becoming increasingly common in many corporations (Lawler, Mohrman, and Ledford, 1992). They have been particularly popular in manufacturing, where they seem to be effective substitutes for hierarchy and to be consistent with an emphasis on speed, quality, and customer service. Many of the same reasons that have led to the use of teams in manufacturing should lead to their use in staff organizations. In some cases, teams represent a good structural response to the performance demands that staff organizations face.

Teams offer a way of organizing around customers and/or processes, a way that can break down some of the functional boundaries that now separate parts of the staff organization (Hammer, 1990). This in turn can lead to high-quality customer service and to lower costs. For example, teams can be created to manage areas (such as employee benefits) where different customers can be identified and a critical service must be delivered. Staff members can be chosen from different areas of expertise (accounting, legal, personnel) and formed into staff teams responsible for delivery of services. Teams are the natural units to use in a contracting process, since teams can be held responsible for costs, quality, and speed.

Careers

The type of staff role that has been described so far suggests that careers in staff work may be quite different in the future. Historically, many large organizations have had individuals who did nothing but staff work throughout their entire careers. They started at the bottom of the staff organization and over time worked their way up the hierarchy. For many, a career meant moving up a staff-function management ladder; for others, it meant becoming more and more technically knowledgeable in particular areas of expertise. In a sense, many staff individuals ended up more cosmopolitan than local in orientation. They knew more about their staff functions and identified more with professionals in those functions than with the businesses and organizations for which they worked. If they left their companies, they typically moved to other large companies in the same staff functions, or perhaps to consulting firms.

In the future, organizations will not need as many individuals who make their careers in staff functions. As noted earlier, there will still be a need for some high-level functional experts in most staff organizations. If consulting firms are used to provide much of this expertise, however, then opportunities for careers as high-level staff experts will be severely restricted. What may become much more common are careers in which individuals spend time both in line and in staff positions within large organizations. Career moves from line to staff, and from staff to line, make much more sense when the staff organization is conceived of as providing customer service. It is crucial to understand what the customer is doing and to be able to put oneself in the customer's place. One way of enabling staff employees to do so is to have them perform a customer role for a period of time. Similarly, one way to help line personnel understand how they can effectively utilize the resources of the staff is to put them in staff positions for a while.

This type of career mobility also makes sense in the context of a world where management layers and levels are being reduced. Level reduction means that fewer upward moves are possible for individuals, and it creates the real danger that individuals will stagnate in their learning and development. Opening the possibility for horizontal moves from line to staff, and vice versa, is one way of reducing the stagnation that can occur in a flattened hierarchy.

Such movement is a potentially useful way of helping staff people get increasingly involved in and committed to the particular business that an organization is in. In the absence of this kind of experience, it can be hard to get staff employees to feel a sense of ownership and commitment to the business. A related problem is getting them to understand the business enough so that they can provide the kind of staff support that the business requires. Time after time, data suggest that staff groups in such areas as human resources are not involved in strategic decision making (Lawler, 1988; Towers Perrin, 1992). A common explanation is that they do not understand the business well enough to contribute to strategic decision making. This may be true if their careers have been totally within the staff organization. The best way to solve this problem is to have staff employees spend time in line management positions.

Moving a line manager to a staff function has the potential advantage of helping to transfer some staff skills to the line organization. As noted earlier, this can have a particularly big payoff if the organization is moving toward a team-based management model. It can help create teams that are self-managing and, in some respects, self-supporting. Particularly if they can be provided with the information technology that will allow them to access the expertise they do not have, they can be substantially self-managing.

Conclusion

The business environment is changing dramatically, and the role of staffs in organizations also appears to be on the verge of dramatic change. The changes include an orientation toward customer satisfaction and quality, a more strategic role, and, ultimately, perhaps a staff organization that is represented not so much by individuals as by particular tasks performed by a variety of individuals who are part of the business unit. The actual evolution of the staff for any particular organization will be determined by the type of business that the organization is in and by the demands that it faces. Nevertheless, it seems safe to conclude that the old ways are going to disappear in most organizations.

The reality is that most organizations simply cannot afford large, centralized staff groups that have high levels of expertise in particular areas. They particularly cannot afford them if the staff groups become insulated from the business, fail to look critically at the value they add to the business, and are not responsive to business needs.

The creation of a world in which staff organizations are flexible and integrated into the business units will require many changes. Such things as the movement of staff groups closer to the business, careers that involve movement between staff and line positions, the extensive use of information technology, and the skillful use of external resources and consulting firms will be necessary. The combined effects of these changes can support a new approach to organizing.

References

Bowen, D. E., and Lawler, E. E., III. "Total Quality–Oriented Human Resources Management." *Organizational Dynamics,* 1992, *20*(4), 29–41.

Choate, P. "Political Advantage: Japanese Campaign for America." *Harvard Business Review,* 1990, *68*(5), 87–104.

Cooper, R., and Kaplan, R. "Profit Priorities from Activities-Based Costing." *Harvard Business Review,* 1991, *69*(3), 130–137.

Ellig, B. R. "Improving Effectiveness Through a Human Resources Review." *Personnel,* 1989, *66*(6), 57–64.

Fayol, H. *Industrial and General Administration.* London: Pitman and Sons, 1949.

Hamel, G., and Prahalad, C. K. "Strategic Intent." *Harvard Business Review,* 1989, *67*(3), 63–76.

Hammer, M. "Reengineering Work: Don't Automate, Obliterate." *Harvard Business Review,* 1990, *68*(4), 104–113.

Irwin, R. A., and Michaels, E. G., III "Core Skills: Doing the Right Thing." *McKinsey Quarterly,* 1989, *25*(3), 4–19.

Lawler, E. E., III. "Human Resources Management: Meeting the New Challenges." *Personnel,* 1988, *65,* 22–27.

Lawler, E. E., III, Mohrman, S. A., and Ledford, G. E., Jr. *Employee Involvement and Total Quality Management: Practices and Results in Fortune 1000 Companies.* San Francisco: Jossey-Bass, 1992.

Mohrman, S. A., and Cummings, T. G. *Self-Designing Organizations: Learning How to Create High Performance.* Reading, Mass.: Addison-Wesley, 1989.

Prahalad, C. K., and Hamel, G. "The Core Competence of the Corporation." *Harvard Business Review,* 1990, *68*(3), 79–93.

Schulz, K. D. "Put Your Corporate Counsel Where Your Business Is." *Harvard Business Review,* 1990, *68*(3), 72–78.

Stalk, G., and Hout, T. M. *Competing Against Time.* New York: Free Press, 1990.

Towers Perrin. *Priorities for Competitive Advantage.* New York: Towers Perrin, 1992.

Willigan, G. E. "The Value Adding CFO: An Interview with Disney's Gary Wilson." *Harvard Business Review,* 1990, *68*(1), 85–93.

Zuboff, S. *In the Age of the Smart Machine.* New York: Basic Books, 1988.

PART TWO

Organizing for Internal Effectiveness

To be competitive, organizations need to demonstrate continuously higher levels of performance. Achieving these new levels often requires dramatic changes in the way that the internal operations of organizations are structured and managed. The old, hierarchical forms cannot produce the necessary improvements in speed, quality, and productivity. This fact has led to a virtual landslide of ideas about how organizations can operate more effectively with less hierarchy, less overhead, and more participative management. This section focuses on these ideas by considering how organizations can operate more laterally, get employees involved in the business of their organization, and operate with more team structures. A number of topics are considered, but the message throughout is consistent: to meet today's performance demands, and compete effectively in global markets, organizations must utilize their employees in different and more significant ways. This is not just a matter of changing individual pieces of organizations; it requires changing all the major internal systems and management practices.

Chapter Four

Organizational Change and Learning

Susan Albers Mohrman
Allan M. Mohrman, Jr.

History books will describe the final two decades of this millennium as the period during which new organizational forms evolved. These forms are suited to the global economy and to the postindustrial, information-rich world of computerization. Weberian bureaucratic design principles and Tayloristic work design are subsumed within a set of design principles that enable simultaneous flexibility and efficiency. The changing geopolitical, world financial, and technological context within which organizations function poses a never-ending barrage of challenges to adapt and to learn new ways of functioning.

Organizational environments have become less benign, more complex, more interconnected, and more dynamic (Mitroff, 1988). These very conditions pose the need for change and at the same time make it difficult to learn and change by overloading the information-processing capabilities of organizational members. Consequently, it is of critical importance to understand how organizations learn and how they change. It is important to the survival of organizations that they become effective learners and that they be able to adapt to the rapidly changing conditions in their environment and to generate the innovations that will give them a competitive advantage and allow them to survive.

The task facing existing organizations goes deeper than a simple expansion of focus to include innovation and problem solving. Certain organizational design features foster innovation, learning, and change. These design features differ from the traditional bureaucratic design that has been "perfected" during this century. Organizations that have been designed for stability actually block the forces for change, and the behavior patterns that they shape stifle learning (Argyris and Schön, 1978). For these organizations to become sufficiently agile for today's environment, they must be able to redesign themselves — to undergo large-scale organizational change.

This chapter describes what we and other researchers have learned about organizational learning and large-scale organizational change. It then extrapolates from these learnings, to predict the nature of the organization that will be able to withstand the winds of change that we believe will continue to characterize the coming decades in the world economy. Our belief, based on our research to date, is that, simply to survive, organizations in the future will have to be able to innovate, to improve their processes, and to redesign themselves. Learnings about the organizational conditions that foster these three processes are briefly described in the following section.

Organizational Learning

Organizing is the arranging of the organizational *elements* (people, tools, and information) required for the ongoing transformation of organizational *inputs* into the products and/or services that constitute organizational *outputs*. Organizational elements must be organized to produce patterns of activity with the requisite variety to respond to the variety of inputs received from the environment and to produce the variety of products and services required by the environment. The arrangement of organizational elements and the recurring patterns of organizational activities constitute the organization.

In addition to the transforming of inputs into outputs, patterns of activities are required that foster the ongoing capabilities of organizational elements. These are the activities that maintain the performance capabilities of human, technical, and informational resources. In a dynamic environment, patterns of activities are also required that enable the organization to respond to changes in the environment. These patterns may enable the organization to process different inputs, to learn new ways of obtaining and securing inputs, or to respond to changing environmental demands for different products or services or for products or services that are more efficiently produced. Organizational learning occurs when the organization is able to alter its performance patterns to anticipate and/or respond to environmental change by adding new patterns of activity, deleting patterns that are not needed, and/or by developing better sensing mechanisms that allow the appropriate matching of patterns of activity to particular environmental events. For an organization to learn, it must have patterns of activities that alter its own patterns of activity.

Some forms of organizational learning occur regularly in many organizations. Human resource development activities, strategic and other planning activities, and the introduction and mastering of new technologies for doing work are three common learning processes. They often do not fulfill their potential for true organizational learning, however.

Organizational learning is more than the sum of the learning of its parts—more than cumulative individual learning. The training and development of individuals with new skills, knowledge bases, theories, and frameworks does not constitute organizational learning unless such individual learning is translated into altered organizational practices, policies, or design features. Individual learning is necessary but not sufficient for organizational learning. It may enable an individual to enact a role in the organization more effectively, but it will not lead to fundamentally altered patterns of behavior. Such behavior is *overdetermined,* it is held in place by a large number of organizational features. For example, many organizations have discovered that training in team skills is not a strong enough stimulus to change individualistic patterns of behavior that are held in place by job design, reward, and appraisal practices and by career systems.

Organizations are the collective and public embodiment of the theories of action of organizational members. Individual-oriented job designs, rewards, and appraisals reflect the fundamental beliefs (theories of action) of organizational members about performance and motivation. The organizational features that constitute the embodiment of the theories of action change through a process of collective inquiry that results in changes both in individuals' theories of action and in their representation in a shared description of the organization, its patterns of activity, and the elements that constitute it (Argyris and Schön, 1978). Teaching an individual teamwork skills will not lead to a different way of enacting a role unless the organization collectively determines that organizational performance is achieved through teamwork and changes the design features of the organization to promote it.

In recent years, the pace of change in organizational environments has led to the implicit recognition of the limitations of individual training and development as an approach to organizational learning. More and more companies are investing in training experiences that develop entire teams or intact units, or they are blanketing the organization with development experiences designed to establish a common theory of action among organizational members. In addition, organizational change activities constitute a component of an increasing number of development experiences. As part of their development experiences, groups of employees are given the opportunity to design and introduce organizational changes that embody some of the theories that they are being taught.

Strategic planning is another organizational activity that can be a form of organizational learning. The systematic examination of the environment and the determination of organizational approaches to obtaining needed inputs and targeting outputs addresses, at the macro level, the matching of appropriate patterns of activity to environmental conditions, trends, and events. Unfortunately, many strategic planning exercises stop short of organizational learning because they specify only the outcomes that are desired and do not identify either the patterns of organizational activity that will have to be established or the organizational design features that will elicit the desired behaviors. They may specify, for example, that the firm must move away from customized, high-margin products and toward low-cost consumer goods, but they may not identify the very fundamental changes that this requires in the assumptions and behavior patterns of organizational members and in organizational activity patterns.

The planning processes adopted by Shell Oil Corporation are often cited as having achieved the goal of "planning as learning." Through the development of scenarios about the future, rather than plans, senior managers expand their mental models of what is possible and begin to identify the implications. Readiness for quick identification of needed organizational change is one product of this learning. Shell is cited as thus having been able to respond more quickly than other oil companies have done to post-OPEC changes in the industry (deGeus, 1988).

The introduction of new technology generally stimulates some organizational learning. New transformation technologies (such as improved machines, automation, and information-processing and telecommunications technology) and new organizational processes (such as planning, coordinating, and control technologies) make new patterns of activities possible and help eliminate old ones, and they often require the reconfiguration of organizational elements. When this is done well, the organization learns to maximize the benefits it receives from the new technologies, and the result is increased organizational effectiveness. Because the patterns of activity required for organizational learning are often not in place, however, organizations frequently adopt new technologies with only partial learning; consequently, they derive only partial advantage from them. For example, many organizations have been slow to derive advantage from the integrative potential of computer-aided design/computer-aided manufacturing (CAD/CAM) technology. The ultimate benefit of CAD/CAM technology comes from the simultaneous processing that is enabled when various organizational members share data bases and their work is linked in real time. Although many organizations have addressed the individual learning required for system utilization, they have not addressed the myriad organizational elements required to foster integration among diverse elements of the organization, including organizational structure, reward systems, and goals. Consequently, the potential benefits in cost, time, and design quality often have not been accrued (Adler, 1990).

In the future, the introduction of new organizational technology may require organizational learning because the technologies that are currently being developed are so flexible that an organization will be able to tailor them to meet its needs and can continue to make modifications as organizational members discover ways to utilize the technologies more effectively (Brown and Duguid, 1991). Xerox's PARC research center, for example, is working on approaches to technology development in which organizations will be coproducers of the technologies that they employ and will have the capacity to reprogram that technology continually to fit developing needs.

Organizational learning requires patterns of activity to be established in the organization that enable collective examination of and changes to its own patterns of activity. The next section examines three approaches to organizational learning and the organizational design features that foster each one.

Three Kinds of Learning

Organizations struggle with three kinds of organizational learning. The first is the learning that is entailed in the process of *innovation,* the "invention" and adoption of new processes, products, and systems. The second kind of learning occurs in *organizational improvement processes,* through which organizations focus on increasing the effectiveness of their work processes. The third is the learning that guides the *redesign* of organizations and organizational subsystems to carry out new strategies and/or to embody new values and to significantly improve organizational performance. It is possible, conceptually, to distinguish among these three kinds of learning processes, but they often coincide in practice. Improvement processes may lead to innovation or to organizational redesign. Innovation may necessitate organizational redesign. A new design may be an innovation. Nevertheless, each process has a different focus and embodies a somewhat different logic.

Innovation

Innovation is a process that generates something new — products, applications, processes, practices, or systems. It is a creative process of seeing new applications for existing knowledge, combining different bits of knowledge to create a new capability, or "inventing" new solutions. Innovation is not a well-controlled process; rather, it relies on the availability of slack resources, redundancy of effort, trial and error, experimentation, freedom from constraints and specified ways of doing things, autonomy, and the ability to be playful. Consequently, a strong organizational control orientation is antithetical to innovation. Bureaucratic controls that limit action, slow down decision making, and slant the organization away from risk taking discourage innovation.

Although we tend to think of an innovation as the brainchild of an "inventor," behind most innovations are teams of people (Pinchot, 1985; Kanter, 1983; Quinn, 1980). They are involved in the many facets of the innovative process, including securing resources, generating ideas, developing the innovation, bringing it to market, and/or implementing it in the organization. Innovations frequently emerge from the blending of multiple perspectives, such as the customer's needs and the designer's knowledge base, or the combination of two different disciplines. Consequently, innovation is fostered in organizations that promote integration of multiple perspectives by linking the various organizational parts more closely and by linking the organization more tightly to its customers.

Innovating often requires changing the mental models of people throughout the innovating organization. Brown and Duguid (1991), for example, discuss numerous creative approaches that are used to open up the imaginations of people throughout Xerox to thinking about new models of the business, models that take advantage of digital copying capabilities. The same techniques are now being used with customers as a way to fashion new technology to fit emerging ways of doing business.

Organizational factors that have been found to promote innovation include the following:

- Rich networks of contacts that cut across functional boundaries
- Flat organizational structures that place innovating teams very close to ultimate decision makers
- Diversity of practices
- Availability of slack resources and redundancy of effort
- Long time horizons
- Rich connections between organizational members and external groups, such as other knowledge-generating groups and customers
- Incentives that promote risk taking
- Teamwork
- An orientation to the future
- A management style that promotes freedom within broad guidelines
- A clear vision

Organizational Improvement

The identification of areas where there are opportunities for enhancing performance and the application of problem-solving processes to make improvements are standard aspects of how organizations learn. In recent years, a number of techniques have become relatively common in organizations. Survey feedback, for example, is a technique for collecting data that focuses problem-solving efforts on areas where there is general agreement that improvement is needed. Quality circles and other problem-solving groups have been utilized to identify problem areas and to go through a systematic problem-solving process in addressing them. More recently, organizations have been utilizing a total quality approach, which includes a focus on controlling and improving the various processes that comprise the organization, the use of sophisticated analytical tools for identifying causes of process failure and generating solutions that will have the greatest impact on quality, and a focus on quality as defined by the needs of internal and external customers (Deming, 1986; Juran, 1989).

Organizational improvement methodologies often involve the establishment of parallel organizations, including problem-solving groups (such as quality-improvement teams, task teams, and steering committees). A parallel organization is intended to solve problems and introduce change. It supplements the regular hierarchical organizational structure, which has been designed to carry out the ongoing work of the organization and operates on the principle of control, stability, and maintenance of the status quo.

Our research has found that the parallel organization, although elegant in theory, often fails in practice (Lawler and Mohrman, 1985). Essentially, it is put into competition with the "regular" organization for the scarce resources that are needed by both organizations — time, money, information, and authority. Parallel structures are frequently seen as "extra," and the regular organization is often resistant both to redeploying resources to support their activities and to implementing the changes that result from their problem solving. The improvement process is frequently viewed as a nicety that gets set aside in the press to accomplish operating objectives. Furthermore, the changes that are suggested by the parallel structure are often perceived as treading on turf, and they encounter resistance from those who see themselves as the keepers of the very processes that have been targets of the improvement efforts.

Successful parallel structures are those that have clearly stated organizational objectives related to accepted business goals, utilize systematic and effective process analysis and group problem solving, and build rich, two-way links to the regular organization. In short, the parallel structure must be well integrated into the regular organization. In the Japanese production system, for example, small teams of workers are also given

the opportunity to meet and solve problems, and individual dis-
coveries about how to improve work processes are quickly sys-
tematized and disseminated (Galbraith, 1990). By continually
pushing the limits of the organizational system, the Japanese
are able to expose problems quickly and use total quality management tools to generate continuous improvement.

Organizational conditions found to be related to the successful use of parallel organizations for organizational improvement include the following:

- Extensive communication and information sharing, to ensure that participants in the parallel structure are well informed about the business and the organization that they
  are trying to improve
- Training and education of organizational members in group
  processes, process and statistical analysis, and other problem-
  solving techniques
- Adequate resources to support improvement processes and
  implementation of change
- Altered role definitions of supervisors, managers, and technical and support staff, including responsibility and accountability for supporting the activities of the parallel structures,
  involving employees, and implementing change
- Interfunctional cooperation and shared goals
- Orientation to internal and external customers
- Incorporation of organizational improvement into the long-
  and short-term goals of the organization and the appraisal
  of performance

Examination of the organizational conditions that foster
innovation and organizational improvement processes reveals
a number of factors in common. Both situations require strong
lateral integration, including close cooperation between different specialties and subgroups and orientation to internal and
external customers. The objective of learning and change requires patience and an adequate time horizon. The new roles
of individuals in problem solving and in sponsoring, champion-
ing, and managing change must be supported by incentives,
goal setting, appraisal, and other human resource practices that

shape such behavior. Quick and easy communication up and down the hierarchy and an open sharing of information about the business and its mission and objectives are required. The processes of learning, innovation, and improvement must be seen as core organizational processes and should be supported as such.

These conditions are not found in many American organizations today, and so they will have to be developed in organizations that see learning, innovation, process improvements, and performance enhancement as critical to enacting business strategies. As can be seen in Table 4.1, every aspect of an organization's design — people, structure, decision making, information systems, human resource practices, and technology — must be aligned with the desired learning behavior. To become learning systems, many organizations will have to redesign themselves. This redesign process is itself an organizational learning process.

Table 4.1. Innovation and Improvement in Organizations.

Conditions That Foster Innovation	Conditions That Foster Organizational Improvement
Freedom from controls	Systemic group process
Playfulness	Analytical problem solving
Redundancy	

Conditions That Foster Both
Innovation and Organizational Improvement
Long-term orientation
Resource support
Organizational vision
Management support
Proximity to decision makers
Interfunctional networks and teamwork
Learning connections with the external environment
Incentives for risk and experimentation

Redesign

Many forces in today's environment are demanding that organizations learn to increase their effectiveness. In addition, the changing nature of the economy is causing strategic redirection in many firms. The design of the organization affects the levels and types of performance that the organization can attain in implementing its strategy. Therefore, organizational design can be a competitive advantage. The term *design* is used here in its broadest sense, to encompass all the manipulable aspects of the organization, including its people, systems, processes, and technology, in addition to its structure. Organizational design provides the framework for recurring patterns of activity. In a rapidly changing world, where the landscape of the competitive marketplace changes frequently and competitive performance levels continue to escalate, the ability of an organization to redesign itself is also a competitive advantage. Mastery of self-design — the process by which an organization learns to change its design features in order to be more effective in its changing environment — will be a critical organizational capability. A key managerial role in the learning organization will be that of designer of the organizational system that is capable of learning (Senge, 1990b).

In our work with organizations that are redesigning themselves to compete in the changing environment, we have observed that successful self-design is an iterative process, which consists of the components illustrated in Figure 4.1 (Mohrman and Cummings, 1989). It is triggered by a change of strategy or by a need for a markedly higher level of performance that can be achieved only through a change in the elements of the organization's design, so as to support the new level of performance. The foundation for self-design includes clarification of organizational values — of the valued human and business outcomes that the organization is striving to achieve. Some of these values come from the strategy; others are expressions of the values of the organization's members. Acquiring knowledge about the principles of organizational design and awareness of alternative design possibilities will provide a framework for the diagnosis of the current organization, as compared with what is desired, and for the creative design process.

The creative tension that leads to learning comes from the gap between the realistic picture of reality (diagnosis) and

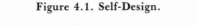

Figure 4.1. Self-Design.

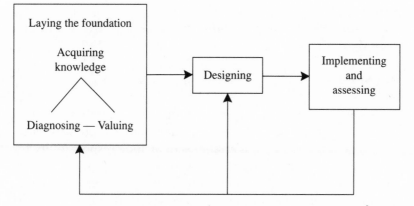

Source: Mohrman and Cummings, 1989, p. 37.

the vision of a desirable future state (Senge, 1990a). The importance of vision has also been stressed by Nonaka (1991), who discusses the knowledge-creating organization as one that continually renews itself as it recreates its world according to its vision or ideal.

The design process entails both minimum specification of the features of the new design and reliance on the implementation process for learning to occur throughout the organization about how to fill in the detailed design features. Implementation is an action-learning cycle of implementing a design, assessing how well it is working, and making design alterations. Through a series of iterations, the organization refines and modifies its design to achieve greater effectiveness. Although portrayed as a neat, logical sequence, the process is actually quite messy. At any particular time, there will be diagnostic activities, design activities, and implementation and assessment being carried out as different organizational subsystems are brought into alignment with the overall strategic direction, and as different parts of the organization proceed through change processes at varying speeds. Such changes as Hewlett-Packard's shift from being a products company to being a systems company, or IBM's shift from being an integrated monolith to encompassing smaller business lines, occur through a gradual process by which all parts of the organization become redesigned to fit the new way of operating.

Organizational conditions that foster effective self-design include the following:

- Multistakeholder participation in design processes
- Ongoing assessment of the efficacy of organizational features
- Open information sharing and the use of data for problem identification and redesign, rather than for punishment
- Redefinition of managerial jobs to include responsibility for design of organizational units
- Leadership that includes strategy clarification and the establishment of clear performance values that can guide organizational members in all organizational units
- A view of structure and design as temporary
- An understanding among organizational members that their continued employment demands ongoing personal learning and change

Organizational redesign can include substantial change in the values that the organization is striving to achieve, the roles that people are expected to play, the assumptions and world view that govern behavior, and the concrete design features of the organization. Such change is truly large scale in the sense that it is pervasive (involving multiple aspects of the organization) and deep (involving change in such fundamental aspects as values; see Mohrman and Associates, 1989). The following paragraphs provide a summary of the major learnings about such change processes that have emerged from our studies and of the consequences for the way change is managed.

1. *Organizational change does not happen unless there is a compelling reason to change.* The reason for change has to be linked closely to the business strategy, although it can and should be accompanied by a strong "people" orientation. Our research has found that changes in human resource management practices are most likely to occur if they emanate from an articulation of the strategic needs of the organization, rather than if they

are the driver of the change process (Lawler, Ledford, and Mohrman, 1989).

2. *Leadership is a critical factor in the change process.* Change will not occur without energy, guidance, and commitment from the top of the organization. Part of the leadership role is articulating, or helping the organization to articulate, the compelling reasons.

One of the dilemmas of change leadership is that change will be continual and will most often be an adaptive response to changes that have occurred or are anticipated in the environment, and yet organizational members look to the leader for a steady course that indicates that the ship is not out of control. Change leadership entails being a continual catalyst for the change process by formulating and updating a compelling change agenda, helping the organization envision the future, unleashing energy and resources to fuel the change process, and helping the organization experience change as success rather than failure.

Change leadership must be diffused throughout the organization. Since change is frequently resisted, the development of a leadership network must be accomplished through alignment of incentives, provision of skills and tools for change, and use of the management succession system. It must clearly be in the best interests of people to change, and they must be provided with information, skills, and resources, just as they are for other organizational responsibilities.

3. *Organizations are systems in which change in one aspect will beg change in other aspects.* The system will be more effective to the extent that its various components fit with one another. Galbraith (1990) has pointed out, for example, that the strength of the Japanese production system lies in the complementarity of factory practices, the work system, and human resource policies, all of which support high performance and continuous improvement. Many of the kinds of changes that organizations face today require systemic realignment, including strategic redirection, globalization, introduction of new technology, accomplishment of performance increments beyond those achievable by "cleaning up" the system, and the transition to a high-

involvement culture. In such situations, *limited interventions will have limited impact.* Change involves organizational redesign, and design capabilities and processes have to be built into the organization.

4. *Change involves both technical design and effective human processes.* These two aspects are two sides of the "change" coin. Failure to progress in either area can prevent a change from happening. Attending to the system design issues of human resource management is necessary but insufficient for dealing with issues of human process. Managing change involves understanding and dealing with resistance, individual and collective learning, and the natural dynamics of transition. These processes of change can be facilitated by such patterns of activity as communication, process consultation, participation, and conflict resolution, but they cannot be avoided.

5. *Major change alters the psychological contract (What am I expected to contribute, in return for what outcomes?) of almost everyone in the organization.* It also involves change in the way people understand their organization and in the assumptions they make about what is desirable and undesirable, as well as qualitative change in skills and behaviors. There will be people who are unable or unwilling to make the transition, and major change does involve some turnover in personnel.

Managing the "people" side of change will involve developing an understanding of what is needed and expected, skills to deliver the new behavior, and reinforcement of change when it occurs. It will also entail the management of people from whom change is not forthcoming. These individuals must be managed in a way that does not undermine the learning norms that the organization is working to establish. This requires a good-faith effort to help people change, a spelling out of the consequences of not changing, and, when possible, permission for people to choose different roles if they do not believe that they can change.

6. *Change involves conflict.* In fact, the essence of change is a process of resolving tension and conflict within a system. Part of the energy for change is unleashed by dynamic resolution of conflict among various stakeholders in the organization. This is the fundamental mechanism by which the assumptions

of the status quo are challenged. Consequently, change involves establishing political mechanisms by which stakeholders can resolve issues. This includes joint resolution between groups that have previously operated independently and the empowerment of stakeholders who have a different frame of reference from the keepers of the status quo.

7. *Change is not an orderly, controlled process.* It involves iteration, messy encounters, resistance, conflict, and surprise. Although change can be partially planned, a great deal will be unplanned. Change will involve opportunistic events and responses to unanticipated consequences. Each change will make other opportunities and other needed changes evident. A major objective of the change process is to develop the new organizational norms that will enable organizational members to deal effectively with complexity, ambiguity, disorder, and frequent reordering and unplanned activity (disruptions of plans). Fortunately, the norms required to deal with the inherently disorderly nature of large-scale change are the same as those required for ongoing organizational learning. The needed norms, values, and assumptions involve learning from mistakes, borrowing ideas from others, taking risks, tolerating and benefiting from diversity, and exposing and dealing with conflict.

8. *Change will be a continual fact of life for organizations in the coming decades.* Much of the change will require the development of capabilities that the organization has never had before. This need for discontinuous change is fueled by rapid technological advances; the unfolding of the global economy; the increasingly heterogeneous work force; changes in local and global financial, economic, and legal frameworks; complex environmental problems; rapidly shrinking time frames; and deregulation.

One new capability that will have to be developed is the capacity for organizations to change themselves. This will include but go beyond what is currently referred to as the *continuous improvement process,* which is a means of improving existing activity cycles. The redesign process will involve the development of new processes and the realignment of organizational elements. The organization will have to become a learning community, capable of redesigning itself through time.

Implications for the Organization of the Future

We have argued that a viable organization in the coming decades will have to be good at the processes of innovation, process improvement, and self-design. In short, effective organizations will become effective learning communities. They will be effective at applying multiple perspectives and kinds of expertise to the complex problems and opportunities that confront them. During the past decade, a number of our best firms had efforts under way in these directions. The total quality movement is one widespread indication of the pressing need of organizations to become competent at changing themselves. The large number of innovation studies and audits is another indication that there is already significant momentum in this direction.

Where is this leading? How will organizations look in the future? Extrapolating from the findings that have come from a decade of studying learning and change in organizations, we predict the following general characteristics of the learning organization:

1. *Organizational design will be understood to be a temporary configuration of components that will change as the organization's strategy and environment change.* Organizations will be much less geared to preserving stability and the status quo and will come to see their systems and structures as strategic tools that can be altered to change organizational capabilities. Management of organizational design will be a key managerial competency.

2. *There will be greatly increased, ongoing application of resources to the development of skills and knowledge, throughout the organization.* Skills and knowledge will be moved downward in the organization, and this will enable those closest to the work to solve complex problems. In addition, much more attention will be paid to developing breadth skills — to cross training and the lateral movement of individuals across various parts of the organization, in order to facilitate the integration of perspectives in innovating, designing, and solving problems. Individuals will secure their employment by increasing their value to the company and their flexibility.

3. *Organizations will be flatter and more agile.* Layers of hier-

archical and staff control that slow down the functioning of the organization, inhibit learning, and add costs will be reduced. In flatter organizations, broad guidelines and management by results will replace tight controls. Much of the skills and knowledge currently housed in specialized staff groups will be moved into line groups, so that their decision making will be informed by a rich constellation of perspectives. This will allow the application of local knowledge to the development of organizational systems and solutions. Wherever possible, organizational units will become self-contained and self-managing. Lateral movement of people will contribute to this mode of control and decision making.

4. *Organizations will become excellent at integrating a rich constellation of task teams, "overlay" organizations, and intergroup networks that complement organizational capabilities and offset the focus of the core structures.* This will enable the organization to address multiple simultaneous focuses (for example, operating efficiently and improving product focus and functional focus). It will also build bridges between these perspectives and their respective knowledge bases, to enable the organization to learn and to address complex systemic issues.

5. *Organizations will be richly connected to a wide diversity of other organizations in the environment, with which they will learn and share learnings.* Consortia, joint ventures, university-industry alliances, and multiorganization symposia will continue to proliferate. Membership in these cooperative efforts will link organizations to the learning that is occurring in the larger environment. This will be important, given the speed at which learning is occurring and new knowledge is being proliferated. Individual organizational members will also have to build rich personal networks of contacts, in order to keep their own knowledge and skills up-to-date and to be able to direct their own development.

6. *Organizations will foster diversity of practices and designs, in order to seed the learning process and enable various parts of the organization to adapt to performance requirements.* They will devote more time and attention to the diffusion process — the sharing of ideas and learnings across organizational units — so that managers who are expected to manage continually improving systems will be ex-

posed to new ideas and ways of doing things. There will be fewer
attempts to "roll out" massive, systemwide changes and more
efforts to encourage units to redesign themselves continually to
be more effective.

7. *The role of top management will be to formulate and communicate a clear vision of the organization's strategy and vision and to continually challenge the organization to achieve excellence in implementing
the direction.* As a corollary, the role of managers throughout the
organization will include translating the strategy and vision into
terms that are meaningful to the units that they manage, clarifying the missions of their units, and empowering them to innovate, improve their processes, and redesign for the best implementation of their missions.

8. *The psychological contract of employment will change irrever-
sibly.* First, organizations will become much more demanding
places to work. Employees will be expected to do the work, think
of ways to improve it, contribute to learning and change efforts,
and manage their own ongoing learning processes. Second, organizations will be much more ambiguous places to work. Careers will not be well specified and secure. To maintain their
flexibility and employability, individuals will have to plan their
own development. The paternalistic era that was possible in the
benevolent period of the 1950s and 1960s has ended, and individuals will have to learn to manage themselves and their careers.
One possible scenario is that people will become, in a sense,
contractors to their organizations. They will be utilized where
they have needed skills and can expect to move from place to
place in their organizations as needs change. The flatter organization, with less emphasis on vertical mobility, will foster the
definition of *career* largely in terms of breadth and depth of skills,
rather than in terms of level in the organization.

Conclusion

This chapter has argued that new organizational forms are evolving, which will be well adapted to a world that requires ongoing organizational learning and change. If our predictions about
the learning organization of the future prove to be correct, it

will differ from the traditional bureaucratic form of organization in fundamental ways. It not only will house ongoing activities to improve its processes and introduce innovation but will also have self-design capabilities, so that it can alter its own design features on an ongoing basis.

The large-scale change process required for an organization to become a learning organization entails second-order change (Bateson, 1972). Such change is not simply learning to do better what is already done (first-order change); it entails a change in fundamental assumptions and organizing principles. For example, structures will be perceived as temporary, improvement and change activities will be seen as primary organizational tasks, and decision making will be made intentionally political by the purposeful exposure of conflict among different perspectives. The relationship between the individual and the organization will change fundamentally. As extreme competitive pressures continue to disrupt the paternalistic patterns of the last three decades, the onus will be on the individual to be a qualified, productive member of the work force.

Adaptation to a rapidly changing environment requires flexibility and agility—the ability to learn rapidly how to produce new products and services and raise performance standards. In the new environment, where technology is readily copied, information can be transferred with great ease around the world, and geography is no barrier to market entry. The organization that learns how to execute effectively will survive. This will require the ability to learn new activity patterns and discard those that no longer fit the circumstances. Learning will be the competitive advantage of the organization of the future.

References

Adler, P. "Managing High Tech Processes: The Challenge of CAD/CAM." In M. A. Von Glinow and S. A. Mohrman (eds.), *Managing Complexity in High Technology Organizations.* New York: Oxford University Press, 1990.

Argyris, C., and Schön, D. *Organizational Learning.* Reading, Mass.: Addison-Wesley, 1978.

Bateson, G. *Steps to an Ecology of Mind.* New York: Ballantine, 1972.

Brown, J. S., and Duguid, P. "Organizational Learning and Communities of Practice: Toward a Unified View of Working, Learning, and Innovation." *Organization Science,* 1991, *2*(1), 40–57.

deGeus, A. P. "Planning as Learning." *Harvard Business Review,* 1988, *66*(2), 70–74.

Deming, W. E. *Out of the Crisis.* Cambridge, Mass.: Center for Advanced Engineering Study, Massachusetts Institute of Technology, 1986.

Galbraith, J. R. "Japanese Transplants." Working paper, Center for Effective Organizations, University of Southern California at Los Angeles, 1990.

Juran, J. M. *Juran on Leadership for Quality.* New York: Free Press, 1989.

Kanter, R. M. *The Change Masters.* New York: Simon & Schuster, 1983.

Lawler, E. E., III, Ledford, G. E., Jr., and Mohrman, S. A. *Employee Involvement in America: A Study of Contemporary Practice.* Houston, Tex.: American Productivity and Quality Center, 1989.

Lawler, E. E., III and Mohrman, S. A. "Quality Circles After the Fad." *Harvard Business Review,* 1985, *63*(1), 64–71.

Mitroff, I. *Business as Usual.* San Francisco: Jossey-Bass, 1988.

Mohrman, A. M., Jr., and Associates, *Large-Scale Organizational Change.* San Francisco: Jossey-Bass, 1989.

Mohrman, S. A., and Cummings, T. G. *Self-Designing Organizations: Learning How to Create High Performance.* Reading, Mass.: Addison-Wesley, 1989.

Nonaka, I. "The Knowledge-Creating Company." *Harvard Business Review,* 1991, *69*(6), 96–104.

Pinchot, G., III. *Intrapreneuring.* New York: HarperCollins, 1985.

Quinn, J. B. *Strategies for Change: Logical Incrementalism.* Homewood, Ill.: Business One Irwin, 1980.

Senge, P. M. *The Fifth Discipline: The Art and Practice of the Learning Organization.* New York: Doubleday, 1990a.

Senge, P. M. "The Leader's New Work: Building Learning Organizations." *Sloan Management Review,* 1990b, *32*(1), 7–23.

Chapter Five

Integrating Roles and Structure in the Lateral Organization

Susan Albers Mohrman

All signs point to the importance of lateral integration in the organization of the future. Galbraith's description, in Chapter Two, of the emerging forms of business units is laced with references to the importance of processes that link people and units across the organization. The traditional organizational model of functional units integrated by the general manager is increasingly being replaced by organizational models with mechanisms for integrating multiple functions, with common focuses on customers, products, projects, or processes.

The increasing salience of lateral processes results from a combination of the performance pressures in today's organizational environments and new information technologies that serve as integrating media. These forces, which were described in the Introduction, are briefly described here:

1. The evolution of the global economy and the atten-

Note: Some of the ideas in this chapter stem, in large part, from the work of Jay R. Galbraith. I have based a great part of my thinking not only on his written work about organizational design but also on insights derived from field projects with him.

dant increase in competitive pressure have put a premium on *organizational learning*. In a world where products are easily copied and processes can be transported almost anywhere, competitive advantage can be sustained only through being first, executing better, and staying ahead. Organizational learning processes inherently involve links across an organization. As described in Chapter Four, organizational learning requires the establishment of lateral links, so that individuals with different functional paradigms and broad systemic exposure to the organization can generate solutions to complex problems and novel approaches to doing work.

2. Pressures for *speed,* such as the need for reduction in time to market and cycle time, require up-front cross-functional planning and optimization of simultaneous processes, such as those found in concurrent engineering. Organizations cannot afford delays due to bureaucratic approvals or to the slow process of escalating decisions through layers of hierarchy.

3. Total quality management approaches that focus on the improvement of *organizational processes* make it evident that key organizational processes do not respect organizational boundaries, and their optimization requires multiple stakeholders' input and changes.

4. *Customer power* requires organizations to have the capability to focus all functions on the customer and to align organizational processes, from start to finish, with customers' expectations.

5. Market demand for *systems solutions* requires the organization to integrate all its own components, to focus on the system that is being developed.

6. *Computer and communications technology advances* enable the real-time linking of diverse parts of the organization with common data sets and computer tools. These new tools know no organizational boundaries. Their optimal use requires norms of shared data ownership and mutual accommodation of the work that is being done in various parts of the organization.

7. Rapid product generation and entry into new markets require the growth, nurturing, and leverage of *core competencies* of the corporation. These scarce resources must be managed

across multiple business units and organizational boundaries (Prahalad and Hamel, 1990).

The combination of these forces has led to a large variety of organizational change and redesign efforts. The difficulty of establishing effective lateral integration in these change efforts has yielded the recognition of a powerful inertia built into our traditional organizations. The logic of differentiation, specialization, hierarchy, and functionalization is pervasive in almost all aspects of organizational design. Furthermore, careers, attitudes, beliefs, and self-concepts are heavily enmeshed with the status quo. Redesigning organizations to promote lateral teamwork will involve a major shift in the orientation of employees and changes in many of the organizational systems that shape behavior. This chapter provides an overview of some key concepts that are relevant to the question of how to achieve lateral integration. It also provides some structural alternatives and process requirements for achieving such integration.

Integration and Differentiation Revisited

The underpinnings of our traditional organizational models are, in large part, a legacy of the scientific management tradition, the bureaucratic form, and administrative rationality. Organizations are differentiated into jobs and units that are specialized and divided into hierarchical layers, with the middle layers providing direction and coordination among specialized subunits and individuals. Standard operating processes are formalized and specify the way in which work is to be done and the sequence by which it proceeds through the system. The key transformation processes of the organization are performed by the technical core, consisting mostly of individual contributors who are managed and controlled by a middle-management group that receives strategic direction from the executives of the organization.

This model of organization is supported by human resource management practices that include job descriptions and job evaluation systems to clearly specify who does what. They are also used to make status differentiations (such as exempt/

nonexempt, labor/management, and bonus eligible/ineligible). Individual performance appraisals and merit pay practices establish the individual as the performing unit. Jobs are defined to minimize the cost of training and maximize the number of productive hours from scarce technical resources. Organizational units are constructed of people performing similar tasks and using similar expertise, in order to create a critical mass and make units easily supervised and evaluated. Job evaluation systems that heavily value size of budget and head-count control reinforce an image of the organization in which the tasks of hierarchical control are valued more than the creation of products and delivery of services. Careers are oriented toward moving up in the hierarchical control structure, rather than toward increasing contributions to the transformation of inputs into products and services.

In an organization that is designed according to these principles, integration is accomplished largely by hierarchically driven processes, such as direction from supervision, rules and procedures, and goals and objectives. Galbraith (1973) has pointed out that in a very simple and static world, these integrative devices are sufficient glue to keep all the parts of the organization heading together in the same direction fast enough to respond to the environment.

Complexity and speed are foes of this simple, machine-like organization. Rapid change undermines the stability of its infrastructure; goals, processes, jobs, and rules must change to meet changing environmental demands. High interdependence that requires on-line coordination of work makes it difficult to segment the work so that individuals and units can be managed independently. The work of a sales organization, for example, is highly interdependent with the administrative support tasks that typically have been housed in a business administration function. Toyota's one-week delivery of cars is made possible by extremely tight coordination between these two functions and the manufacturing line.

Extreme performance pressures put a premium on speed and efficiency and preclude the handling of complexity through organizational buffers and other forms of organizational slack

(Galbraith, 1973). Just-in-time delivery to customers, for example, is considerably more cost-effective than the stockpiling of large inventories, but it can be achieved only through a close working relationship between the customer and the supplier. Even the external boundary between organizations and their environments is beginning to blur as new forms of lateral integration emerge between organizations.

The environment faced by organizations today is characterized by complexity and extreme performance pressures. The challenge facing the organizations of the next decade is to simultaneously do the following:

- Achieve multiple focuses (on product, market, customer, and geography) without dysfunctionally segmenting the organization
- Align individuals and groups that are task-interdependent in a manner that fosters teamwork in pursuit of shared overall objectives
- Enable quick, low-cost, high-quality performance while responding to a highly dynamic environment that calls for ongoing change
- Respond to ongoing increases in competitive performance standards by learning how to be more effective
- Attract, motivate, develop, and retain employees who are able to operate effectively in such a demanding organizational environment

An organization's design must seek to jointly optimize its business, technical, and human performance. The organization must be capable of making conscious trade-offs. To do this, forums must be created where people with diverse organizational perspectives develop solutions to complex problems and opportunities. For example, an effective new-product development process must determine an optimal balance among considerations of market characteristics, cost, time to market, and technical product characteristics. The structures and processes of new-product development must create the integration of the diverse perspectives required to define this balance for each product. Systemic solutions to complex, multifaceted choices can be developed only through lateral integrative processes.

The processes that integrate the lateral dimensions of organizations are achieving importance equal to that of the hierarchical processes that have dominated much of the traditional literature on organizational structure and design. Systemic images of organizational design are beginning to replace the predominantly analytical design principles of the past. Systemic organizational designs retain the imperative to reduce complexity wherever possible by creating differentiated units, but they attend much more clearly to the simultaneous need for different functions to work together. They acknowledge the role of hierarchy but distinguish between integrative tasks appropriately conducted hierarchically (such as overall portfolio development and business strategy) and those best done laterally (such as working out trade-offs between design sophistication and manufacturability).

Self-directed teams are an excellent example of the kinds of structures that are becoming more prevalent. They are a form that facilitates both integration and differentiation, and they have implications for both the hierarchical and the lateral nature of the organization. Self-directed teams are becoming more common on the factory floor (Lawler, Mohrman, and Ledford, 1992). They combine a group of people responsible for all the tasks involved in doing a whole, identifiable, measurable piece of work. The hierarchical implications of this form of management are that fewer management layers are needed; the traditional role of the supervisor changes from hands-on coordination and direction of work to a coaching role and to translation of organizational strategic direction and its implications for the teams (Pasmore, 1988; Manz and Sims, 1989). Team members perform self-management tasks that were formerly done by the supervisor.

The lateral work-design implications of self-directed teams are also interesting. The skills required to do the work are combined in the same unit. Tasks that were previously done by external support groups or by managers are moved into the unit, and individuals on the teams are cross-trained, so that they can perform multiple tasks and schedule and coordinate themselves flexibly. Thus, a team is made self-reliant (differentiated) when it is given control over as many aspects of its performance as possible. Integration occurs within the team, laterally. This model requires a number of key changes in human resource practices, so as to enable people to advance within a team through the mastering of multiple skills and the achievement of a broader scope of contribution. A team of team representatives often performs coordinating functions among teams, makes organizationwide decisions, and influences decisions made within the management hierarchy.

Self-directed teams embody three key principles: the team and the individuals on it are multiskilled (the team contains all the skills to do the whole task), lateral coordination occurs within the team, and some management tasks and decision making are moved down into the team. To the extent possible, the team is bounded (differentiated from the rest of the organization), so that it can function independently. The need for integration is met by building into the team's composition the multiple perspectives and skills necessary for doing the task and solving problems. The traditional boss-subordinate hierarchical coordination role is diminished; coordination occurs laterally, to the greatest possible extent. The team is integrated into the larger organization and its hierarchy through representation on teams that address larger systems issues.

Although self-directed teams have been used mainly in manufacturing settings, many organizations are now exploring their applicability to white-collar work. In the response to pressures for lateral integration, the principles embodied in the self-directed team will probably become more prevalent, although the organizational forms that embody them will be diverse. Organizations will search for ways to link the various parts of the organization more tightly, in order to promote coordinated functioning. They will also create smaller, highly motivated, self-sufficient units. There will be an escalation in the use of teams, minibusinesses within businesses, and multiskilling, and there will be further flattening of the organization.

In complex and dynamic situations, the need for integrative

devices increases dramatically (Lawrence and Lorsch, 1967). These devices may be structural (for example, self-contained teams and other integrative structures, such as task teams and councils). Special integrator roles, such as those of product or process managers, may be used. Shared information systems, goal setting, and measurement systems can also link units laterally. The remainder of this chapter examines the various structural and process design features that facilitate lateral integration and that can be expected to characterize organizations increasingly in the future.

Integrating Structures and Roles

Lateral integration has many purposes, and it can take many forms. In the future, an important part of the skill set of an organization will be the knowledge and ability to design itself so as to optimize its strategy. A working understanding of various integrative approaches and the management challenges that they present will be critical to the designing and redesigning that will be required as the organization tries to sustain a competitive advantage in a rapidly changing environment. The following sections present a framework for conceptualizing the design issues related to the lateral integration of the organization. A continuum of integrating mechanisms will be discussed, and particular design features (teams, integrating roles, and the use of a hierarchy of teams) will be described.

A Continuum of Integrative Design Approaches

The importance and the difficulty of integrating the various parts of an organization increase when the organization is required to make trade-offs, solve problems, and make adjustments to work on the basis of information from knowledge that resides in different parts of the organization. The work of the organization requires simultaneous focuses, so that work is not easily broken down into independent departments and units. For example, in a technical firm there is a need to focus on functional technical expertise and on the multifunctional process of new-product development. Firms may make delicate and dynamic trade-offs between the development of global products and the optimization of geographical markets. Service organizations have to focus simultaneously on the development of functional excellence and on the provision of service to diverse customers with idiosyncratic needs. Galbraith and Kazanjian (1986) have posited a continuum of integrating mechanisms that can be employed to integrate and coordinate work between groups; a modified version appears in Figure 5.1. Such organizational processes as standard procedures, goals, measures, and plans provide a

Figure 5.1. Integrative Mechanisms.

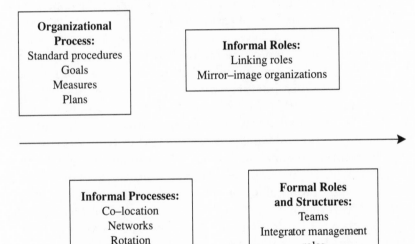

foundation for coordinated activities. When uncertainty and dynamic conditions make it impossible to plan coordinated activities, ongoing adjustment between individuals and groups is required. The approach that involves the least amount of organizational investment in new roles and structures is to encourage such integration to occur informally, through such means as colocation, the purposeful establishment of rich interpersonal networks, and the rotation of individuals through multiple disciplines. These methods do not require special structures or roles;

they create a context in which integration of work is the "natural" response. They can be successful only to the extent that the individuals and groups who must cooperate are working in a context where goals, plans, and measures are aligned, so that people are not pitted against one another.

Complex interdependence calls for more formal organizational approaches. Integrative tasks may be assigned as part of the roles of specific individuals. The designation of an official "linkage" person creates a special role, with responsibility for integrating with other departments, although it is a role with informal influence. Mirror-image departments (see Chapter Two) identify people from different departments who are task-interdependent, thereby making it easier to identify the appropriate contacts for working out such interdependence. For example, in an aerospace firm, every department may have someone working on the design of the aircraft's wing, the fuselage, and so forth. By clearly specifying and shrinking the size of the set of people who must interact with one another around a particular component, this arrangement makes integration easier.

The strongest integrative design formalizes responsibility for integration in management roles and/or team structures. These approaches increase the organizational investment of resources for supporting the integrative processes. For example, the designation of a team of individuals from the different departments that have responsibility for the wing or the fuselage represents a further formalization, beyond the mirror-image organization. It also entails the additional organizational cost of the time to build the team and resolve issues. Another approach is to create a formal managerial role, such as that of a product, market, or process manager responsible for integrating the work of the various contributors.

An organization can use these integrative roles and structures to shift influence toward the focus that represents its most strategic concern. For example, product managers and product development teams that integrate various functions can be designed to yield more or less influence vis-à-vis the functions. At one end of the continuum, the function has most of the power, and the integration of functions is largely informal. The integrative structures do not have resource control or decision-making authority. Product managers, for instance, would have integrative responsibility but not control over the human resources that work on the project. The product development team might be a loosely defined group of members from different functional units, with diverse reporting relationships. This would be appropriate if functional, technical excellence were the key strategic variable for the organization. At the other end of the continuum, the product wields primary power (has resource control and decision making authority), and functional integration is more informal. For example, technical resources would report to product teams or minibusinesses. Issues of development and coordination of technical specialties across business units might occur through technical councils. This approach would be appropriate if new-product development were the key strategic variable and did not rely heavily on rapid advance of highly specialized fields or on careful, organizationwide management of scarce technical resources.

Between these two extremes is shared influence, in which both function and product share resource control and authority. This may take the form of a matrix organization characterized by dual reporting and authority. Creating the matrix entails another organizational cost — the additional time required to arrive at joint decisions and make explicit and often difficult trade-offs. These costs may be justified, however, if functional excellence and new-product development are equally vital strategically, and if the organization is required to continually weigh both these concerns and make trade-offs.

Thus a continuum of integrative devices can be used to integrate the efforts of individuals and groups, ranging from the use of formal and informal processes that create the context for integrative behavior to the use of informal and formal organizational roles and structures. Research has demonstrated that in highly complex, dynamic situations, all these integrative approaches are likely to be in place (Galbraith and Kazanjian, 1986; Lawrence and Lorsch, 1967). Organizations that use integrative roles and structures are also likely to use formal and informal organizational processes to foster integration.

The design of appropriate integrative approaches is extremely important in today's environment. These mechanisms not only must enable adequate integration but also must result in balanced influence of the various viewpoints required for effective accomplishment of tasks. Managing the influence balance is a key organizational imperative in an environment where organizational success is determined by the ability to excel simultaneously in several interdependent arenas and when the strategic importance of these focuses changes through time.

A Team Typology

Although diverse integrative approaches are possible and necessary, the use of teams is becoming increasingly prevalent, partly because many functional organizations find reliance on less formal integration techniques inadequate when functional power is deeply ingrained in the culture and design of the organization. Functional criteria drive behavior, often in spite of the cost of suboptimization. In addition, if speed is a key competitive variable, the push toward parallel processing puts a premium on person-to-person resolution of interdependence and on agreement about overall project goals. Forming a team with shared objectives and agreements about task performance strategies and roles is one way of addressing these issues. Time can be saved if it is not necessary to go through a hierarchical approval process — if authority to make decisions resides in the team.

A different form of team for resolving problems and improving processes has been advocated in the literature on total quality management (Deming, 1986; Juran, 1989; Scholtes, 1988). Quality improvement teams are set up for that special purpose; they are not the primary organizational structural unit.

There has been a tendency in the organizational literature to deal with teams as if they were a homogeneous phenomenon, whereas there are actually many kinds of teams, each with its own design and management requirements. Teams that are improperly designed and managed will not achieve their purpose. In the next ten years, organizations will have to become facile at designing and managing different kinds of teams.

Teams vary along three key dimensions (see Figure 5.2). First, their *purpose* or *mission* can be either to perform the work

Figure 5.2. Types of Teams.

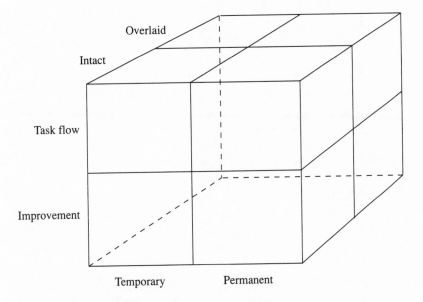

of the organization (product development, customer service, software support) or to improve the processes of the organization (quality improvement teams, task teams, quality circles). A work team operates directly to transform organizational inputs into the products or services of the firm, or it performs functions relevant to supporting, controlling, or directing the organizational transformation. These units can be measured and evaluated against goals for the products or services that they produce. Participation in the work team is generally the primary organizational responsibility of its members. Improvement-oriented teams, by contrast, have as their mission the task of increasing the effectiveness of the organizational processes by which work is accomplished. Their effectiveness must be measured in terms of improved results from the processes that they alter, processes that must be adopted and executed by their co-workers. The work of the improvement team is often not the only or even the major responsibility of the team members. The differences between work teams and improvement teams are managerially significant. Their tasks are defined differently and must be managed and evaluated differently. It is possible for the same team to be both a work team and an improvement team. For example, self-managing work teams may track trends, analyze processes, and make changes in work processes to improve performance. This dual mission is best achieved, however, if the group has clear "switching" rules for going from one mode to another and if the team is recognized and supported for performing both functions.

Time defines the second dimension. Teams can be either permanent or temporary organizational structures. Temporary structures are established for a task, such as a project, that has a finite life. Quality improvement teams, task teams, project teams, and new-product development teams are generally temporary. Customer-service teams, work teams, and product-line teams are examples of permanent teams. They are set up as ongoing organizational units, and dissolving them would be considered a restructuring of the organization. The dynamics and management of these two kinds of teams are quite different. The finite-life team has a recognizable beginning, middle, and end, and its life cycle conforms to the work it does. It is best managed according to this life cycle. Its ultimate performance measure is the success of the project that it was set up to accomplish. The permanent team goes through measurement and management cycles that are artificially prescribed. Yearly, quarterly, and monthly reports, reviews, and assessments punctuate an ongoing stream of tasks. Goals and objectives reflect targets and trends in performance measures.

The third dimension reflects whether the team is part of or overlaid on the organization's primary *authority structure*. In a functional organization, for example, a functional unit is the major organizational unit; a cross-functional quality improvement team or a new-product development team is overlaid. In a product organization, the product team is the major structural unit; the functional specialty group that cuts across products would be overlaid. The members of a team that is a primary structure of the organization report through the same hierarchical structure; members of an overlaid team report through different channels. The difference between the two teams has significant implications for design and management. The overlaid team faces issues of ambiguity of authority and priority. Its members may experience conflicting directions from different reporting structures. Such a team must operate by creating a consensus among the many groups that control the resources that it needs. Overlaid product development teams, for example, must have resources allocated by a number of functional and service groups. The design of such teams must include mechanisms to effectively influence and develop consensus in the organization. Planning processes must provide a forum for agreeing on direction and making difficult trade-offs.

Organizations are increasingly utilizing teams that fall into multiple segments of the cube illustrated in Figure 5.2 for different purposes. Most of the current approaches to managing performance are suitable for permanent work teams that are part of the main authority structure of the organization. Less is known about successful approaches to managing improvement teams, teams that are temporary, and those that are overlaid structures. Successful functioning of these teams depends on the organization's developing approaches to managing them and learning how to house and manage very different kinds of teams.

In addition to these three dimensions, teams vary in the extent to which they can be bounded. In many organizations, interdependence makes it difficult or impossible to design teams that house or control all or even most of the inputs required to get tasks done. Consequently, a clean boundary cannot be drawn around what is in the team and what is not. In such organizations, "teaming" behavior is critical, but it does not occur in easily identifiable teams.

All the types of teams illustrated in Figure 5.2 must have permeable boundaries to the extent that their work is interdependent with other teams and individuals beyond their bounds. A project team, for example, may rely heavily on support from centers of excellence or other shared resources. An improvement team may require data and technical assistance from organizational members and units not represented on the team. Such unboundedness increases the importance of the relationships that the team establishes with parts of the organization beyond its bounds. It also puts a premium on the use of such organizational processes as objectives setting and rewards, to tie people's fates together and point them in the same direction. This reiterates a point made earlier: even when teams exist as formal entities, formal *and* informal integrative processes are required.

Integrating Roles

Integrating roles, like integrating structures, can be designed to be weak or strong. Informal roles, such as those of designated contact people, are the weakest, since they generally carry with them no sources of formal empowerment. Creating formal roles, such as those of team leaders, systems managers, or project managers, differentiates those roles from others and may convey greater legitimacy to the integrator. Such roles can be further empowered if they entail formal decision-making authority and budgetary control. In the strongest integrating role, the people who are being integrated report to the integrator. The more these sources of power are vested in the integrator's role, the more likely it is that systemic interests and shared interests of the team, rather than the functional interests of the members, will be optimized.

It should be noted that the selection of integrating structures (such as teams) and the selection of individual integrating roles are somewhat independent design choices. Formal and informal integrating roles, such as liaisons and project managers, can be used whether or not there is a team structure in place. A team is itself an integrative device that may or may not require the establishment of a special leadership role for purposes of integration. For example, the creation of a self-contained cross-functional team does not automatically call for the creation of a strong individual integrator role. The team could be leaderless. In some companies, such a team reports to a higher-level cross-functional team, which exists to integrate functions at a more strategic level. The technical integration task may be so complex, however, that special roles are created. In some new-product development teams, for example, a systems integration role may be held by a team member who may be responsible for integration within the team or between the team and units outside its boundaries. Even where there is an empowered project manager, a complex project generally includes a number of other informal and formal coordinating roles and structures. Organizations that exist in highly complex environments, and in those where work is highly interdependent, house a wide variety of integrating mechanisms. It is not uncommon to see numerous overlapping and fluid structures, as well as many different kinds of general and specialized integrating roles. Clarification of roles and avoidance of costly redundancy are key process imperatives in such organizations.

Hierarchy of Teams

Teams can be established at any level of the organization where integration of effort is required, and they can be composed of those contributors whose work needs to be integrated. Work teams, for example, often consist of individual contributors who perform the transformation task. They may be functional or cross-functional, project-focused, customer-focused, or geographically focused. Management teams may exist at the top or the middle of the organization if it is necessary to integrate across the units that are conducting the transformation task. A top-level management team, for example, may create a framework to integrate businesses, geographies, or functions, according to the macrostructure of the organization (Nadler, Gerstein, and Shaw, 1992). Middle-level management teams may exist to integrate the various functions required for conducting a division's business, the various products that constitute a business line, or the various countries that must sell the division's products.

The more compelling the imperative for lateral integration in the operations of the organization, the greater the need for a hierarchy of teams that deal with increasingly aggregated levels of the organizational system. Knowledge of the bigger picture, required for lateral resolution of issues, can to some extent be built into the lower levels of the organization, but complex trade-offs are often strategic in nature. If the business units are relatively independent, then the functionally integrated strategy can be forged at the lower levels. For example, if two business units develop and manufacture unrelated products, then they can be managed with little integration between them. If, however, the units are highly interdependent because they share resources, technology, or customers, then it is important for the business direction, within which the operating teams are functioning, to be clearly forged, so that the units that have to cooperate are not put in conflict.

If the products of the two units must fit together in a system, then technical interaction will be required, and a common technology and product strategy must be forged. Furthermore, when issues cannot be resolved laterally, it is important that a decision maker be readily available to align various participants behind the decision. In the absence of higher-level teams, such decisions must often go to a general manager. A cross-functional team that has reached an impasse, for example, may have to move an issue up through several different functional chains before reaching a level with authority over all the parts of the organization that have to contribute to the success of that team. A second-tier cross-functional team can resolve many issues in a single escalation.

If integrating structures exist at multiple levels, two hierarchies may exist. If this is the case, then determining the roles and authority of each is critical. For example, many aerospace firms have a project or program hierarchy side by side with a functional hierarchy. The role of the program hierarchy is to integrate various functions that have to contribute to program success. This is made difficult if authority is not clearly delineated and if processes for planning and resolution are not spelled out. Overlapping membership and shared accountability systems can help.

This issue also arises when there is a hierarchy of parallel structures, such as are found in the nested council or steering committee of total quality management or union-management cooperative efforts. Higher-level teams provide a context for operational-level teams and can also serve as approval and decision-making bodies. The effectiveness of this design depends on clarity of the respective roles and responsibilities of the two hierarchies. Otherwise, the parallel structure is likely to generate decisions, plans, and improvements that the main organizational structure has no will to implement.

The lateral integration of an organization involves far more than setting up stand-alone teams or creating integrating roles. It requires that lateral integration occurs at multiple levels, and that the various structures and roles fit with one another and with the processes that are established. Ironically, lateral integration requires vertical integration, as illustrated by the concept of a hierarchy of teams.

Need for Balance

It is evident that an organization can quickly become overwhelmed by the complexity of its own integrative mechanisms and by the costs of integration. Therefore, it is structurally important to try to identify the units that are to be differentiated from the rest of the organization and allowed to optimize themselves, unshackled by unnecessary constraints from the larger organization. For example, some businesses may be truly independent of others and should not be burdened with the need to be part of lateral integrative devices that cut across businesses. Within a larger business, minibusiness units may be effectively decoupled from one another through built-in self-sufficiency, even if that implies some redundancy of resources. Some units may be coupled through a contracting mechanism that approaches a vendor-customer relationship, whereby an economic, market relationship allows relatively independent functioning, with specifications and pricing mechanisms as the integrators.

The motivational impact of creating a clearly measurable and accountable unit, with authority over the elements necessary to do its work, is great. Indeed, striving to create such empowered units is a basic principle of high-commitment work systems (Lawler, 1986; Lawler, Mohrman, and Ledford, 1992;

Walton, 1985). This arrangement is best achieved if the unit is constructed to include all the different skill bases that affect results, so that it can be bounded and somewhat decoupled from its context.

A decoupling strategy will not work, however, unless the principle can be adhered to rather rigorously. If the unit is dependent on other units of the organization for resources key to its own goal attainment, and if integrative or market mechanisms are not established, then the lack of coordination can be far more costly, in terms of redundancy, missed deadlines, rework, and unnecessary work, than the cost of integration. This issue is evident even in relationships with vendors, where we increasingly see a more permeable boundary, with overlapping teams and liaison roles to ensure that technical and business interdependence are addressed. The art of management is to walk the tightrope between too much and too little integration.

Integrating Processes

If there are strong pressures for lateral integration, complex interdependence and organizational trade-offs, then a complex assortment of lateral structures and roles will be present. As illustrated by Figure 5.1, the most fundamental form of integration is established by the integrating processes. Integrative structures and roles cannot be fully effective if these processes are not in place. Integrating processes include the following:

- The setting of mission, strategy, and values to guide overall organizational direction
- Objectives setting and budgeting to guide operations
- The connection of various parts of the organization and individuals through the integrative use of information systems
- Career paths and development approaches that develop the ability of employees to perform in laterally integrated organizations
- Performance-management practices that motivate individual, team, and organizational effectiveness

Mission, Strategy, and Values

The establishment of mission, strategy, and values is the over-arching integrative task of the organization. These provide the direction, the priorities, and the criteria to guide organizational decision making and help resolve conflicts. Responsibility for making sure that these exist, are current, and embody the guiding direction of the organization lies with top management. A wide variety of participative (integrative) mechanisms can be utilized to ensure buy-in and take various stakeholders' perspectives into account.

The cascading of the mission, strategy, and values throughout the organization often takes the form of the development of customized but congruent versions for different organizational units and various system levels. This is intended to prevent organizational units from working at cross-purposes and to make the organizational direction meaningful to organizational participants. The cascading process allows participants to be more specific about unit-level mission, strategy, and norms.

Objectives Setting and Budgeting

Operational alignment is achieved through the process of setting long- and short-term objectives and the allocation of resources to support those objectives. Hierarchically nested objectives-setting processes (such as management by objectives) have been common, but mechanisms for the lateral integration of objectives are less developed and less frequently practiced. In most organizations, for example, process improvement objectives that require the concurrent focus of multiple organizational units often have been perceived as "extra" and have not been officially funded. Objectives that cut across have often relied on a cumbersome "tin cupping" process, in which various individuals and organizations ante up to support a common concern, or they have relied on tapping pots of money controlled by top managers.

Formal processes for lateral planning, objectives setting, and budgeting will become more common in organizations.

Companies such as Hewlett-Packard, Florida Power and Light, and Procter & Gamble utilize a policy-deployment planning process (also called *hoshin* planning). Such planning is a component of a total quality management system. It is a multifunction, multilevel process of identifying objectives that are aligned with a strategic direction, laterally integrated, and supportive of process improvement. A key component is an explicit process for sharing objectives laterally and ensuring that interdependent groups have mutually supportive objectives. Generally, a team is responsible for making sure that this happens. At the project level, quality functional deployment (Hauser and Clausing, 1988) is a cross-functional planning tool. It is a data-based process for planning and committing each function to its required contribution in meeting customers' expectations.

Budgeting processes must reflect these laterally determined objectives and fit the lateral structures that have been established. In an organization where the key processes and structures are cross-functional, relying solely on functional budgeting works against the logic of the work flow. At a minimum, cross-functional input to budgeting trade-offs is required because budget cuts in one part of the organization can prevent the execution of plans in other parts.

Development and Careers

Effective performance in a laterally integrated organization puts a premium on the ability to work in teams, be part of multiperspective problem-solving efforts, communicate effectively across disciplines and boundaries, and make judgments about trade-offs. Effective performance requires a more systemic understanding of the organization, based in part on career exposure to more than one part of the organization. This can be achieved through job rotation or through the judicious use of temporary assignments (such as represented by membership on cross-functional special-purpose teams).

One development focus is on preparing individuals for cross-functional moves and bringing them rapidly up to speed in new areas. Much development will occur in teams and will happen concurrently with task performance. A key benefit of cross-functional improvement teams is the cross-training that goes on as functions share their frameworks and perspectives. The goal is to make sure that specialists have a broad understanding of the organization and to develop generalists with a number of specialist backgrounds.

Laterally integrated organizations continue to have a need for experts — highly trained specialists — especially in technical organizations. The preservation and development of core competencies (Prahalad and Hamel, 1990) requires the ability to attract, nurture, and retain people with skills and knowledge critical to the organization's strategy, as well as to deploy them where they will have the largest strategic impact. Core competencies often represent the nexus of several technological skills. They are integrative in nature. For example, core competencies at 3M include adhesives and coatings; at Honda, a core skill is engine manufacturing.

The integration of employees with depth skills and core competencies into cross-functional tasks and projects presents a special challenge. Organizational units will be complex mixtures of generalists and specialists, who may be related to their units in quite different ways. Highly developed depth skills and core competencies, for example, may reside in an excellence pool and be integrated into projects in a consulting capacity. A similar relationship may exist for members of highly specialized staff support groups, which reside in a centralized group but provide customized consulting services to various business units. Careers may involve movement between generalist and specialist roles, thus enabling individuals to keep up with needed skill bases and apply multiple skills in a generalist capacity.

Performance and Reward Systems

Many common approaches to the management of performance in organizations rest on the assumption that the individual is the performing unit. Work is broken down into individual jobs. Individual accountability is the ideal, and *equity* is defined as the basing of appraisals and rewards on clearly defined individual responsibilities, good measures, and fair comparisons between people. This approach puts a premium on behavior that optimizes "my piece of the work."

In the laterally integrated organization, much more of the focus of performance management is on the connections between performers. Teamwork, communication, multiskilling, and participation in the problem-solving process are increasingly valued and become explicit reward and promotional criteria. Teams are increasingly acknowledged as performing units, and performance-management practices begin to focus on defining team tasks and responsibilities and on appraising and rewarding teams (Mohrman, Mohrman, and Lawler, 1992). Attention is paid to how the team's work fits into the larger organizational context, as well as to key stakeholders with whom integration is required. The focus on the identification of internal and external customers, advocated by proponents of total quality management, is one manifestation of this phenomenon.

Individual performance requirements and roles are increasingly defined in the context of the team and the larger organization, often by team members and stakeholders of the individual's work. For example, as teams become more self-directed, the breakdown of tasks within them is increasingly done by the team members themselves and is based on priorities and requirements for meeting team objectives and customers' requirements. Multistakeholder input into team and individual appraisals is becoming more common.

Rewards such as gain sharing, target-based bonuses, profit sharing, and stock ownership will increasingly be based on team and organizational performance. These approaches tie the self-interest of interdependent performers together and align them with the performance of the organizational system. Fixed-pie merit pay systems, which inherently pit team members against one another, will be altered to be less disruptive of cooperation. Such practices as basing the size of merit pools on team performance and having co-workers determine individual merit pay are incentives to cooperation.

A second trend is toward person-based (skill- and competency-based) rather than job-based pay. This approach explicitly rewards lateral movement, cross-training, and the resulting increased exposure, broader understanding, and flexibility. In the past, this form of pay has been primarily utilized in production settings, but we are seeing increased application among knowledge workers (see Lawler, Mohrman, and Ledford, 1992). Person-based pay explicitly acknowledges individual value to the organization but in a manner that is compatible with teamwork. It encourages development and application of multiple competencies and does not pit individuals against one another in competition for a fixed pot of "merit money." (Chapter Nine deals more extensively with these trends.)

Connectivity

Shared information systems and data bases, computer networks, distributed information, and common languages are important integrative mechanisms. Idiosyncratic languages and systems work against integration and protect the power bases of individuals and specialized groups.

The use of technology offers powerful possibilities for process integration. For example, optimally utilized CAD/CAM systems entail the development across functions of the common standards, decision criteria, and notation that enable parallel processing and on-line integration. Such systems can be linked to suppliers, to enable just-in-time parts delivery; to billing, to enable automatic accounting and bill generation; and to customers, to enable quick order entry, product customization, and delivery. Effective achievement of these integrative benefits requires and enables organizational integration. The integrative information system must be based on a consensually developed model of the business enterprise that includes data bases, languages, distributive capabilities, and access rules.

Use of Processes, Roles, and Structures for Integration

To some extent, processes can substitute for structures. For example, strategic planning processes that provide a framework for aligned objectives among various organizational units, and reward systems that acknowledge overall performance, may be adequate to guide those units in the same direction, without the creation of cross-unit teams. The difference between process and structure may be semantic, however, since it will be necessary to create a mechanism to do the strategic planning that links the different units' perspectives. That mechanism may be an overlaid structure, such as a strategic planning council, that is essentially a team.

In general, it has been our observation that different mixtures of integrating processes, structures, and roles can be used. As the need for integration increases, however, all three have to be used more frequently. Processes must fit with the structures and roles that are established.

As increasingly sophisticated communications technology and information systems link people, our images of teams and team structures will become more ethereal. Teams may be composed of individuals spread throughout the world, linked up by information technology and integrated by a project manager who does not reside with the team members. "Virtual teams" (Savage, 1990) will be linked by distributed information, shared goals, and agreed-to protocols and will entail fluid membership and temporarily close (although perhaps physically distant) working relationships. Rigid definitions of how things are done will give way to customized organizations designed for the task at hand and utilizing structures, roles, and processes appropriate to its optimization.

Changing Role of Management

The laterally focused organization poses a new set of managerial challenges. The effectiveness of such lateral structures as teams and councils rests on their ability to decide on common courses of action and on their authority to make decisions and commit resources. The operation of lateral mechanisms is not cheap. Considerable amounts of time and energy are tied up in these processes. This redirection of energies is best accomplished if the hierarchical structure has been streamlined. If the lateral mechanism merely duplicates hierarchical responsibilities, then costly redundancy, conflict, and inertia are built into the organization. For example, if the decisions of a cross-functional team have to go up several levels of multiple functional hierarchies for approval, then those decisions may as well be made at a higher level, by a cross-functional team or a general manager. This implies not only a change in the organization's shape but also a change in the role of management. As the lower levels of flatter organizations are increasingly populated by individuals with considerable tenure and experience, authority can be moved downward.

One key management role is that of providing a context for effective functioning at these lower levels by ensuring a common direction coming from its own level. The development and cascading of a strategy are critical management tasks. The importance of communicating that strategy, in order to provide an umbrella for effective lower-level decisions, is enhanced. Management must also provide effective channels for issues that cannot be resolved at lower levels.

Another key role of management is to participate in ongoing design and redesign of the organization. Lateral integration occurs through a fluid set of integrative mechanisms. Particularly in dynamic environments, and wherever continuous improvement is a competitive imperative, change will be the order of the day. Managing change requires continual attention, so that incentives are aligned, development occurs, and processes meet the needs of the organization. Lateral organizations are oriented toward processes and projects and are tailored to the task at hand. Ensuring that these organizational forms are tailored, modified, established, and discontinued is the key to their effective functioning and to ensuring that integrative tasks do not overwhelm the organization.

Yet another key role of management will be in the people-management processes of the organization. Here, the role will change substantially. The one-to-one, all-powerful supervisor-subordinate role will change. The management of performance requires active involvement by a larger network of people who are stakeholders and co-workers. The manager's role will be to orchestrate that involvement and provide guidance and coaching in helping employees respond and develop. Managers will also be expected to ensure that teams are effectively developed and to orchestrate the process for team appraisal and rewards. Another key people-management role will be to ensure that a human resources strategy is enacted—that core skills and key talent pools are attracted, retained, and developed. This will no longer be the exclusive purview of a highly specialized human resources group; it will be a responsibility shared with line managers.

Organizational Tensions

A number of tensions and trade-offs are inherent in the transition to a more laterally oriented way of organizing. These are briefly described in the sections that follow.

Function Versus Process

Many traditional organizations have promoted functional excellence and adhered to a logic of discipline-based expertise. In fact, these continue to be essential in laterally oriented organizations. There will always be a need for the ongoing revitalization of functional excellence, which may be attended to by functional organizations or by councils or other overlaid organizations that provide focus on this issue.

The notion that an organization has to protect its core competencies goes even farther. There are certain competencies in which world leadership is strategically desirable. The organization must be designed to protect excellence in these areas, as well as to promote integration of these skills into the business units that need them. The balance between specialists and generalists is a key design issue and involves a number of trade-offs.

Individual Versus Team Orientation

U. S. society is highly individualistic. Personal equity, advancement, and feedback are key attractors and motivators in organizations. Engineering and other technical disciplines rest on an analytical knowledge base that has been reinforced by the individual work-breakdown processes utilized in organizations. In human resources, practices have striven for clear delineation of individual accountability and objective measures. Our studies have indicated that people want to know where they stand, and that individual rewards and recognition are related to job satisfaction and feelings of personal equity (Mohrman, Mohrman, and Worley, 1990). Hierarchical progression, individual performance appraisal, and merit increases have been experienced as confirmation of self-worth.

The movement toward a culture of teamwork will be uncomfortable for many individuals, especially during the transition period. Given our cultural orientation, it is likely that this transition be effected only if organizations attend to the need for personal acknowledgment and sense of accomplishment. Mechanisms must be developed for building in acknowledgment of personal value while reinforcing teamwork. This implies emphasizing contributions to the team in definitions of personal performance. It also implies rewarding teamwork and developing ways for team members themselves to recognize clearly superior contributions.

Definition of Productive Work

The staffing patterns in most organizations have assumed a commodity theory of expertise—that is, that people should be assigned to tasks in such a way as to maximize the number of hours of their applying their expertise directly to tasks. "Process," hours, such as those involved in team meetings, team development, planning, coordinating, and joint problem solving, have been viewed as nonproductive time. This is formalized in such industries as aerospace and defense, where there is no account against which to "charge" those hours. Furthermore, many of these process activities have been placed in the jobs of specialized staff experts and managers.

The movement toward lateral integration will require the belief that "process" hours are productive, and that they lay the foundation for coordinated effort, higher quality, higher speed, and lower cost. Nevertheless, the establishment of lateral mechanisms where integration and coordination are not required is a waste of valuable time. When a team is required, it is essential that its members become efficient at team information processing. Effective lateral integration does not imply that all work is now done in groups. The skill of management (or self-management) will be to create the most efficient mix of team and individual performance.

Every effort must be made to expedite team processes and lateral integration mechanisms so that they do not consume unnecessary hours. Technological methods, such as using shared computer systems and teleconferencing, will be helpful in integrating dispersed contributors. Broadly held team skills, aligned incentives, and effective conflict-resolution mechanisms will also be absolutely critical.

A constant challenge will be to optimize the process gains that are achieved by establishing teams and to minimize the process losses that result from inappropriate or ineffective teams and from the establishment of teams that are not empowered to make decisions. Managers will have to be knowledgeable about design and able to make appropriate choices among integrating mechanisms. Organizational members will have to become effective team participants, and team process skills will have to be widely dispersed in the organization.

Costs of Change

For many organizations, the costs of changing to a lateral focus are high. The change process must alter the logic that has been built into every aspect of the hierarchically, individually oriented organization. Ultimately, it will essentially alter the game of organizational success for employees and require new skills, new concepts of career, and new concepts of self-worth.

The barriers to such change are substantial. Existing jobs, departments, career paths, and authority distribution define a status quo in which a large number of people have considerable vested interest and entrenched power. Current performance-management practices define a well-understood game for employees. Although they see its dysfunctional aspects, they know their own place within it. Replacing it with the unknown constitutes a considerable threat.

The resources required for the development of teaming skills are considerable, and the current individual-development paradigm will have to be significantly altered so as to focus more on the development of teams and groups. Executive leadership and modeling of lateral integration at the top of the organization will be a keystone of the change process.

Conclusion

This chapter has argued that the lateral aspects of organizational functioning are becoming more important to organizational success in a highly interdependent, competitive world. Speed, quality, organizational learning, and continuous improvement require effective work across an organization.

This lateral emphasis is influencing the design of business units at the macro level and the way work is done at the micro level. Lateral structures and integrating roles must be carefully designed to ensure that the organization achieves balance among its multiple focuses. Basic processes will be redesigned to support a more lateral and less hierarchical view of the organization.

The impact on individuals will be substantial. The most fundamental change will be that their competence in teamwork skills will be critical to their contributions to organizational effectiveness. Careers will look different in organizations that are flatter and more lateral in orientation. Organizations will face the challenge of promoting a teamwork culture while preserving the individual's sense of meaningful contribution and self-worth.

Although these changes are well under way in many organizations, most organizations are at the beginning of a change that will eventually alter all their processes, as well as the assumptions built into organizational functioning. People will envision organizations, and their careers within them, in a fundamentally different way.

This whole arena is a true organizational frontier. Our learning about the lateral organization is at a very early stage. There are no off-the-shelf designs and solutions. A great deal of academic and practical learning about the lateral organization will take place over the coming years. Meanwhile, organizations will have little choice but to learn by doing.

References

Deming, W. E. *Out of the Crisis.* Cambridge, Mass: Center for Advanced Engineering Study, Massachusetts Institute of Technology, 1986.

Galbraith, J. R. *Designing Complex Organizations.* Reading, Mass.: Addison-Wesley, 1973.

Galbraith, J. R., and Kazanjian, R. *Strategy Implementation: The Role of Structure and Process.* (2nd ed.) St. Paul, Minn.: West Publishing, 1986.

Hauser, J. R., and Clausing, D. "The House of Quality." *Harvard Business Review,* 1988, *66*(3), 63–73.

Juran, J. M. *Juran on Leadership for Quality.* New York: Free Press, 1989.

Lawler, E. E., III. *High-Involvement Management: Participative Strategies for Improving Organizational Performance.* San Francisco: Jossey-Bass, 1986.

Lawler, E. E., III, Mohrman, S. A., and Ledford, G. E., Jr. *Employee Involvement and Total Quality Management: Practices and Results in Fortune 1000 Companies.* San Francisco: Jossey-Bass, 1992.

Lawrence, P., and Lorsch, J. *Organization and Environment.* Boston: Division of Research, Harvard Business School, 1967.

Manz, C. C., and Sims, H. P. *Superleadership: Leading Others to Lead Themselves.* Englewood Cliffs, N.J.: Prentice-Hall, 1989.

Mohrman, A. M., Jr., Mohrman, S. A., and Lawler, E. E., III. "The Performance Management of Teams." In W. Bruns (ed.), *Performance Measurement, Evaluation, and Incentives.* Boston: Harvard Business School Press, 1992.

Mohrman, A. M., Jr., Mohrman, S. A., and Worley, C. "High Technology Performance Management." In M. A. Von Glinow and S. A. Mohrman (eds.), *Managing Complexity in High Technology Organizations.* New York: Oxford University Press, 1990.

Nadler, D. A., Gerstein, M. S., and Shaw, R. B. *Organizational Architecture: Designs for Changing Organizations.* San Francisco: Jossey-Bass, 1992.

Pasmore, W. A. *Designing Effective Organizations: The Sociotechnical Systems Perspective.* New York: Wiley, 1988.

Prahalad, C. K., and Hamel, G. "The Core Competence of the Corporation." *Harvard Business Review,* 1990, *68*(3), 79–93.

Savage, C. *5th Generation Management: Integrating Enterprises Through Human Networking.* Bedford, Mass.: Digital Press, 1990.

Scholtes, P. R. *The Team Handbook.* Madison, Wisc.: Joiner Associates, 1988.

Walton, R. E. "From Control to Commitment in the Workplace." *Harvard Business Review,* 1985, *63*(2), 76–84.

Chapter Six

Employee Involvement: Lessons and Predictions

Gerald E. Ledford, Jr.

This chapter has two purposes. First, it attempts to summarize the key lessons from a decade of research on employee involvement at the Center for Effective Organizations (CEO). Second, it looks to the future and offers a set of predictions about where employee involvement practices are headed.

Employee involvement has been a central theme in our work at CEO since the center's inception. We have conducted research on participation groups, quality circles, and self-managing work teams; union-management employee involvement processes; reward systems that support employee involvement, such as skill-based pay and gain sharing; and the human resource systems (such as for selection and training) that are needed to reinforce employee involvement activities. We have studied the

Note: Although I am the author of this chapter, it summarizes the work of a group of researchers, including Ed Lawler, Sue Mohrman, Monty Mohrman, and Susan Cohen of the Center for Effective Organizations and Tom Cummings, Dave Bowen, Barry Nathan, and others from the USC faculty. I am responsible for specific statements made in this chapter, but the general perspective represented here is that of the larger group of researchers to which I belong.

high-involvement organization as an organizational form. We have examined the installation of employee involvement practices in retrofits of traditional organizations and in start-up or "green field" organizations. We have studied the processes used to implement and maintain employee involvement at the group level, the plant level, the division level, and the corporate level.

What Is Employee Involvement?

We define employee involvement as extension of the power to make decisions and of business information, rewards for performance, and technical and social skills to the lowest levels of the organization (Lawler, 1986). Employee involvement is a complex concept, according to this definition. In our view, each of the four elements of the definition is integral to the concept of employee involvement. Without the power to make decisions, employee participation is superficial or even trivial. Without adequate information about the business and other relevant matters, involvement is naïve and potentially harmful. Without rewards for performance, employee motivation will not be aligned with organizational objectives, in the long run. Without skills, employees will not have the technical and social knowledge they need to participate effectively.

This concept of employee involvement is obviously deeper than the dollop of influence or participation that constitutes employee involvement in many laboratory experiments and field studies. For this reason, much writing and research about employee involvement are irrelevant to the concept as we define it. Much of the existing work on employee involvement is limited because it is concerned only with changes in the amount of influence employees feel, rather than with real changes in decision-making authority. In other cases, the changes in involvement that have been studied are so inconsiderable that they should not be expected to have strong effects on employees and organizations.

Our definition indicates that employee involvement is a property of organizational systems, not of individuals. Employee involvement is reflected in the way organizations are structured

and managed, not simply in the beliefs and attitudes of individual employees. We argue that it is important to ask what
structural mechanisms channel participation and what organizational systems support or limit involvement.

Our definition of employee involvement also implies that
a variety of basic organizational practices must be congruent
with high levels of involvement (Lawler, 1992). As will be discussed in Chapter Seven, these practices include organizational
structures and job designs, which move decision-making power
down into the organization; pay systems, which link rewards
with business performance; management information systems,
which deliver information; and training, which builds skills.
These management practices also include those human resource
practices that symbolize the common fate of different employee
subgroups (such as the all-salaried work force) and that facilitate the realization of employee involvement (such as the selection system). Employee involvement practices may also extend
to the elimination or reduction of special management perquisites and status symbols.

In defining what employee involvement is, it is important to identify what employee involvement is not. Among other
things, employee involvement is not simply quality improvement, union avoidance, or "Japanese-style management."

Employee Involvement and Total Quality Programs

Quality improvement may be — and, indeed, often is — a result
of employee involvement practices (Ledford, 1988). Employee
involvement groups, usually on the order of quality circles or
task forces, are often created as part of quality improvement
efforts. The quality movement has led to increased emphasis
on providing employees with good feedback from customers (one
type of business information) and with group problem-solving
skills (one important type of skill). These developments certainly
are consistent with our definition of employee involvement.
Nevertheless, the gurus of the quality movement are engineers,
statisticians, and consultants who, in our view, often are naïve
about human behavior. The writings of Philip Crosby, for ex-

ample, make the innocent assumption that workers will be motivated to improve quality if only they are told more clearly what to do and how to do it (Cole, 1989). In general, contemporary quality approaches do not make employee involvement, as we have defined it, a central feature of the strategy for quality improvement. The typical quality program is top-down, in all important respects, and usually does not involve such deeper forms of employee involvement as changing job designs to permit greater worker discretion over quality. Indeed, some quality improvement tactics, such as some forms of just-in-time inventory management, may reduce employee involvement by leaving little room for worker autonomy or discretion about the work. It is possible to emphasize both quality improvement and employee involvement in the same organization, but some common practices recommended by quality experts either represent limited forms of employee involvement or represent barriers to employee involvement.

Employee Involvement and Union Avoidance

Organizations with very high levels of employee involvement tend to be very difficult for unions to organize, and so companies sometimes view employee involvement as a strategy for union avoidance. This rationale for employee involvement is the basis for the skeptical attitude of some union leaders toward employee involvement. Employee involvement is not necessarily a union-free approach, however. Indeed, even the most intensive current forms of employee involvement are found in both union and nonunion settings. For example, the General Motors Saturn operation uses a high-involvement design that includes work teams, skill-based pay and gain sharing, intensive training each year, and extensive sharing of business information. This organizational design was created by a joint union-management design group. More generally, virtually every major union in the United States has been involved in joint union-management employee involvement efforts in at least some locations.

Focusing on an intensive employee involvement process

as a means of avoiding unionization not only is misguided but also sets management's sights too low. There are easier and less expensive ways for an antiunion management to avoid unions in today's environment. Employee involvement can and should be pursued on its own merits, as a means of increasing organizational effectiveness. If the focus is on avoiding unions, rather than on organizational effectiveness, management may well stop short of creating an employee involvement effort that can significantly improve organizational performance. Instead, management may be satisfied with piecemeal efforts that it credits with helping avert union organization.

Employee Involvement and "Japanese-Style Management"

The phrase "Japanese-style management" is deceptive. Such management practices as consensus decision making and lifetime employment are often assumed to be almost universal in Japan and in Japanese-owned organizations in the United States. In fact, however, there appears to be considerable variation in the use of particular human resource practices in Japan, and many practices that are relatively common in Japan appear to be rare in Japanese-owned operations in the United States. It is easy to overstate the degree to which employee involvement practices are used in Japanese organizations.

Some observers argue that there is a fair degree of employee involvement in one form of Japanese management — specifically, the Toyota production system (also termed the *lean production model;* see Adler, 1991; Womack, Jones, and Roos, 1990). This approach does provide workers with much more job-skills training than is typical in conventional U.S. manufacturing operations. It also provides them with information about organizational performance and sometimes provides organization-level rewards for business performance (such as profit sharing and greater job security). Employees do not have much autonomy in making decisions, but their suggestions for improvement in the production system are actively encouraged through quality circles and other means.

Overall, however, there is no evidence that Japanese managers are more committed than U.S. managers to providing lower-level employees with real decision-making authority. Indeed, job involvement and high involvement (defined below) are rare and perhaps even nonexistent in Japanese-managed organizations. In our view, Japanese management essentially embodies a more rational version of the traditional, control-oriented management model that dominates U.S. management thinking (Lawler, 1992).

Types and Prevalence of Employee Involvement

Three different types of employee involvement can be distinguished. These are suggestion involvement, job involvement, and high involvement (Lawler, 1988).

Suggestion involvement entails the power to make suggestions for change, but not the power to make decisions. Suggestion involvement usually is provided by means of special structures, such as quality circles, that are parallel to the formal organization and are dependent on it for the implementation of changes. It is the most limited of the three forms of employee involvement. It can be installed without major changes to the key design elements of the normal organization.

Job involvement comprises changes in the design of work, so that employees have more control over the day-to-day decisions relevant to their jobs. These changes are accomplished through job enrichment for individuals, or through the creation of work teams (which also may be called self-regulating teams, autonomous work teams, or self-managing teams). One of the key design elements of the organization — namely, work design — is automatically changed in this approach. Other elements may or may not be changed.

High involvement encompasses job involvement and suggestion involvement but goes farther, to stress the involvement of employees in managing the business. High-involvement organizations use a wide variety of congruent organizational design elements to reinforce and facilitate employee involvement, including a whole range of innovative power sharing, information sharing, skill building, rewards, and related human resource

practices. The best-known examples are new showcase manufacturing plants built by such companies as Procter & Gamble,
General Mills, Anheuser-Busch, Digital Equipment Corporation, Mead, and many others.

While none of these three types of employee involvement
is easy to implement effectively, job involvement is more complex and more difficult to implement than suggestion involvement. High involvement is the most complex and difficult of
the three.

Employee involvement practices in U.S. corporations tend
to be broad rather than deep. The more limited approach of suggestion involvement is the most common form of employee involvement, and even this form of employee involvement is typically not extended to the majority of the corporate work force.
Two studies of the employee involvement practices of Fortune
1000 corporations (Lawler, Ledford, and Mohrman, 1989; Lawler, Mohrman, and Ledford, 1992) found that over 80 percent of
these corporations use some form of employee involvement. Relatively few companies, however, make extensive use of power-
sharing practices. The most popular power-sharing practices were
the parallel-organization forms, such as quality circles and employee participation groups. These do not fundamentally change
the level of decision-making authority extended to the lowest levels
of the organization. In both studies, only 1 percent of companies claimed to include half of the work force in a typical job involvement practice: self-managing work teams.

The high-involvement organizational form has been mostly
restricted to a few innovative manufacturing plants. Estimates
on the number of such organizations vary, from a few hundred
to perhaps a thousand. In percentage terms, this represents a
tremendous increase over the past twenty years. Measured in
terms of the percentage of U.S. organizations or even U.S.
plants, however, the percentage organized as high-involvement
organizations is relatively small.

Advanced Forms of Employee Involvement

An overwhelming percentage of major companies report that
they have tried at least some form of employee involvement and

that their employee involvement efforts are successful in enhancing organizational performance. Yet the use of employee involvement practices remains relatively limited, even in most companies that have directly experienced the effectiveness of high-involvement designs. Why? Even more important, why have the most advanced forms of employee involvement not been tried more extensively, despite evidence that even the more limited forms are successful to some degree?

This pattern would be understandable if job involvement and high involvement were relatively rare because these approaches had limited payoffs, as compared with those of more limited forms of employee involvement. These forms of employee involvement do not appear to be rare because of poorer cost-benefit ratios, however. The research evidence shows that suggestion involvement is a limited intervention with limited effects (Ledford and Mohrman, 1988; Ledford, Lawler, and Mohrman, 1988; Mohrman and Novelli, 1985). The evidence also suggests that job involvement often has strong effects on performance and employee attitudes (Guzzo, Jette, and Katzell, 1985). For example, our study of self-managing teams in a telephone company (Cohen and Ledford, 1990) found that they outperformed a matched set of control groups on most indicators of performance and quality of work life.

The available data also strongly suggest that high-involvement organizations are very effective in general, even though the evidence is more limited than we would like (Lawler, 1986). Internal studies by Procter & Gamble, General Foods, and General Mills have found that their high-involvement plants are 20 to 40 percent more productive than comparable plants. A study of ninety-six high-involvement organizations (Ledford, Cummings, and Wright, 1992) found that about three-fourths outperformed their industries on a variety of measures. Hard performance data from a large subset of the sample found that the high-involvement organizations outperformed their industries on return on sales by an average of 532 percent and on return on investment by an average of 388 percent. There certainly are examples of high-involvement organizations that have failed; for example, Perkins, Nieva, and Lawler (1983) studied a less than successful implementation of a high-involvement design. The overall success rate, however, appears to be quite high for high-involvement organizations.

Employee Involvement and Managerial Ideology

If advanced forms of employee involvement are not rare because they are ineffective, then why are they rare? Perhaps the reason is that the employee involvement movement is relatively recent, and deeper forms of employee involvement will spread in the long run. We are not convinced that this is the case, however. We believe that advanced forms of employee involvement are rare because they are inconsistent with the dominant management ideology and the fundamental design principles of most contemporary organizations.

Modern organizations are designed to ensure hierarchical control and internal stability — two basic virtues of the bureaucratic form of organization. Intensive employee involvement efforts are often resisted by managers because of threats to control and stability, even if they seem to produce improvements in performance.

Intensive forms of employee involvement imply a new world view, or paradigm, of the management of human resources in organizations. This paradigm is based on the assumption that maximizing employees' ability to respond to business challenges and changing technical conditions is the key to maximizing organizational effectiveness. Widespread adoption of this paradigm will depend on the extent to which managers adopt new ways of looking at the world and become familiar and comfortable with new practices and behaviors. There is some evidence that an employee involvement paradigm may be emerging in U.S. corporations (Mohrman and Lawler, 1985).

There are indications that managers increasingly accept the rhetoric of employee involvement. It is the rare manager today who cannot recite the popular wisdom about why employee involvement is desirable. No consultant or author needs to tell managers about the changing work force, increasing foreign and domestic competition, "Japanese-style management," changing technology, and the many other forces that usually are claimed to create the need for employee involvement. Consultants often seem to be preaching to the converted when they tell managers that more employee involvement is needed. In every company we have surveyed on employee involvement in recent years, most managers at all levels express verbal support for whatever employee involvement efforts are being tried within their companies.

This acceptance of the desirability of employee involvement represents a change in espoused managerial philosophy but cannot always be accepted at face value. Managers who openly oppose employee involvement these days are considered "Neanderthals" or "dinosaurs" — not an acceptable characterization for managers in this era of corporate delayering and downsizing.

Rhetoric Versus Behavior

This does not mean that managers who espouse employee involvement are truly comfortable with it. First, senior managers in favor of employee involvement often see few implications for their own behavior; they see employee involvement as "something the top tells the middle to do to the bottom" of the organization (Nadler and Lawler, 1983). Second, and more important, managers repeatedly show the ability to redefine employee involvement in ways that correspond to whatever styles of management they already practice. Several studies of communication styles in employee involvement groups of various kinds have found that managers often foster pseudoparticipation by the use of such techniques as loaded questions and mixed messages (see Fairhurst and Chandler, 1989). In such situations, employees have little trouble discerning the real messages about employee involvement.

We saw this very clearly in a Fortune 500 company that was attempting to adopt employee involvement as a day-to-day mode of doing business. Twenty-five managers, in an area of the company where employee involvement efforts were concentrated, were asked to define employee involvement and to say whether they practiced that style of management. All twenty-five claimed to practice employee involvement, and most said they were relieved that the company had finally endorsed the style of management that they had privately accepted all along. Nevertheless, the managers also provided twenty-five different, inconsistent definitions of employee involvement, ranging from sharing decision-making power to smiling a lot and otherwise being friendly to employees.

Changing Managerial Behavior

The preceding discussion indicates that a manager's response to employee involvement initiatives may be to redefine employee involvement as something that requires no change. It misses the point, however, to say that managers are insincere or that nothing can be done other than to replace veteran managers. We suspect that, regardless of whether they claim to practice employee involvement, most managers do not know how to manage in a manner that fosters and is consistent with employee involvement. Like other human beings, they have difficulty breaking out of old frames of reference. The perspectives and behaviors that are required to support high levels of employee involvement simply go beyond the experience of most managers.

Ways must be found to define employee involvement as something that requires real change, yet this must be done without hopelessly alienating the managers who ultimately must make it work. Managers cannot be trusted to define employee involvement completely on their own; it must be defined for them. Yet the concept must also inspire their interest and commitment. This suggests the importance of vision and leadership, two elusive concepts that are difficult to realize in practice.

Organizations adopting employee involvement need good methods for the selection, training, and coaching of managers. Selection, training, and on-line coaching are the ways in which an abstract vision is translated into day-to-day behavior. This is not to say, however, that enough is known about how to do these things well. Much remains to be learned about how to foster effective management behavior in employee involvement–oriented organizations.

Implementation Strategy Goals

Some proponents of employee involvement argue that it should be used because it is the moral way to manage, not necessarily because it affects organizational performance (see Sashkin, 1984). Our research suggests, however, that employee involvement efforts that are not focused on organizational performance are less effective, both for employees and for the organization. We have found this to be true among employee involvement groups (Mohrman and Ledford, 1985) and among companies that are implementing employee involvement efforts (Lawler, Ledford, and Mohrman, 1989).

Organizational performance goals legitimize the employee involvement effort and help provide it with the guideposts by which success can be assessed. Indeed, there is evidence that companies that adopt employee involvement primarily in order to improve performance are more effective both in improving performance and in improving employees' quality of work life than are companies that adopt employee involvement primarily for value-related reasons or to improve the quality of work life (Lawler, Ledford, and Mohrman, 1989).

Rate of Implementation Success

The number of organizations attempting to gain a competitive advantage through employee involvement dwarfs the number successfully implementing major employee involvement initiatives. This is disappointing, in some respects. Companies are implementing employee involvement practices for hard-nosed business reasons, and senior managers see employee involvement as fitting well with other changes that they are implementing, which are intended to lead to performance improvement, greater flexibility, new technologies, and new business strategies (Lawler, Ledford, and Mohrman, 1989). Nevertheless, the thin veneer of employee involvement that exists in most companies is rarely enough to alter the level of overall corporate performance, even when there are local successes (Lawler, Mohrman, and Ledford, 1992).

Most organizations probably do not yet know how to increase employee involvement effectively. This conclusion is suggested by the fact that very few companies have adopted employee involvement practices throughout the firm, as well as by the scarcity of high-involvement organizations. In addition, few companies have experimented with new forms of employee involvement that go beyond replication of their own initial successes and imitations of other companies' efforts. This is another sign of a movement in its early stages.

We also note, however, that many organizations do seem to learn how to implement employee involvement more effectively over time. Many companies seem to learn what types of employee involvement work in their particular situations. They often progress from simpler to more complex and more effective forms of employee involvement, and they learn how to improve their implementation of employee involvement. Companies that are able to learn in this way often devote special effort to learning from experience and to the diffusion of knowledge about employee involvement from one part of the company to another (see Ledford and Mohrman, 1993, for an example of such a learning process within a large division of a major company.) Thus, although we have been critical of the level and types of employee involvement practiced in contemporary organizations, our experience suggests that many companies do seem to learn about employee involvement over time.

Nevertheless, we worry that contemporary pressures for fast improvement in performance will cause the current wave of employee involvement activity to crest prematurely. In general, employee involvement must be regarded as a long-term investment, for which the return is realized over a period of years. Even when employee involvement efforts are perceived as successful in the short term, a long-term focus is necessary, especially at the corporate level. Before significant results can be expected, employee involvement efforts must be diffused enough to create a critical mass within the firm. There is a learning curve for implementing complex social system interventions, which can be shortened only so far. Pressures in the current economic environment for short-term performance improvement are worrisome in this regard. Some companies do make the long-term investment needed to realize a corporate advantage from employee involvement, just as some companies make long-term investments in research and development on new products. Pressures to trim such expenditures, however, are never far from the surface. By a wide margin, short-term performance pressures were the number one barrier to employee involvement cited by companies that had implemented employee involvement programs in two studies of Fortune 1000 companies (Lawler, Ledford, and Mohrman, 1989; Lawler, Mohrman, and Ledford, 1992).

Goals Versus Methods

Proponents of employee involvement have long argued, partly on the basis of their own values, that employee involvement should be implemented with methods that are compatible with it. Paradoxically, however, this is not always necessary. The *strategy* used to implement employee involvement need not necessarily employ the *methods* of employee involvement (Lawler, 1987). It may be possible to change a traditional organization by utilizing traditional management methods, at least initially. Many companies have successfully used such methods, coercing or firing managers who will not or cannot practice the new management methods. Executives at Ford, for example, have often said that employee involvement is voluntary except for managers. Many companies use imposed activity goals, such as a requirement that pilot employee involvement efforts be under way within specified periods of time.

These methods for creating employee involvement have their limitations, however. Unless, at some point, managers embrace the employee involvement goals that have been set for them, and unless they experience employee involvement for themselves, the employee involvement effort will lack the capacity to evolve and develop effectively. Management need not have a high degree of ownership in order for an employee involvement process to begin, but management will need a high degree of ownership for the process to succeed and be diffused.

Which Form? Under What Conditions?

Despite its popularity, we believe that the parallel-organization model is distinctly limited as an employee involvement strategy. The parallel organization is too fragile to constitute an effective long-term strategy for employee involvement in other than exceptional cases. In any case, the parallel form does not go very far along the spectrum of employee involvement possibilities (Lawler and Mohrman, 1985; Ledford, Lawler, and Mohrman, 1988). It usually involves only a small percentage of the work force, and the topics around which employee involvement is possible are too limited. The parallel model also lacks the supportive organizational design features (pay systems, job designs, training, information systems) that are needed to sustain it and make it maximally effective. The model creates self-destructive dynamics that cause most parallel organizations to die out within a few years.

Nevertheless, there are some situations in which restricting employee involvement to a small parallel organization can be advantageous. The parallel model may be all that top management is willing to accept, and it may allow managers to get their feet wet with the concept of employee involvement. Although parallel-organization forms of employee involvement often die out, it is possible for the parallel-organization form to evolve into deeper forms of involvement (see Lawler and Mohrman, 1987).

The high-involvement model is more difficult to implement and therefore has a lower adoption rate than the parallel model does. It probably has a higher success rate, however, and it certainly has higher potential payoffs for employees and for the organization (Lawler, 1986, 1992).

What is not always appreciated is that the lower adoption rate, the higher success rate, and the greater payoffs of the high-involvement model are all related. High-involvement organizations embody a collection of mutually reinforcing design elements, each of which is nontraditional and each of which encourages employee involvement. High-involvement organizations obviously look different from traditional organizations; high involvement cannot be confused with minor, incremental changes. Because the change is more radical, the adoption rate is lower. The network of complementary design elements also makes these models more powerful, however; in the right conditions, they are more successful at achieving high performance.

We believe that the high-involvement form has great potential for success, but it is also important to recognize that high-involvement designs are probably unsuited to many organizations (for example, see Cummings and Blumberg, 1987). Unsuitable conditions include a technology that is extremely routine, a technology in which employees' attitudes are not directly related to business performance, an external environment that moves at a glacial pace, and management that is unwilling or unable to move relentlessly over time in the direction of greater employee involvement. Such conditions are particularly lethal to enriched job designs, to many pay innovations, and to a number of other key elements of employee involvement design. In these conditions, the parallel-organization model may represent the only appropriate form of employee involvement. Since the conditions that are inhospitable to high-involvement design are fairly widespread, it is clear that the parallel model is potentially superior to the high-involvement model in many organizations.

High-Involvement Management and "Lean Production"

So far, we have suggested that, under *favorable* conditions, the high-involvement model is a superior form of employee involvement. Here we will explore a relatively new perspective that challenges this conclusion. This perspective arises from studies of the "lean production" model, also called the "Toyota production system."

In their massive study of the world's auto industry, Womack, Jones, and Roos (1990) make a strong case that the "lean production" system of producing automobiles results in significantly higher quality and productivity rates than conventional management approaches do. The "lean production" model, which was pioneered by Toyota around 1950, is used primarily but not exclusively by Japanese firms. The model incorporates some aspects of employee involvement but remains a bureaucratic system at its core.

Womack, Jones, and Roos (1990) make a direct attack on the high-involvement model in their discussion of Volvo's famous plants, which permit small teams of workers to build entire cars at their own pace in small work cells. They argue that these plants are a "step backward," aimed at restoring the craftsmanship of the last century rather than taking advantage of the benefits of mass production. They also argue that productivity rates in these plants are hopelessly low, as compared with those in plants using "lean production" methods. In evaluating these arguments, two points should be kept in mind.

First, the Volvo production system was not designed, first and foremost, to maximize productivity. It was motivated by the need to attract more Swedish workers to Volvo factories. The combination of high taxes and welfare-state benefits greatly reduced the value of high wages as an inducement for Swedes to take factory jobs. The work itself had to be made appealing. On this score, the Volvo system seems to have worked.

Second, it is inappropriate to conclude that productivity differences between Volvo plants and "lean production" plants result from obvious differences in the production methods. The basic lesson of these researchers' study is that the entire system of auto production, not just any one part, determines productivity and quality performance. Just-in-time inventory management, engineering and the product development process, relationships with supplier firms, relationships with customers, and other aspects of company management critically affect the plant's performance. This overall system ensures, for example, that the product is relatively easy to manufacture, that component parts are of high quality and appear when needed, and that consumer demand is stabilized. The appropriate test, which is not yet possible, would compare plants using Volvo production methods with those using "lean production" methods, within a firm that used all the other advantageous management innovations that comprise the "lean production" system. It is quite conceivable that the Volvo production methods would prove superior in these conditions.

The debate over the merits of the "lean production" system raises, once again, the issue of the conditions in which different types of employee involvement may be more or less effective. It may be that the form of employee involvement embodied in the Toyota production system is superior to the high-involvement model as used in mass-production assembly, where the technology is very routine and relatively little ongoing decision making is needed from workers. It may be that the high-involvement model is especially suited to technologies where a high level of worker skill and decision-making authority is necessary for understanding the overall production process and making rapid adjustments that keep the process under control. Most well-known high-involvement organizations are in industries (such as food, chemical, paint, and paper manufacturing) that use continuous-process technologies. Future research will be needed to demonstrate which models of employee involvement are most effective for different technologies.

Studies of "lean production" methods perform a useful function by helping to reframe the nature of employee involvement in advanced manufacturing technologies. Adler (1991) points out that employee involvement in the Toyota production system is not aimed at increasing worker autonomy. Employees are not encouraged to do the job in any manner that suits them; in fact, they are expected to do things in exactly the way that has been found to be most efficient, through a highly formalized system of work-methods specification. Even though employees may not have much direct control over their behavior on the job, however, they are encouraged to influence improvements in the system that governs their behavior. The important point, which is relevant regardless of the level of employee autonomy encouraged by the organization, is that the focus of employee involvement shifts from the individual to the production system. We believe that this is a useful reorientation for employee involvement in a wide variety of technologies.

Overall, we believe that studies of the "lean production" model show that it has a clear advantage over traditional production methods in the auto industry. Indeed, part of its superiority comes from its provision of greater employee influence, knowledge, information, and rewards than are provided in conventional management systems. Womack, Jones, and Roos (1990) have tended to make overblown claims, however, about the universal applicability of the "lean production" system. We do not think that the high-involvement model has yet received a fair test in comparison with the relevant parts of the "lean production" approach, and we suspect that the type of employee involvement associated with "lean production" may be most useful in highly routine assembly-line technologies.

Installation in New Organizations Versus Conversion

It is commonly assumed that high involvement needs a "green field" to succeed; that is, it is argued that high-involvement organizations (HIOs) should be established in new plants, or even in new companies, because conversions from traditional designs to HIO designs are unlikely to succeed. Newer evidence suggests that this is not necessarily true, however.

New organizations do have one key advantage over conversions in the creation of high levels of employee involvement practices: there are fewer old truths and old habits to unlearn in order to implement the new organization design. Therefore, the transition from the old to the new is shorter when new organizations are being created. There is much less resistance to pushing employee involvement as far as possible in new organizations, because there is much less vested interest in traditional patterns of behavior. Partly for this reason, high-involvement organizations that are newly created ("green field" plants) tend to look different from conversions. Their designs tend to push farther in the direction of the classic HIO model (Ledford, Cummings, and Wright, 1992).

New organizations usually have disadvantages, however, which are often overlooked when they are compared to conversions. During the past ten years, CEO has worked with a number of new high-involvement plants. Almost without exception, the first year or two in such plants can be characterized as chaotic (see, for example, Ledford, Tyler, and Dixey, 1991). The technology never seems to work well at first. Everything needs to be done at once, there is constant performance pressure, and the working hours seem endless. Early in the history of the organization, employees may not have developed the skills needed to participate fully in the organization. These conditions represent the obverse side of the advantages of newness. By contrast, conversions are usually somewhat more stable. The technology tends to be better understood, or at least under better control; organizational members know each other better, and employees may have developed considerable participative skills. These factors argue in favor of conversions. Among managers who are frustrated by the slow pace of change in traditional organizations, the advantages of conversions may not seem obvious except to those who have worked in new high-involvement organizations. Conditions make well-planned incremental changes much less problematic in conversions, if the momentum for change can be sustained.

So far, we have been considering the nature of employee involvement and have reviewed a number of issues related to the design and implementation of employee involvement efforts. Now we will be more speculative and will consider a set of predictions about the employee involvement movement over the next ten years.

The Future of Employee Involvement

1. *Employee involvement will be a growth industry in the 1990s.* Virtually all the specific employee involvement practices that we have considered in this chapter were invented decades ago; no major new employee involvement practices were invented during the last decade. Nevertheless, there has been a dramatic change in adoption patterns. Specifically, there was a tremendous surge in the adoption of employee involvement practices by U.S. corporations during the 1980s.

Data from two Fortune 1000 studies (Lawler, Ledford, and Mohrman, 1989; Lawler, Mohrman, and Ledford, 1992) bear out our contention that employee involvement was a management phenomenon of the 1980s. We asked about the period of time that the companies had used each of seven power-sharing practices. In the first study, the median number of years of use was five or fewer for all seven practices, and the majority of users had employed each practice for five years or less. Between 65 and 85 percent of companies using job enrichment, quality circles, union-management quality-of-work-life committees, minienterprise units, and self-managing teams had adopted these practices within the previous five years. Only survey feedback had been used by as many as 15 percent of users for more than ten years. Data from the second study are consistent with this pattern.

None of the forces that led so many companies to adopt employee involvement practices during the 1980s are likely to abate in the 1990s. Firms will find continued incentives in the needs for more competitive performance, increased organizational adaptability to change, better responses to the demands of the work force in an era of greater labor scarcity, and more effective functioning with fewer managers and staff people. These needs will continue to encourage the adoption of employee involvement practices.

Our research suggests that the overwhelming majority of U.S. corporations have some experience with employee involvement, and large numbers also believe that their employee involvement efforts have improved organizational performance. In an era of relentless pressure for better corporate performance, this is a recipe for increased use of employee involvement practices. So far, however, adoption has been broad but not deep, in terms of numbers of employees affected. In 1990, for example, 68 percent of the Fortune 1000 reported that their spending on employee involvement efforts would increase in the next fiscal year, 30 percent reported that spending would remain about the same, and only 2 percent reported that spending would decrease (Lawler, Mohrman, and Ledford, 1992). Our conclusion is that employee involvement practices will continue to be adopted at an accelerating rate by U.S. companies. A major question remains, however: Which practices will be adopted?

2. *The most popular forms of employee involvement will continue to be the safest ones and those with the least impact.* Although corporate management will turn increasingly to employee involvement as a means of improving organizational performance, the ambivalence about employee involvement in contemporary manage-

ment ideology will not disappear. Managers will continue to worry about how much decision-making power can be given to lower-level employees. We predict that managers will be more likely to favor the adoption of those practices that are least threatening to managerial beliefs, prerogatives, and powers but that offer some promise for affecting organizational performance. Therefore, we expect that the parallel-organization model will continue to find the most favor with organizations seeking to increase employee involvement during the 1990s. This prediction is consistent with trends shown in the two Fortune 1000 studies.

Comparisons between the two Fortune 1000 data sets suggest some change in which practices are growing most rapidly (Lawler, Mohrman, and Ledford, 1992). Respondents to both surveys were asked to predict future implementation of various power-sharing practices over the next two years. In the first study, four of the five highest-rated practices were examples of the parallel-organization model. More than six out of ten firms predicted that they would implement more employee participation groups and survey feedback, and four in ten predicted greater use of quality circles. Only the least drastic high-involvement practice — job enrichment — was predicted to be used to the same degree as the parallel-organization practices (48 percent predicted increased use). Less than one-fourth of the firms predicted increased use of self-managing work teams and minienterprise units. By the time of the second survey, the situation had changed. Six out of ten firms predicted increased future adoption, not only of employee participation groups but also of job enrichment and self-managing teams.

Nevertheless, the more radical power-sharing practices are being adopted from such a low base that it will be many years, at current adoption rates, before job enrichment, self-managing teams, and minienterprise units are as common as parallel-organization practices. This pattern, together with what we know about the parallel-organization model, suggests an inverse relationship between the depth of employee involvement practices and their likely rate of use in the future.

3. *The quality movement will repeat many of the mistakes of the*

quality circles movement. In general, when the leaders of the quality movement have anything to say about employee involvement, they embrace the parallel-organization model. This trend has permitted the quality circle movement, which once appeared to be in jeopardy, to merge with the quality movement. "Quality circles" have been resurrected as "quality action teams" or similar bodies, but the basic group design has remained the same. Once again, managers see the need for some form of employee involvement, in response to organizational performance problems, and they turn to the easiest and most conservative form of employee involvement. There is a legion of consultants and trainers ready to help them with well-packaged programs for establishing quality teams.

We expect that managers will rediscover, in the long run, that employees cannot and will not provide the help needed to solve quality problems unless the organization itself is changed. Employees will need power to make decisions about quality. They will need information to make good decisions. They will need meaningful rewards, not just trinkets or their pictures on the wall. They will need enough training to truly understand quality issues. As management responds to these needs, it will be faced with the necessity of rebuilding the organization in a way that weaves quality improvement into the fabric of the organization. This will bring them back to the choice between the more limited parallel model and the deeper, high-involvement model.

4. *The high-involvement organization will become a much more common organizational form.* We do not expect the number of corporations using the high-involvement organizational form to rival the number using the parallel-organization form at any point in the near future, but we do expect the high-involvement organization to become far more common than it is today. We predict that the number of sites organized as HIOs will at least triple, to perhaps several thousand during the 1990s.

For many organizations, compelling performance advantages will provide the rationale for the creation of new high-involvement organizations. For example, the track record of high-involvement organizations in new manufacturing plants using continuous-process technologies will be so strong that companies not using a high-involvement organizational design for new plants will probably be considered unwise.

Normal patterns in the diffusion of innovations will account for some of the increase. Companies that have some successful HIOs will develop others. Companies that do not have HIOs will imitate successful competitors, suppliers, customers, and others that do. HIOs eventually will become much more common in new industries and new technologies as relevant exemplars appear. For example, if the new General Motors Saturn operation fulfills the aspirations of its creators, it may serve as a model for the auto industry and, more generally, for firms with assembly-line technologies.

Management innovations can take decades to diffuse widely; often, the most drastic changes are the slowest to diffuse. That is one reason why we do not expect to see the HIO as the typical model of American management in the near future. It is useful to remember, however, that Procter & Gamble became the first major U.S. company to use this model, as recently as thirty years ago. If the adoption of the HIO form continues to increase even at its current rate, the total number of HIOs will be much more impressive a decade from now.

One development that could lead to rapid increase in the number of HIOs is a wider managerial conviction that traditional organizations can be converted successfully to the HIO design. As long as the HIO design is restricted primarily to new plants and other new organizations, the number of HIOs will be limited. There is some evidence that more conversions are appearing. In our study of ninety-six high-involvement organizations (Ledford, Cummings, and Wright, 1992), approximately half the sites in the sample were conversions, rather than organizations that had used the HIO model since start-up. The percentage of conversions was far greater than we would have expected just ten or fifteen years ago.

5. *Advanced forms of employee involvement will spread beyond the manufacturing sector in the 1990s.* More advanced forms of employee involvement, including work redesign and high-involvement organizational design, have been mostly limited so far to

the manufacturing sector of the economy (Lawler, Mohrman, and Ledford, 1992). If advanced forms of employee involvement are to become truly widespread, they must penetrate service organizations, which currently represent almost three-fourths of the private sector.

We see no barrier to the extension of high-involvement practices to the service sector. The manufacturing sector has led the way in adopting such practices, which is the usual pattern with management innovations, but many of the same factors that make high involvement applicable to manufacturing also make it increasingly relevant to the service sector. Indeed, there are very few differences between manufacturing and service firms in the factors that represent facilitators or barriers to employee involvement (Lawler, Mohrman, and Ledford, 1992).

Our own experience as consumers continually reminds us that many service organizations are managed in a way that makes outstanding customer service impossible, because employees do not know enough or care enough to solve customers' problems. Service organizations are managed on the basis of an outdated, factory-oriented model, with excessive division of labor, top-heavy management, and so on. Employee involvement appears to be one logical strategy for many service organizations to use in improving customer service. We see three reasons to believe that the use of HIO models in the service sector will increase greatly over the next ten years.

First, the service sector is facing unprecedented domestic and foreign competition. Decreased regulation of such industries as banking and financial services, transportation, and telecommunications has changed the competitive landscape. Perhaps even more important is the relatively new threat of foreign competition. Some services, by their nature, are likely to remain immune to foreign competition; restaurant meals, haircuts, and gardening services probably cannot be delivered successfully from abroad. In the age of electronic information processing, however, a surprising range of services can be successfully imported, including engineering, advertising, finance, and accounting services. Often the highest-value-added services are those that are most threatened. Just as manufacturing firms turned to high involvement as one means of meeting the ever intensifying domestic and foreign competition of the last decade, increasing competition in the service sector may give management in service industries a powerful impetus for adopting broader and deeper forms of employee involvement.

Second, as advanced forms of employee involvement are increasingly accepted as good management practice in the manufacturing sector, these forms are likely to spread to the service sector as well, since service organizations tend to imitate the management practices of leading manufacturers. This pattern of imitation is rooted in the intangible nature of service outputs. Service organizations (such as hospitals, universities, and public utilities) often do not have clear measures of critical outputs. Good health care, good education, and first-class customer service cannot be measured strictly by objective indicators; these outcomes reside partly in the subjective experiences of consumers. This makes it difficult for service organizations to know whether changes in management practices lead to greater organizational effectiveness. As a result, service organizations tend to rely on external definitions of what constitutes good management practice. To the extent that advanced forms of employee involvement are increasingly synonymous with good management in society at large, service organizations can be expected to adopt more employee involvement.

Third, those successful service organizations that have adopted high-involvement practices are increasing in prominence. Financial service organizations (such as AT&T Credit Corporation), insurance firms (such as Aid Association for Lutherans and Shenandoah Life), retail outlets (such as Home Depot), and airlines (such as SAS) are examples of service organizations that have made effective use of high-involvement practices that are quite analogous to those found in the manufacturing sector. As such exemplars become better known, they can be expected to help convince other service organizations that high-involvement practices are relevant to them as well.

6. *We will see high-involvement companies by the end of the decade.* High-involvement units have existed in some major cor-

porations for about thirty years. In some cases, these units have spread, so that there are more than just one or two oases of high involvement in an entire firm. Procter & Gamble has converted essentially all its manufacturing operations to the high-involvement model and now has several dozen high-involvement plants, both start-ups and conversions. Herman Miller, Motorola, and General Mills are examples of other companies that have implemented high-involvement practices in many parts of the firm. Still, no large company has yet been designed so that the logic of high involvement is applied successfully throughout the entire company. As far as we know, no company has successfully pushed high involvement simultaneously throughout its professional work force, corporate headquarters, clerical staff, manufacturing, and service-delivery work force.

We expect to see one or more organizations try to do just that during the next decade. We do not yet see any particular large company that is ready for such a move. Indeed, it is likely that any such radical move would come from a new corporation, one that may not yet exist. Such a company probably will face an extremely challenging environment, and it will have determined that it is going to seek a major competitive advantage over its more traditional competitors through its innovative management of human resources.

There are a great many unanswered questions about how to manage high involvement on such a scale. What forms will high involvement take once it moves outside the factory? Will it create problems in the coordination of effort across different parts of the firm? How will commitment to the high-involvement model be sustained in the face of the business problems that every organization confronts? How will corporate growth affect the organization's ability to manage with a high-involvement model? Such questions move the organization into uncharted territory. We hope to be lucky enough to observe the first hardy pioneers.

Conclusion

Our predictions suggest that we will see more of the same— much more—from the employee involvement movement during the next ten years. We expect some form of employee involvement to penetrate the quality movement, the service sector, and new parts of old organizations. We also expect to see many more high-involvement organizations, including the first large companies built around high-involvement principles. If these predictions are borne out, the 1990s will be the most important decade so far in the history of U.S. employee involvement activity.

References

Adler, P. S. "The 'Learning Bureaucracy': New United Motor Manufacturing, Inc." Unpublished working paper, School of Business Administration, University of Southern California, 1991.

Cohen, S. G., and Ledford, G. E., Jr. "The Effectiveness of Self-Managing Teams in Service and Support Functions: A Field Experiment." Paper presented at the Academy of Management annual meeting, San Francisco, Aug. 1990.

Cole, R. E. "Large-Scale Change and the Quality Revolution." In A. M. Mohrman, Jr., and Associates, *Large-Scale Organizational Change.* San Francisco: Jossey-Bass, 1989.

Cummings, T. G., and Blumberg, M. "New Manufacturing Technology and Work Design." In T. D. Wall, C. W. Clegg, and N. J. Kemp (eds.), *The Human Side of New Manufacturing Technology.* New York: Wiley, 1987.

Fairhurst, G. T., and Chandler, T. A. "Social Structure in Leader-Member Interaction." *Communication Monographs,* 1989, *56.*

Guzzo, R. A., Jette, R. D., and Katzell, R. A. "The Effects of Psychologically Based Intervention Programs on Worker Productivity: A Meta-Analysis." *Personnel Psychology,* 1985, *38,* 275–291.

Lawler, E. E., III. *High-Involvement Management: Participative Strategies for Improving Organizational Performance.* San Francisco: Jossey-Bass, 1986.

Lawler, E. E., III. "Transformation from Control to Involvement." In R. H. Kilmann, T. J. Covin, and Associates, *Corporate Transformation.* San Francisco: Jossey-Bass, 1987.

Lawler, E. E., III. "Choosing an Involvement Strategy." *Academy of Management Executive,* 1988, *2*(3), 197–204.

Lawler, E. E., III. *The Ultimate Advantage: Creating the High-Involvement Organization.* San Francisco: Jossey-Bass, 1992.

Lawler, E. E., III, Ledford, G. E., Jr., and Mohrman, S. A. *Employee Involvement in America: A Study of Contemporary Practice.* Houston, Tex.: American Productivity and Quality Center, 1989.

Lawler, E. E., III and Mohrman, S. A. "Quality Circles After the Fad." *Harvard Business Review,* 1985, *63*(1), 64–71.

Lawler, E. E., III and Mohrman, S. A. "Quality Circles: After the Honeymoon." *Organizational Dynamics,* 1987, *15*(4), 42–55.

Lawler, E. E., III, Mohrman, S. A., and Ledford, G. E., Jr. *Employee Involvement and Total Quality Management: Practices and Results in Fortune 1000 Companies.* San Francisco: Jossey-Bass, 1992.

Ledford, G. E., Jr. "Organization Development for Organizational Performance." In G. N. McLean and S. DeVogel (eds.), *The Role of Organization Development in Quality Management and Productivity Improvement.* Arlington, Va.: American Society for Training and Development, 1988.

Ledford, G. E., Jr., Cummings, T. G., and Wright, R. W. "The Design and Effectiveness of High-Involvement Organizations." Working paper, Center for Effective Organizations, University of Southern California at Los Angeles, 1992.

Ledford, G. E., Jr., Lawler, E. E., III, and Mohrman, S. A. "The Quality Circle and Its Variations." In J. P. Campbell, R. J. Campbell, and Associates (eds.), *Productivity in Organizations: New Perspectives from Industrial and Organizational Psychology.* San Francisco: Jossey-Bass, 1988.

Ledford, G. E., Jr., and Mohrman, S. A. "Attitudinal Effects of Employee Participation Groups: How Strong, How Persistent?" Paper presented at the Academy of Management annual meeting, Anaheim, Calif., Aug. 1988.

Ledford, G. E., Jr., and Mohrman, S. A. "Self-Design for High-Involvement: A Large-Scale Organizational Change." *Human Relations,* 1993, *42*(3).

Ledford, G. E., Jr., Tyler, W. R., and Dixey, W. B. "Skill-Based Pay Case No. 3: Honeywell Ammunition Assembly Plant." *Compensation and Benefits Review,* 1991, *23*(2), 57–77.

Mohrman, A. M., Jr., and Lawler, E. E., III. "The Diffusion of QWL as a Paradigm Shift." In W. Bennis, K. D. Benne, R. Chin, and K. E. Corey (eds.), *The Planning of Change.* (4th ed.) Troy, Mo.: Holt, Rinehart & Winston, 1985.

Mohrman, S. A., and Ledford, G. E., Jr. "The Design and Use of Effective Employee Participation Groups: Implications for Human Resource Management." *Human Resource Management,* 1985, *24*(4), 413–428.

Mohrman, S. A., and Novelli, L., Jr. "Beyond Testimonials: Learning from a Quality Circles Programme." *Journal of Occupational Behaviour,* 1985, *6,* 93–110.

Nadler, D. A., and Lawler, E. E., III. "Quality of Work Life: Perspectives and Directions." *Organizational Dynamics,* 1983, *11*(3), 20–30.

Perkins, D.N.T., Nieva, V. F., and Lawler, E. E., III. *Managing Creation: The Challenge of Building a New Organization.* New York: Wiley, 1983.

Sashkin, M. "Participative Management Is an Ethical Imperative." *Organizational Dynamics,* 1984, *12*(4), 5–22.

Womack, J. P., Jones, D. T., and Roos, D. *The Machine That Changed the World.* New York: Rawson Associates, 1990.

Chapter Seven

Creating the High-Involvement Organization

Edward E. Lawler III

Will the adoption of employee involvement continue to grow? What will employee involvement look like as it matures and becomes a more developed approach to management? The previous chapter presented broad answers to these questions. This chapter considers, in more detail, how employee involvement is likely to develop and where it is likely to be adopted as a management practice during the next decade. It also considers the types of organizational designs and organizational practices that will be associated with effective approaches to employee involvement.

Growth in Employee Involvement

There is every reason to believe that organizations will increasingly use employee involvement as a management style. As the previous chapter noted, there was substantial growth in its use during the 1980s, and a number of surveys indicate that organizations plan to increase their adoption of employee involvement (see, for example, Lawler, Ledford, and Mohrman, 1989; Lawler, Mohrman, and Ledford, 1992). The unknown factor is whether adoption will continue to concentrate on the less radical employee involvement practices, such as quality circles and problem-solving groups, or whether it will increasingly include high involvement or total employee involvement. To answer this question, we need to look briefly at some of the forces that are likely to encourage organizations to move toward the utilization of employee involvement as a management approach.

Other chapters have considered the substantial changes occurring in the business environment. Globalization, for example, has dramatically raised the level of competition in such industries as automobile, steel, glass, and chemical manufacturing. It is also clear that management style and organizational design can be sources of competitive advantage (Porter, 1985; Lawler, 1992). Japanese companies have demonstrated this in industry after industry. In many respects, Japan is a country that lacks any strong advantage in natural resources or geographical positioning, yet it has achieved dominance in a number of industries, simply because its societal and management systems operate more effectively than is true of organizations based in many other countries. This has created a significant challenge for many American and European organizations, which need to be able to organize and manage their work forces in ways that will compete effectively with Japanese companies.

Increased competition does not necessarily mean that organizations will choose to adopt employee involvement. There are other management approaches that may offer improvements over what they are currently realizing from the traditional command-and-control approach. There is reason to believe, however, that employee involvement is the right approach in a number of industries. A look at the performance characteristics that can be expected from successful employee involvement will help point out where it is the right approach.

Speed of Decision Making

Speed of decision making is particularly critical in environments where products change rapidly and in service organizations where customers demand quick responses to their requests. Organizations that move significant power to the lowest levels can respond more rapidly to changes in the environment and to changes in customers' demands than can those that are highly control oriented. Top-down organizations require that decisions be moved through an elaborate hierarchy of checks and balances. In most cases, this means slow response time.

Flexibility

The degree to which an organization pushes decisions downward, and supports this practice with systems that deliver critical information to individuals, determines how flexible the organization is in customizing its products and services to particular customers. Unlike traditional top-down organizations, which tend to have standard policies and procedures for dealing with issues, high-involvement organizations can make decisions that deal effectively with particular environmental issues or particular customer demands, and so they have the chance to be both more flexible and faster in their decision making. They end up serving customers' needs and demands better.

Overhead Costs

An organization characterized by high levels of employee involvement almost always has a flat and lean structure, which can provide a competitive cost advantage because it eliminates highly paid managers and executives. More than this, it can also eliminate a considerable amount of work if the organization looks critically at whether all the activities in which it is engaged are critical organizational functions (Tichy and Charan, 1989). In many cases, a critical look reveals that much of the work of line managers and employees is simply done to help staff (management) groups and senior managers provide a kind of direction that they do not need to provide if decisions are pushed to a lower level (Lawler, 1992). Labor costs are reduced when the organization is flattened and decisions are pushed downward. In many cases, time is freed up at lower levels too. Individuals do not have to respond to many of the requests for information that come from higher levels of the organization. Overall, in situations where labor and overhead costs are a critical determinant of organizational success, employee involvement may be the preferred management approach.

Knowledge Work

It is increasingly apparent that employee involvement is a preferred management style in situations where the majority of the workers are engaged in knowledge work. This is true, for example, of more complex, automated factories. Traditional management yields poor results in these settings because the type of control it exercises is rendered obsolete by the type of work that individuals are doing. Traditional supervision—based on observing work, and on a supervisory staff that understands the work as well as or better than the employees—is simply no longer possible.

When employees are the ones who understand the work best, and when much of the work is mental and intellectual, it is hard to observe when an employee is working effectively or ineffectively. Only when results appear is the quality of the employee's work evident. In many cases, however, it is not even evident then to a supervisor, because the supervisor does not have the technical knowledge to judge the quality of the work. Problems are likely to become evident, however, once the ultimate consumer of the work has a chance to examine or use it.

Control and coordination of work increasingly must be done by the individuals who are carrying out the work. They are the ones who know how hard they are working and what constitutes effective methods and products. The obvious conclusion is that employee involvement is the preferred management style for knowledge work because it is much more likely than a control-oriented approach to produce employees who are committed to the goals of the organization and to doing their work effectively. It also allows employees to coordinate their work with the work of others, so that complex products and processes do not have to be coordinated by layers of management overhead.

There is one other feature of knowledge work that favors

employee involvement. It appears that there is going to be increasing competition for skilled knowledge workers (Johnston, 1987, 1991). Therefore, any management style that they prefer should yield a competitive advantage. According to the research on employee involvement, there seems to be little question that it is a preferred management style (Lawler, 1992). It follows that when employees are difficult to recruit, there may be a real competitive advantage in employee involvement, simply because it attracts more talented people and reduces turnover, which is extremely costly in the case of skilled workers.

Capital-Intensive Technologies

Employee involvement seems to offer a particular advantage to organizations that are in capital-intensive industries. Such industries as petroleum, chemicals, paper, glass, and food processing increasingly have complex control-room-type manufacturing situations. Many electronic plants and even auto plants are increasingly moving in this direction, and this move is creating work that simply does not fit the control-oriented approach to management. Similar movement is taking place in many service businesses because technology, particularly information technology, is advancing. As a result, a different type of employee is needed. This is particularly evident in financial services, where "one-stop shopping" requires that employees make a range of service and selling decisions.

In capital-intensive businesses, labor costs typically represent a low percentage of the total cost of doing business. The key cost is capital. Therefore, a high premium is placed on the ability of the organization to function effectively in certain areas. The key effectiveness determinant is the ability of an organization to utilize its capital. Utilizing capital often means employing a relatively small number of very skillful and knowledgeable employees, who are committed to and capable of seeing that capital is utilized effectively. Control-oriented management typically proves to be poor in these situations because, first and foremost, the employees are knowledge workers and are difficult to supervise. Beyond that, however, much of the work requires problem solving and flexible behavior on the part of employees. Again, control-oriented approaches to management cannot produce this type of behavior. What is needed is a group of employees who are committed to the effectiveness of the organization and are therefore willing and able to do what is required to keep the capital operating. This often involves working flexibly, as well as coming up with creative solutions to difficult technical problems.

Future Directions

An overview of the conditions that seem to favor employee involvement — rapid decision making, flexible approaches, knowledge work, and capital-intensive processes — leads to the conclusion that these are the characteristics that exist in many of the leading industries in the United States and the rest of the developed world. Indeed, all these elements are becoming increasingly characteristic of the industries that dominate the U.S. economy. Businesses that do not have these characteristics are typically moving to less developed countries — unless, of course, they are in the service sector and it is too difficult to move offshore. Car washes, gas stations, and fast-food restaurants do not have most of these characteristics, but they cannot be moved offshore, and so they are still in the United States. Fast-food restaurants ultimately may cease to belong to this group of industries: retail locations are increasingly automated and are becoming more and more capital-intensive. As such, they may become better candidates for employee involvement.

Because the United States is increasingly characterized by work that fits the high-involvement approach to management, this approach ought to enjoy substantial growth because it offers a competitive advantage. What employee involvement will look like, however, is only partially known. In many respects, its implementation and the research on it are still at an early stage. New participative plants are good examples of a total and deep approach to installing employee involvement in the manufacturing parts of large organizations, but they do not represent organizationwide adoption of employee involvement (Lawler,

1978, 1990a; 1991). Few organizations actually do use organizationwide employee involvement (Lawler, Mohrman, and Ledford, 1992).

A few large organizations have begun to move in this direction, however. For example, Motorola has made a corporatewide commitment to using the employee involvement approach. This fits with Motorola's businesses, since most of them are characterized by rapid change, knowledge work, capital-intensive operation, and cost-competitiveness that is influenced by the amount of overhead incurred. Although Motorola has moved to a corporatewide employee involvement approach to management, it cannot at this point be characterized as an organization that has completed the change process. Indeed, no large organization qualifies as having accomplished this.

Even though there is no clear example of a corporatewide employee involvement approach to management, it is possible to talk about some of the characteristics that an organization would have if it practiced high-involvement management on a corporatewide basis. In the previous chapter, employee involvement was defined as moving substantial amounts of power, information, knowledge, and rewards to the lowest levels of an organization. This can be done only if all the important characteristics of the organization's structure are designed to make this happen. In the sections that follow, I will look at the major features of an organization and indicate how they should be designed and managed in order to create the effective movement of information, power, knowledge, and rewards to the lowest levels.

High-Involvement Organizations

In many ways, the concept of a high-involvement organization represents an evolution of the thinking that began in the organizational psychology literature of the 1940s and 1950s. At that time, such writers as Lewin, McGregor, Argyris, and Likert stressed the desirability of organizations' being managed in a more participative and democratic manner. This led to a long series of studies showing the advantages and disadvantages of democratic leadership styles. These studies were frequently done in traditional organizations that were structured in a hierarchical manner. Some of the earlier writing also focused on issues of work design and pay systems and did indeed argue for change, not just in leadership style but in other features of the organization's design. Theory Y, as presented by McGregor (1961) put the values of participative management into a philosophical context.

The problem with the early writings on participative management was that, although some people read them, few organizations adopted the practices suggested by them. There are a number of reasons for this, including the fact that the authors were not presenting a complete organizational model that could be adopted; in many cases, they were simply arguing for new leadership and communication practices. Perhaps more fundamental was the fact that there was little reason to change. Reports did show that the traditional top-down structures produced relatively low levels of job satisfaction and damaged individuals' mental and physical health (*Work in America*, 1973), but U.S. organizations were highly successful. As a result, most corporations felt little need to change their management style.

When the dominance of American management and American organizations began to disappear, in the 1970s, some organizations began to take a much more serious look at the whole idea of participative management (Lawler, 1986, 1992). This was partially spurred by the success of companies like Procter & Gamble, with their team approach to manufacturing, and by the perception, accurate or not, that the Japanese use a more participative management style. In any case, during the 1970s and 1980s some large U.S. corporations looked seriously at the idea of a more employee involvement–oriented approach to management and decided that it was the right management style for them. Companies like Motorola, TRW, and Xerox turned to participative philosophies of management and have implemented them in their organizations.

Most large organizations, however, do not provide useful models for how an organization should be designed in order to create a high-involvement management approach. Their reward systems, work designs, information systems—indeed, all their systems—tend to be designed to accomplish just the opposite. A possible model is provided by the new participative plants (Lawler, 1978). The problem with them is that they operate within the context of larger, traditionally managed organizations. Therefore, many of their systems are typical of the larger organizations, not of what is optimal from the standpoint of employee involvement. In discussing what an organization should look like if it is to optimize employee involvement, it is necessary to be speculative about what practices should be in place, since no operational example exists of a high-involvement organization. The effectiveness of the high-involvement approach therefore remains untested on an organizationwide basis. Nevertheless, it is worthwhile and important to develop a model of what this organization should look like, so that the model can be implemented, tested, and assessed.

Characteristics of High Involvement

Discussions of organizational design typically begin by pointing out that all organizations are made up of multiple systems and the congruence among them. For example, it is not good enough to have a well-administered reward system if the reward system does not fit the structure of the work, the information system, and so forth. Little research data exist to support the congruence argument, but it has an inherent logic, as noted in the Introduction, which has led to its widespread acceptance in the organizational theory literature (see Galbraith, 1977; Nadler and Tushman, 1988).

Although congruence is argued for, what actually constitutes congruence among the different organizational systems is rarely specified in any detail. Such issues as the type of information system that fits enriched jobs, or the type of leadership behavior that fits a decentralized organization, are often discussed, but there is little specification of what a totally congruent, overall set of organizational practices would be, and few tests are specified for determining congruence or fit. The closest thing to a model is the thinking presented in Chapter One, where different structural models were considered.

Most views of organizational design identify different key features. Models range all the way from those that represent only four features or systems to those that specify seven to ten. The approaches that identify fewer systems typically have incorporated some systems from the more detailed approaches into fewer categories. For example, some models refer to human resource management systems; others refer to separate systems for selection, training, and rewarding individuals. In discussing what a congruent high-involvement organization looks like, I will examine eight organizational features, so that I can be relatively complete in specifying what the major features of a high-involvement organization are.

The overall organizational principle central to the high-involvement model is that information, power, knowledge, and rewards should be located at the lowest practical level in an organization. Congruence comes from locating all four of these factors together in an organization. This should lead to an organization where individuals who have the power to make decisions also have the information and knowledge to make them well and are rewarded on the basis of how their performance affects the organization's performance.

Organization and Work Design

The literature on organization and work design gives a rather clear picture of what an organization must look like if it is going to be consistent with a high-involvement strategy (see Hackman and Oldham, 1980; Lawler, 1992). Table 7.1 summarizes this literature in terms of themes and actual design practices. The table argues that, to foster involvement, jobs and the overall structure of the organization must deviate from those of the traditional hierarchical approach. Through teams or job enrichment, individuals have to be given some say over how their particular work is done and how their work areas operate. Through flattening of the organizational structure, the organizational levels chiefly responsible for control and direction should be eliminated.

The overall organizational structure has to focus more on products, services, and customers than on functions. This

Table 7.1. Organization and Work Design.

Themes	Practices
Involvement in business	Teams or enriched jobs
Ownership over product, service, and customer	Flat, lean structure
Felt responsibility	Product-, service-, or customer-based activities
	Task forces, diagonal-slice policy groups

is crucial to giving individuals an opportunity to receive feedback and to making them accountable for the effectiveness of their business areas. This is where many of the new participative plants fail. Because these are usually stand-alone manufacturing facilities, most employees are not involved in such areas as sales, marketing, and new-product development. As a result, lateral integration (see Chapter Five) has to be achieved through the creation of a hierarchy.

For individuals to be able to participate in such larger issues as business strategy and policy development, the use of task forces and policy groups is called for. An extension of this approach is the idea of putting employee representatives on boards of directors. Task forces and employee board members are not present in most organizations, even in those that may have gone to flat structures and team-based job design. They are included here, however, because they involve individuals participating in important decisions that affect their work lives, and they are a way of facilitating horizontal coordination of work. Otherwise, employees can end up simply executing tasks and having little or no say in the overall strategy, direction, and operation of their organizations.

Taken together, these organizational and job-design practices should locate a great deal of decison-making power, information, and knowledge in the hands of the employees who produce products and deliver services. None of these are new or unproved ideas, as far as organizational theory and job-design research literature are concerned. They represent an important part of what constitutes a high-involvement organization.

Physical Layout and Design

Closely related to the issue of organizational and work design is the physical layout of the organization. Virtually everyone is familiar with the typical layout of hierarchical, top-down organizations. Careful gradations in status symbols exist, and such symbols are allocated on the basis of hierarchical position. This practice clearly reinforces an internal culture where power rests at the top of the organization, and where power is vested in positions, rather than in individuals. It also strongly encourages individuals who want status symbols to orient their careers toward moving upward. In many cases, the physical layout also separates functions from one another by putting them in different locations or parts of the building. The focus is on functional identity, not on identification with a business, product, or service.

As Table 7.2 shows, the key to creating a high-involvement organization includes a physical layout that minimizes status differences. The argument in favor of an egalitarian physical layout stems from the view that, in a high-involvement organization, power should move around the organization to those individuals who have the knowledge and information to exercise it; it should not simply move to the highest level. Such things as egalitarian perquisites and facilities are a symbolic as well as a practical way to encourage individuals to treat each other on the basis of what they have to contribute to a decision, rather than on the basis of their particular positions.

Table 7.2. Physical Layout Design.

Themes	Practices
Egalitarianism	Equal access to parking, dining, entrances
Support of job design	
Facilitation of communication	Use of similar offices
	Layout around team structure
Encouragement of a focus on business, product, or service	Meeting areas, few walls
	Co-location of business units

Physical layout should also support job design, particularly if teams are used. It can do this by encouraging face-to-face interaction and by providing teams with a physical environment that allows them to meet, solve problems, and gather the information they need. It can also lead to the kind of informal social contact that facilitates socialization and builds group cohesiveness. Where possible, the layout should also encourage cross-functional coordination by co-locating members of business units and product teams.

Information System

The information system is critical to the success of any organization. Traditional systems are oriented toward providing information about performance upward and directions downward. As shown in Table 7.3 the orientation is very different in a high-involvement organization. The key is to structure the information system so that it provides a free flow of information and provides the people who are producing a product or serving customers with a good sense of the organization's direction and performance. The information system must also provide individuals in higher-level jobs with data about the condition of the human system of the organization and about how effectively the organization is operating from the standpoint of decision making, information processing, and culture. One way to do this is to make regular use of attitude surveys.

Table 7.3. Information System.

Themes	Practices
Openness	Use of distributed technology; on-line capability; user-friendliness
Two-way communication	
Local ownership	Regular financial reviews
Performance orientation	Competitive benchmarking
Human system orientation	Suggestion processing system
	Attitude surveys
	Performance feedback against goals

The organization has to be sure that it has ways of processing suggestions, providing employees with good data about how the organization is functioning, and developing informal communication links. Quality circles and other suggestion-type programs are a way to assure a good upward flow of ideas and suggestions. Much of the communication of performance data has to be done on a face-to-face basis, so that individuals can ask questions and become comfortable with interpreting business information.

In many cases, the key to developing an information system consistent with high-involvement management is the use of new forms of information technology. Computer networking creates the possibility for much greater amounts of information to be delivered to and obtained from any employee (Zuboff, 1988). Input to decisions can be obtained easily; attitudinal reactions can be gathered. It also becomes possible for employees to handle much of the necessary coordination and information exchange, without using a hierarchy or a supervisor to link different pieces or parts of the organization. The information system is an important piece of technology that makes a more involvement-oriented management style possible in large, complex manufacturing operations and in many multilocation and large-location organizations.

Managerial Role

The traditional managerial role in an organization involves controlling, directing, and setting priorities. In a more participative environment, very different behaviors are required. As shown in Table 7.4, managers need to be in more of a leadership role and to engage in a number of practices that empower people and lead to their being involved in the management of the business and of their own jobs (Bennis and Nanus, 1985). Managers also need to place a great deal of emphasis on monitoring the effectiveness of the organization and the external environment. They, more than anyone else, are in a position to sense changes in the environment and, from a competitive point of view, to help position the organization effectively.

Table 7.4. Managerial Role.

Themes	Practices
Leadership	Monitoring the culture
Vision	Managing symbols
Empowerment	Sharing power and information
Enabling	Setting goals
Participation	Modeling good decision-making process
	Developing values/philosophy statement and using it
	Benchmarking performance
	Monitoring the environment

Perhaps the hardest part of the managerial role in a high-involvement organization is developing high-performance teams. This team-building role is difficult because it requires the ability to manage teams and to monitor their decision processes and operations (Hackman and Walton, 1986). Teams must be developed over months or years, so that they can be increasingly effective and self-managing. The manager needs to walk a very fine line between abdication and overcontrol. It is not all right for a manager to stand back and say, "The group decided, so there is nothing I can do, even though I disagree with the decision or think the decision was poorly made." Similarly, it is wrong for the manager to preemptively reject group suggestions and ideas about how things should be done. The right approach is to focus on how decisions were made and be sure that the group used a good decision process and made thoughtful, well-considered decisions.

If the manager strongly disagrees with a decision and can clearly say why, then it may be reasonable to override the decision, but this should be done only in extreme cases. There is no excuse, however, for a manager's allowing decisions to be based on a poor decision process or made in a way that reflects bias or unfairness. If this is happening, the manager needs to intervene and correct the decision process.

The second feature of the manager's role, particularly important in a high-involvement organization, is the need to act more as a leader. Managers have to do more than simply carry out day-to-day administrative duties. Particularly crucial is the ability to articulate the management philosophy of the organization and the role of individuals within it. Managers have to provide vision and manage symbols in ways that lead employees to understand the goals of the organization and to be inspired by them (Bennis and Nanus, 1985). These skills are often difficult to develop. Nevertheless, a successful participative organization needs managers who are visionary, inspirational leaders.

Reward System

The reward system in a high-involvement organization must emphasize and support the idea that information, knowledge, and power are located at the lowest organization levels. It can do this by rewarding all employees for developing their skills, by facilitating the movement of information downward in the organization, and by balancing power with rewards that depend on performance. It is particularly important for individuals who are empowered to have rewards that are contingent on how effectively they exercise their power (Lawler, 1990b). In a traditional organization, it makes sense for individuals at the senior levels of management to have a great deal of their compensation based on the effectiveness of the organization, for they are the ones who have the power to influence organizational performance, and they are clearly given that power. Once power has moved downward, however, it follows that rewards for organizational performance should also move downward, through the use of profit-sharing plans and broad stock ownership. Failure to do this constitutes a mismatch between power and rewards.

Table 7.5 lists themes and practices consistent with moving information, power, knowledge, and rewards to lower levels. Some of the practices listed are relatively new; others have been around for some time. For example, gain sharing, profit sharing, and all-salaried work forces have been used for decades in some organizations (Lawler, 1981; 1990b); skill-based pay and flexible benefits have become popular only in the last ten years (Lawler, Mohrman, and Ledford, 1992). The key is to combine them all into a single reward system that is intended to

Table 7.5. Reward System.

Themes	Practices
Individualized rewards	Skill-based pay
Performance-based rewards	All-salaried work force
Egalitarian rewards	Gain sharing
Growth-oriented rewards	Employee ownership
Open and participative administration	Flexible fringe benefits
	Participative management and design
	Openness of information
	Few perquisites
	Individual and team recognition

support a high-involvement approach. There also should be recognition events that acknowledge outstanding performance on the part of the organization and individuals.

Training and Development

High-involvement management, of necessity, places strong emphasis on training and development. If information and power are moved downward, it is vital that the knowledge and skills to use them be moved downward as well. In Table 7.6, which enumerates the educational practices consistent with high-involvement organizations, there is an emphasis on training. Individuals not only need to understand the economics of business but also need to be provided with training that supports their understanding of and control over work process and work flow. This increasingly must include training in quality control. People also must be trained to participate in problem-solving groups, teams, and task forces. Skills assessment is critical as well. It is the key administrative procedure that an organization needs in order to ensure that individuals are able to exercise power and deal with the information they are given.

Because of the importance of training, it makes sense to

Table 7.6. Training and Development.

Themes	Practices
Lifetime learning	Economic education
Economic literacy	Team-skills training
Teamwork	Skills assessments
Personal growth	Peer input
Understanding of the business	Problem-solving training
	Horizontal and vertical training
	Regular training for all employees
	Total quality control skills and techniques

give employees access to all they need, by requiring that they spend a certain amount of time in training each year. An alternative is to have a healthy training budget and ask individuals to take responsibility for planning their own programs for skill and career development.

Staffing

Not everyone is capable of or interested in working in a high-involvement organization; therefore staffing decisions need a great deal of attention. Table 7.7 shows selection practices designed to ensure that individuals know what is expected of them and to ensure that the individuals who are selected have the motivation and ability to succeed in a high-involvement organization. The selection process must include a realistic preview of the work

Table 7.7. Staffing.

Themes	Practices
Careful selection	Realistic preview
Mutual commitment	Employment security
Support of the culture	Peer input
Personal growth	Extensive testing and interviewing
Understanding of the business	Open job posting
	Testing for technical and social skills
	Promotion from within

and the way the organization operates, so that individuals can decide for themselves whether this type of organization is for them. Simulations can be helpful here, as can more traditional tests. The realistic preview can be handled by having individuals do the work and then be interviewed by work teams, so that they have a sense of what it is like to operate in a team environment. The preview should also include an extensive testing procedure, in which individuals are tested for their ability to do the job and to handle the social and decision-making aspects of the organization (Bowen, Ledford, and Nathan, 1991).

Once individuals are hired, the key issues concern how promotions are handled and how job openings are filled. Here, the emphasis is on participative decision making. Peers and subordinates should be asked for their input on promotion and placement decisions, and strong emphasis should be placed on promotion from within.

High-involvement organizations ask individuals to commit a great deal of time, effort, and energy to developing an understanding of their organization and the skills that are necessary within it. These skills may not be transferable, and they are difficult for an organization to build and replace. Therefore, a policy of high employment security and stability makes a great deal of sense from the point of view of the organization, which needs to retain its valued human resources. It also makes sense from the standpoint of the individual. Employment security and stability are congruent with asking individuals to make a substantial commitment to developing skills specific to the organization.

Personnel Policies

Personnel policies must support a high-involvement approach not just in their content but also in how they are developed. They represent one area where, even from the beginning, most individuals can participate meaningfully in organizational decisions. Thus, as shown in Table 7.8, it is very important for employees to participate in the design of the personnel policies and in their administration. Policy committees, grievance com-

Table 7.8. Personnel Policies.

Themes	Practices
Participative design	Task forces to develop personnel policies
Participative administration	Ongoing personnel committee
Individual choices	Grievance committee
Encouragement of social interaction	Flex time
Development orientation	Telecommuting
Support of the family	Celebrations
	Special events
	Activities that include the family
	Financial support for education
	Maternity and paternity leave
	Child care

mittees, and other cross-sectional groups of employees are the best means of involving employees.

Because of the emphasis in high-involvement organizations on individual responsibility and trust, personnel policies should allow individuals considerable choice. Whenever possible, such practices as flex time and telecommuting should be used. It is also important that the family responsibilities of employees be taken into account. A great deal is demanded of employees in high-involvement organizations, and so help with child care, elder care, and other family responsibilities is very important.

As part of the process of getting individuals involved in the organization, it is helpful for the organization to emphasize social events that encourage interaction. In situations where technology tends to isolate people, social events and opportunities for social interaction are particularly important because they can help to develop a sense of community and group cohesiveness and to offset isolation.

Conclusion

The practices described in this chapter are generally congruent with an organizational design that pushes information, knowledge, power, and rewards downward. Taken together, these practices constitute a radical departure from traditional management and open up a number of interesting new areas for organizational researchers. There are numerous issues that concern the effectiveness of such new practices as skill-based pay, flexible benefits, work teams, information technology, and employment security. There are perhaps even more interesting issues that concern the interfaces between different systems. Are the systems congruent with each other? Do they support each other and lead to organizational effectiveness? These questions warrant research and can lead organizational researchers toward new paradigms.

The high-involvement organization seems to represent an important new way of operating. It clearly is not appropriate for everyone, but it may have the effect of making work more satisfying for many individuals and making many organizations more effective. High-involvement management may help retain work in the United States that otherwise might be sent to other countries. More than any other approach, it takes the democratic, participative characteristics of American society and puts them into organizations, from a managerial systems perspective. Therefore, it may represent a way for U.S. organizations to be simultaneously congruent with societal values and competitive internationally. At this point, it is premature to declare this approach a success. Nevertheless, there are reasons for optimism.

References

Bennis, W., and Nanus, B. *Leaders: The Strategies for Taking Charge.* New York: HarperCollins, 1985.

Bowen, D. E., Ledford, G. E., Jr., and Nathan, B. "Hiring for the Organization, Not the Job." *Academy of Management Executive,* 1991, 5(4), 35–51.

Galbraith, J. R. *Organization Design.* Reading, Mass.: Addison-Wesley, 1977.

Hackman, J. R., and Oldham, G. R. *Work Redesign.* Reading, Mass.: Addison-Wesley, 1980.

Hackman, J. R., and Walton, R. E. "Leading Groups in Organizations." In P. S. Goodman (ed.), *Designing Effective Work Groups.* San Francisco: Jossey-Bass, 1986.

Johnston, W. B. *Workforce 2000.* Indianapolis: Hudson Institute, 1987.

Johnston, W. B. "Global Workforce 2000: The New World Labor Market." *Harvard Business Review,* 1991, *69*(2), 115–127.

Lawler, E. E., III. "The New Plant Revolution." *Organizational Dynamics,* 1978, *6*(3), 2–12.

Lawler, E. E., III. *Pay and Organization Development.* Reading, Mass.: Addison-Wesley, 1981.

Lawler, E. E., III. *High-Involvement Management: Participative Strategies for Improving Organizational Performance.* San Francisco: Jossey-Bass, 1986.

Lawler, E. E., III. "The New Plant Revolution Revisited." *Organizational Dynamics,* 1990a, *19*(2), 4–14.

Lawler, E. E., III. *Strategic Pay.* San Francisco: Jossey-Bass, 1990b.

Lawler, E. E., III. "The New Plant Approach: A Second Generation Approach." *Organizational Dynamics,* 1991, *20*(1), 5–14.

Lawler, E. E., III. *The Ultimate Advantage: Creating the High-Involvement Organization.* San Francisco: Jossey-Bass, 1992.

Lawler, E. E., III, Ledford, G. E., Jr., and Mohrman, S. A. *Employee Involvement in America: A Study of Contemporary Practice.* Houston, Tex.: American Productivity and Quality Center, 1989.

Lawler, E. E., III, Mohrman, S. A., and Ledford, G. E., Jr. *Employee Involvement and Total Quality Management: Practices and Results in Fortune 1000 Companies.* San Francisco: Jossey-Bass, 1992.

McGregor, D. *The Human Side of Enterprise.* New York: McGraw-Hill, 1961.

Nadler, D. A., and Tushman, M. *Strategic Organization Design.* Glenview, Ill.: Scott, Foresman, 1988.

Porter, M. E. *Competitive Advantage: Creating and Sustaining Superior Performance.* New York: Free Press, 1985.

Tichy, N., and Charan, R. "Speed, Simplicity, Self-Confidence: An Interview with Jack Welch." *Harvard Business Review,* 1989, *67*(5), 112–120.

Work in America: Report of a Special Task Force to the Secretary of Health, Education and Welfare. Cambridge, Mass.: MIT Press, 1973.

Zuboff, S. *In the Age of the Smart Machine.* New York: Basic Books, 1988.

Chapter Eight

New Approaches to
Teams and Teamwork

Susan G. Cohen

Will organizations expand their use of teams and teamwork mechanisms over the next ten years? This chapter examines the current use of teams and internal networked designs and predicts that their use will grow because they are basic to the implementation of the new approaches to organizing and managing work. I will briefly review the competitive and technological forces that have led to a surge of interest in teams and teamwork mechanisms, and then I will discuss four types of team designs and the organizational and management practices that enable them to work.

Forces Encouraging the Use of Teams

Teams and teamwork are in. Organizations have experienced a resurgence of interest in using teams and teamwork mechanisms as the basic building blocks of performance. Although organizations have used teams to solve problems, coordinate activities, and accomplish tasks for quite some time, what has changed and will continue to change is the integration of teams into the organizational structure, as well as their increasing scope of authority (Drucker, 1988).

What has created this increased interest in teams and teamwork? At the most basic level, teams are established to create synergy — to increase the coordinated application of specialized knowledge, so that the performance of the whole is greater than the sum of its parts (Ancona and Nadler, 1989). Competitive challenges and information technology demand the synergy that can be achieved through teamwork.

Competitive Challenges

The current competitive environment requires flexibility and speed. Flexible organizations place decision-making authority in the hands of those close to sources of information and those who have the expertise to interpret and act on it. This is rarely an individual task, because changing technologies and markets have different impacts on organizational functions and disciplines. Cross-functional product development teams can enable an organization to achieve a competitive advantage through speed by simultaneously developing products and manufacturing processes (Takuchi and Nonaka, 1986). When time is short, individuals cannot accomplish much, and organizations must use teams.

Of course, organizations still need to improve the quality of goods and services and increase operating efficiencies. The quality movement has identified "continuous improvement" of organizational processes as the key organizational strategy (Masaki, 1986). Continuous improvement is frequently accomplished through the use of teams: problem-solving teams, quality improvement teams, and cross-functional task forces. Self-managing teams have been used to improve efficiency, particularly in manufacturing settings. They take over many functions performed by first-level supervisors, thereby increasing the supervisory span of control and reducing costs.

Information Technology

Advanced information and automation technology transforms much work into knowledge work. The knowledge worker uses specialized information and skills to analyze data and make decisions. Computer analysis, computer-aided design systems, interactive technology, and expert systems extend the judgment, capabilities, and creativity of decision makers (Applegate, Cash, and Mills, 1988). Computer technology extends the firm's capabilities to add value to products or services. For example, Toyota has a Monday-to-Friday design-to-delivery program, in which a customer "designs" his or her car on a computer terminal on a Monday, and the factory automatically receives the specifications and has the manufacturing completed by Friday of the same week (Davidson, 1990).

The opportunities for synergistic decision making are significant. Specialists will need to collaborate, in order to perform such specific organizational tasks as the introduction of new products or the design of customized services (Drucker, 1988). They will work on self-managing task-focused teams that disband once the job is done (Applegate, Cash, and Mills, 1988). Computer technology makes information widely available and distributes the ability to make informed decisions throughout an organization (Zuboff, 1988). Work becomes location-independent. Those with complementary skills can work together, even though they are geographically dispersed. The information and communication systems will permit input to be obtained, decisions to be made, and results to be tracked without a team's co-locating. Coordination among multiple task teams can occur through the use of computer and people networks. The networked organization links potential contributors (Savage, 1990).

Future Directions

We can expect the competitive pressures demanding flexibility, speed, quality, and efficiency to intensify, thus requiring organizations to accelerate and broaden the implementation of team designs. These forces will cause organizations not only to expand their use of teams but also to modify team designs. In general, organizations will move toward giving teams greater authority over their tasks. Team designs will rely more heavily on self-management. Self-management speeds up organizational

decision making by permitting those with task-relevant expertise and information to make decisions and not waste time refer-
ring decisions up an organizational hierarchy. As discussed in
previous chapters, self-management is also favored by the American work force. Organizations will provide teams with more autonomy because it is a source of competitive advantage.

Team designs will be modified in two countervailing directions. Relatively permanent, self-managed teams will be established wherever work can be self-contained and organized around
products, customers, or services. These teams will be the way
that organizations get work done. They will be the basic performance units for specified outputs. The reliance on relatively
permanent self-managed teams to produce products or serve customers will eliminate overhead costs, because some supervisory
and managerial positions will be able to be eliminated. Organizations are likely to dramatically increase their use of temporary
teams and loosely bounded networked structures, however. In
a world that is rapidly changing, much work is temporary and
nonroutine. More of an organization's work will be handled with
task forces and project-oriented teams. Because information technology enables teamwork to occur without team co-location,
bounded teams will not have to be established before synergy
can be derived from teamwork. New collaborative structures
will be generated through links on distributed information networks. These structures will be highly fluid, flexible, and responsive to change.

In general, organizations will increase their use of teams
and collaborative designs, in order to be competitive. In the sections that follow, four different types of teams and networked
designs will be discussed, as will ways to design and manage
each team type for team and organizational effectiveness.

Types of Team Designs

Organizations use four types of collaborative and team designs.
The first type is the collaborative networked design, which consists of the interactions and relationships among interdependent
contributors or teams of contributors who cooperate to achieve

an explicit purpose. The second is the parallel team structure, which exists separately from regular work activities, with teams being responsible for recommending performance and quality improvements and for solving business problems. The third type is the project and development team, which is assigned responsibility for completing projects to fulfill users' requirements in a defined but typically extended period of time. The fourth type is the work team, which is responsible for producing a product or service.

As discussed in Chapter Five, these designs can be arrayed on a continuum, from less formal and temporary to more formal and permanent. Networked designs build on the informal organization and support task-focused collaboration. Links are temporary and change over time. Parallel team structures are usually temporary and supplement the formal organizational structure. Project and development teams are either overlaid on a functional structure or integrated into a project organization; although temporary, they tend to have a long life span. Work teams are integrated into the formal structure and are permanent.

Networked Designs

Networked designs consist of the interactions or relationships among interdependent contributors or groups of contributors who cooperate to achieve a purpose. A network may be viewed as consisting of nodes or positions (occupied by individuals or groups) and links or ties (manifested by interactions among the positions). Networks may be tight or loose, according to number, intensity, and type of interactions among members (Thorelli, 1986). Not all pairs of nodes are directly linked; some are joined by multiple relationships (Tichy, Tushman, and Fombrun, 1979), and nodes and links change over time. The purpose of a network is its reason for existing and may involve strategies, goals, objectives, or problems to be solved (Lipnack and Stamps, 1987).

Networked designs differ from other team structures in

their lack of clear boundaries between the network and the organization. In contrast to the other team structures, networks are not self-contained. Membership is fluid and diffuse. Members cannot reliably identify the other members of the network and may be aware only of the participants with whom they have direct links. Work teams or project teams may comprise nodes of a network, but the network extends beyond team boundaries.

Examples of networked designs can be found in such professional service companies as investment banks or consulting firms and in high-technology companies — organizations that perform complex tasks and must adjust rapidly to changing market conditions and customer needs. Eccles and Crane (1987) describe the organizational design of investment banks as a dynamic and flexible network consisting of multiple client teams, with functional specialists working on several teams and professionals having overlapping and shared responsibilities, dual reporting relationships, vague roles and responsibilities, and careers that involve cross-departmental movement. These characteristics all contribute to the formation of network ties.

Digital Equipment Corporation has conceptualized its organization and technology as comprised of networks — intelligent nodes linked for a purpose. It describes the successful and timely introduction of the 6200 series of midrange VAX as attributable to its organizational networked design, a distributed core group of forty to fifty people in fourteen locations, with several thousand more participating indirectly, having firm agreement on the goal and a distributed leadership structure.

Although several authors have suggested that networked designs are the wave of the future (Drucker, 1988; Miles, 1989; Naisbitt, 1982; Savage, 1990), no studies have estimated their prevalence or evaluated their effectiveness. Therefore, the following discussion of the design features required for effectiveness is speculative.

Characteristics of Networked Designs

The overarching purpose of the network should be explicit, clearly articulated, and engaging. Its purpose needs to be aligned

with the organization's strategic objectives, so that the project
fits within the organization's broader goals. Because the individuals and groups within the network (its nodes) will work on
parts of a project, it is critical that they understand the relationship between their tasks and the network's overall objective.
Without a clearly defined and articulated purpose, individual
and group effort will not be integrated, and suboptimization will
be the result.

The final output from the network should be identifiable
but may be distant from specific activities and links in the network. For example, investment bankers spend considerable time
with one another and with clients, to make sure that they can
provide significant amounts of information on market prices and
trends, financing mechanisms, and mergers and acquisitions.
Their major task, however, and the basis for payment, is the
completion of investment deals. To increase the exchange of
information, many investment banks define and measure desired
output as total revenues earned from customers across deals over
a period of time (Eccles and Crane, 1987).

The composition of a network must be fluid and responsive to changing business and informational requirements.
Changes in business conditions may require links to be made
or broken, strengthened or weakened, and so the organization
must support and manage a flexible allocation of human capital. The members of the network should have the specialized
expertise to contribute to the network task but should also be
willing to cooperate across disciplines and functions. Members
have to be brought into a network as their expertise is required
and leave when they are no longer needed. This fluidity changes
the concept of a job.

The network may consist of core and peripheral members, with tighter boundaries defined for core members. Core
members are likely to have greater responsibility for accomplishing the network objective, while peripheral members provide
information, advice, or support. Core members of the network
are likely to be located closer to the center of the network, with
more links among them. Given their centrality and their access
to information and resources, core members will be the most

influential participants. In general, network members are part-time and are not co-located, although core members are occasionally full-time and co-located, according to the complexity of the network project. Organizational members may participate in multiple networks simultaneously, according to their level of involvement.

The links forged for a network should build on the informal organization. Contributors are most likely to coordinate with others whom they know, respect, and trust. They will seek the advice and assistance of those they perceive as influential, knowledgeable, and supportive. Personal relationships can help solidify links in a network.

Networks have multiple links between those in the network and external constituencies, such as customers, suppliers, and people providing professional support. The links are distributed, and network members must be responsive to their key stakeholders, making sure that appropriate external communication occurs. Internal network ties depend on external links and can change quickly when business conditions or technologies change.

Network members need to take the initiative and the responsibility for forging necessary relationships, sharing information, resolving conflicts, and achieving interdependent goals. In other words, the nodes of the network—individuals as well as small groups—must be self-managing.

A networked design would intensify coordination costs and be unwieldy if it did not distribute authority. Those with task expertise should be empowered to make critical business decisions, without relying on hierarchical intervention, and so the locus of decision-making authority must reside at the nodes of the network. Self-managing contributors have the responsibility to resolve problems with other self-managing contributors. They need to be responsible for monitoring their progress in the context of the overall purpose. They should be responsible for self-design by forging new links as necessary, discontinuing other links, and making sure that appropriate information exchanges occur.

The authority for establishing the overall purpose or conceptual framework for the network belongs to the organization's hierarchical decision-making structure or to a specially constituted network governance structure. High-technology companies frequently constitute special governance structures for managing complex efforts at product development. For example, a "systems team," composed of a core group of managers from product engineering, manufacturing, customer service, support engineering, and product management/marketing, is given responsibility for overseeing the development of a new computer, from its inception as a new-product idea through its introduction to the market. This group determines the initial high-level specifications for the product and is ultimately responsible for its business success.

Network leadership tends to be multiple and distributed, although a variety of mechanisms can be used. A governance structure, such as a "systems team," may be responsible for establishing the overall direction and developing the shared conceptual framework. Network leadership may be collectively shared by members of this governance structure, or the organization may require an integrating role to be assigned, such as that of a project or network manager. This person assumes general management responsibilities for coordinating key decision processes. He or she may need to act as a tie breaker, to speed decision making.

Multiple leaders may direct different activities in the network. Leadership may be based on knowledge and task expertise, functional experience, and managerial position. Leadership may shift according to project phase, technical requirements, and customer requirements. Leadership structures must reflect the distributed composition and task assignments of the network.

The systems for performance management and rewards must support cooperative and self-managing behavior on the part of organization members. Cooperative or collaborative behavior should count in individual performance reviews. Making decisions at the source (with appropriate others) should also be considered in performance reviews. Networked performance-management systems should recognize and reward collaborative behavior among interdependent performers. Because the final output from a network is likely to be distant from the specific activities and links required for task accomplishment, performance-management systems need to recognize in-process activities, links, and accomplishments. Of course, final network accomplishment can also be recognized and rewarded.

Developmental activities should focus on building interdisciplinary expertise and increasing network ties. Job-rotation training programs and lateral career movement develop general management perspectives and contribute to the formation of network ties. Individuals who have made lateral career moves become conduits of information between old and new departments.

Education and training programs should help participants form ties and integrate activities across interdependent disciplines, functions, levels, and locations. Problem-solving, conflict-resolution, and intergroup-relations training are helpful if provided in forums involving participants from multiple departments, disciplines, regions, countries, and so forth.

Skills in project management and time management may also be critical to effective network participation. Individual contributors are likely to be involved with multiple projects and to belong to multiple networks at the same time.

Information systems make network designs possible. People can communicate with one another and work together without having to co-locate. Electronic mail and video conferencing enable networks to be formed rapidly as "virtual organizations," with no investment in physical space or administrative support. These "virtual organizations" can be dissolved rapidly when the work is completed. Electronic mail and computer conferencing also permit coordination to occur, without the need to develop new reporting relationships. Communication through electronic media tends to diminish attention to status differentials and helps decision making occur on the basis of task expertise (Eveland and Bikson, 1989).

Information technology reduces the need for face-to-face interaction but does not eliminate it. In the early stages of a project, when network members need to clarify the conceptual framework, goals, and methods, extensive face-to-face communication is required (Galagher, 1990). Studies have suggested that participants prefer face-to-face interaction over computer-mediated communication at the initiation stage of a project (Bikson and Eveland, 1990). In the later stages of a project, however, participants rely on computer-mediated mechanisms that permit them to transmit textual or graphic information in a form that can easily be understood and acted on. Although participants may still need to meet occasionally during the project's execution, the need for face-to-face interaction is significantly reduced.

Information systems must contain global data bases in order to be useful to a dispersed network. It becomes important to define a limited core set of data elements that can be used by different functions. Network participants can identify additional core data elements that can be merged into an integrated data architecture, thereby expanding the architecture and developing agreed-upon meanings for key terms (Savage, 1990). The use of a shared data base forces network participants to be explicit about conceptual frameworks and approaches, thereby integrating their efforts and potentially speeding up progress on projects.

Shared global data bases enable connections to be made between participants from multiple disciplinary backgrounds and organizational "homes." Multiple organizational logics can be integrated through the process used to define the shared global data bases. In this way, networked designs use information technology as a substitute for the dual reporting structures found in matrix organizations. Rather than depending on dual authority structures to integrate different organizational logics (for example, product and function), information technology connects people from multiple structural bases and forces them to integrate their efforts in pursuit of common goals.

Shared data bases may also be helpful in communicating with external constituencies. They provide real-time on-line information exchanges with customers, suppliers, and other key stakeholders. Network participants can respond quickly to external changes if they are linked through technology to their key stakeholders.

Computer-assisted decision-aiding technologies, such as

project management systems, expert systems, and group and cooperative work systems, extend the capability, creativity, and judgment of interdependent contributors. These tools enable dispersed self-management. More effective decision making can take place where the task expertise resides — at the nodes and links of the network.

In summary, networked designs depend on collaboration among self-managing, interdependent contributors. They build on the strengths of the informal organization. They maximize the exchange of information and are flexible and responsive to business and technological changes. Networked designs can connect those with relevant task expertise, independently of geography or organizational structure.

Their dispersed structure makes them difficult to control, however. Because networks frequently include participants from multiple locations and organizations, managers may be threatened by their inability to direct activities or provide hands-on supervision (Miles, 1989). Managers are likely to have difficulty keeping track of network activities. Participants may suffer from information overload. Managers may find it frightening both to be responsible for outputs and not to have people and processes under their control.

Effective networks do not happen automatically. They have to be designed, managed, and led. Without an integrating purpose and objective, networks may fragment. Without supportive performance management, education, and information systems, the participants will not be empowered to make effective decisions. Organizations must create the conditions that support interdependent, collaborative work. If the environment is turbulent, the benefits of enhancing flexibility are worth the costs.

The Future

More organizations will intentionally create, manage, and support internal networks. Linking people with the right skill sets will be critical in developing core competencies and will be perceived as too important to be left to the vagaries of the informal organization. Information and human technologies will be developed to enhance the establishment of links and successful collaboration among disparate contributors. The links will extend, to include customers, suppliers, distributors, and other external partners. Organizations will struggle with adapting their formal structures and systems to support (and not obstruct) the networks' accomplishments. The organizations that are successful in managing multiple task-focused networks will achieve a competitive advantage. The networked organization will be perceived as an information-age alternative to bureaucracy.

Parallel Team Structures

Parallel team structures supplement normal work structures and are usually temporary. They carry out functions that the regular organization is not equipped to perform well (Mohrman and Lawler, 1988; Stein and Kanter, 1980). Examples of parallel structures include problem-solving teams, quality circles, quality improvement teams, productivity improvement groups, employee participation teams, and task forces. In contrast to networked designs, parallel team structures have clear boundaries. Members both inside and outside a team can identify the team and reliably distinguish members from nonmembers. Parallel team structures may be established to make recommended improvements or solve specified business problems.

These teams typically make recommendations that are considered by the hierarchical decision-making structure. No change results unless the recommendations are approved by the hierarchy (Lawler and Mohrman, 1987). This process takes time, adds to overhead costs, and places the locus of decision-making authority far from those with task expertise. These teams usually meet regularly (every week or two) and may follow defined processes for problem solving or quality improvement. Participants are trained in the use of the processes and skills that the organization adopts (for example, in problem solving, quality improvement, or group interaction).

Organizations now tend to implement parallel team structures more frequently than other team-based designs. A study

of the employee involvement practices in Fortune 1000 companies indicated that approximately 86 percent of the companies
sampled use quality circles or employee participation groups;
their use tends to be limited to less than half of the work force
(Lawler, Mohrman, and Ledford, 1992). Almost all organizations use task forces to solve special problems, but only a small
percentage of employees are involved in task forces at any given
time.

The widespread use of parallel team structures has occurred because they are easy to install and require no shifts in
managerial power and authority or changes in organizational
structure. Nevertheless, parallel teams have difficulty achieving organizational legitimacy, and most compete with the regular
organization for time, money, information, and other resources.
They are difficult to sustain and may introduce conflict between
those who are involved in these teams and those who are not.
In many organizations, middle managers and staff professionals,
who are required to respond to recommendations and implement them, often have not been involved with the teams, have
competing objectives, and perceive these recommendations as
treading on their turf (Lawler, Ledford, and Mohrman, 1989;
Lawler and Mohrman, 1987). By contrast, Japanese companies and transplants implement a much higher percentage of
quality circle suggestions than their American counterparts do
(MacDuffie, 1988). Despite the testimonials for their success,
as reported in the practitioner literature, there is little empirical evidence regarding the performance effectiveness of parallel team structures, and the empirical evidence that exists is
equivocal (Ledford, Lawler, and Mohrman, 1988).

Task forces are parallel structures, but they differ from
quality circles or problem-solving teams in four ways. First, task
forces are typically asked to recommend solutions to specific business problems, rather than given a general mandate to generate ideas for improving quality. Second, membership may be
assigned rather than voluntary. Third, they usually have specific deadlines for accomplishing their tasks, and they are established as temporary groups. Fourth, task forces are used at
any level in the hierarchy; managers are just as likely as rank-

and-file employees to be members of business task forces, and so task forces tend to be more integrated into an organization's functioning than other parallel structures are.

Organizations frequently use task forces because they are a relatively easy way of obtaining the synergy required in departing from routine ways of doing things. They bring together those with the necessary expertise and provide opportunities for development and organizational learning. They enable an organization to focus on time-limited tasks. They are flexible and responsive to change.

Characteristics of Parallel Team Structures

The research on quality circles provides a picture of the design features that contribute to effective parallel team structures (Ledford, Lawler, and Mohrman, 1988; Mohrman and Ledford, 1985). Parallel teams must consist of members who have the expertise to successfully address the issues they choose. Because most parallel teams are made up of volunteers, training and the availability of expert resources are both critical. Organizations that provide extensive training and encourage their professional and support staffs to meet with teams, as needed, have the most successful parallel team structures. The typical problem-solving or group-process training should be supplemented by business and economic education, so that employees will generate recommendations that make economic sense. To minimize in-group and out-group tensions, organization should provide opportunities for everyone to join parallel teams. This does not mean, however, that members cannot be selected for task forces on the basis of their expertise and backgrounds. If organizations make wide use of task forces, employees will eventually have the opportunity to serve on them, and membership opportunities will be perceived as open.

Parallel teams should make sure that their activities are closely linked to performance goals. This is important both for teams that determine which issues they will address and for teams that are assigned specific problems. Task forces that address non-routine problems should work to define objectives and measures that will help to align task forces' activity with customer and business requirements.

Because parallel team structures can only make recommendations, it is critical that the organization set up an explicit mechanism to respond to them. This is likely to be a management-level group or steering committee for a quality circle or quality improvement team; it can be the management sponsors for a task force. The team should know the criteria for evaluating its recommendations and should know who the decision makers will be. Although this is obvious, it is not always done.

Leadership requirements include facilitating meetings, coaching team members, providing links to management and outside constituencies, and obtaining training and other resources. Parallel teams frequently use facilitators to perform these functions, although supervisors and managers also take these roles.

Financial rewards are usually not offered to participants in parallel team structures, but such rewards as gain sharing could be used to reinforce team activities (Lawler and Mohrman, 1987). Recognition in the form of lunches, T-shirts, plaques, and pins is frequently used and has some motivational value. Management's responsiveness to parallel teams' recommendations is the most critical support for participation in parallel teams.

Communication is critical. It is important for parallel teams to communicate their progress to sponsors and other interested stakeholders. Parallel teams need to keep good written records, such as meeting agendas, minutes, and action items. In general, written records help teams use time efficiently, track progress, and have effective meetings.

Finally, temporary parallel structures that have specific deadlines for task completion must manage time. Gersick's (1988) study of eight task forces found that they established an initial direction at the first meeting, which they followed until half their time had elapsed. At midpoint, they changed their work patterns, re-engaged with outside managers, developed new understandings of their work, and made dramatic progress. Her study suggests that managers need to plan carefully for a task force's first meeting, because that meeting will set a lasting precedent for how the task force goes about its work. It suggests also that the midpoint is a time when the team will be especially open to outside assistance and information, and this input can help the team revise its framework and generate a final product aligned with the organization's objectives. Parallel team structures require ongoing care and nurturance, but they can be useful mechanisms for expanding participation, generating ideas for improvement, and solving problems.

Future Directions

Organizations will continue to expand their use of parallel team structures. Quality improvement teams, problem-solving teams, employee participation teams, and task forces will be used throughout organizations. Although the use of quality circles is waning, the use of quality improvement teams will continue to grow. The quality movement is still on the upswing in the United States. Regardless of which quality program an organization selects, teams are used as the vehicles for recommending improvement ideas. The use of task forces will also grow. Organizations will continue to have problems that cannot be addressed by the normal structure and require special attention. The flexibility of the task force's structure makes it particularly suitable and efficient in turbulent environments: when a problem is identified, a task force can be established; when the problem is resolved, the task force disbands. Few doubt that organizational environments will only become more turbulent in the next decade.

New types of parallel structures may emerge, focused on increasing decision-making speed and responsiveness to internal and external customers. New problem-solving technologies and tools intended to enhance decision-making speed and execution will be developed. These will be based on computer technologies. "Groupware" business programs are already being developed to enhance the decision making of business support teams (Johansen, 1988). The new automated tools will complement such existing quality improvement tools as statistical process analysis. Although particular forms or names may change, organizations will continue to use parallel team structures to supplement their normal decision-making processes.

Project and Development Teams

Project and development teams have been used by organizations for some time. Members — typically white-collar professionals, such as engineers, designers, and reseachers — are brought together to conduct projects for fulfilling users' requirements in a defined but typically extended period of time. Examples include new-product development teams, information systems teams, research and development teams, and new-factory design teams.

Project teams are assigned unique, uncertain tasks, and are expected to create nonroutine products. Therefore, they cannot rely on standardized procedures, because they are creating something new (Gersick and Davis-Sacks, 1990). Their products are identifiable and measurable, but measurement may be difficult because of the output's uniqueness. For example, the degree to which a new product meets the requirements of customers may not be known for several years.

Project teams usually have broad mandates and considerable authority. They are assigned responsibility for key decisions within broad strategic parameters. Within these parameters, they typically are free to define the conceptual framework for the project, project objectives, and methods for accomplishing tasks. Thus project teams are self-managing. It is impossible to solve nonroutine problems or create innovative products without the autonomy to exercise judgment.

A project team also responds to the requirements of its sponsor and the customers for its work, however. Thus it balances its needs for independent thinking with responsiveness to key stakeholders and makes sure that appropriate external communication occurs (Ancona and Caldwell, 1988; Gersick and Davis-Sacks, 1990). If the project team's decisions are not aligned with the firm's strategic objectives and its customers' requirements, then it is unlikely to be successful.

Project teams differ from task forces in three ways. First,

their work tends to be integrated into the work flow of the enterprise (for example, new-product development is a basic business activity of all high-technology companies). Second, they tend to have the authority to make decisions, not just recommendations. Third, their life span tends to be longer than that of the prototypical task force. Therefore, project teams are usually not parallel structures.

These distinctions may not hold up in actual practice, however. If a task force's work is integrated into the actual business, and if it has the authority to make decisions rather than recommendations, then it is more like a project and development team than a parallel structure. Many task forces fall in the middle of a continuum between parallel structure and project and development team. Task forces are strengthened if they are designed and managed as project teams are.

Characteristics of Project Teams

In general, organizations can build and sustain effective project teams by providing contextual supports and helping teams deal with the values and technical conflicts that arise from heterogeneity of membership. A project team's members typically do not work together but come together from different jobs, roles, departments, functions, and business units to perform the team's task (Gersick and Davis-Sacks, 1990). The composition of project teams should be relatively fixed, with most of the necessary competencies located within the team. Members can either be full-time or part-time, and the project team can consist of a combination of a few full-time core members and a majority of part-time members (Galbraith, 1973). According to the project and the size of the team, members may or may not need to be co-located.

The function and role of the project leader will depend on the group's authority, the nature of the project, and the culture of the organization. In general, the project leader should be able to help the team understand its direction, help the team align its efforts with the organization's strategic objectives, help to make sure that appropriate expertise is brought to bear, and make sure that appropriate links with key stakeholders exist.

The leader may also have to act as a tie breaker, to speed decision making. Therefore, the leader should have organizational credibility, appropriate expertise, and access to information and resources.

A variety of leadership mechanisms can be used. If organizational credibility depends on rank, and if the group has decision-making authority, a senior-level project manager will have to be assigned. A less senior project manager will suffice for less critical tasks, or in organizations where rank is less critical in getting the job done. Some project teams may be able to select leaders from inside the group, and leadership can change according to the task. In general, what matters is not the position as such but whether the project leader enables the group to complete its work by its deadline and obtain support from key organizational stakeholders.

The organization's performance-management and reward systems will communicate a message about the value of project work. At the minimum, project participation should count in individual performance reviews and rewards. Group performance can be recognized and rewarded as well. Group performance goals have to defined and outcomes must be evaluated. The relatively clear objectives and timelines inherent in a project team's activity offer a performance advantage by motivating the members and structuring the work (Hackman, 1990). The organization should use its performance-management system to capitalize on this feature of a project team's work.

The training for project participants can build on the training provided for parallel structures. Indeed, problem-solving skills and group-interaction skills are appropriate for helping individuals work effectively in groups. Nevertheless, project teams that cut across functional and disciplinary areas may need special training, so that members will appreciate their differing perspectives and communicate effectively across disciplinary, functional, and geographical lines to resolve conflicts. The ability to resolve conflicts quickly can be a competitive advantage.

Project teams must have the information they need for their projects. Although this is a commonsense notion, it is frequently overlooked (Galbraith, 1973). Organizational information systems need to provide useful project data, which may include information about task requirements and constraints, available resources, and technical requirements. Reconfiguring an information system to support projects can be a huge investment if the information system has been designed to support the functional organization.

Project teams need to manage schedules and times. Because of the complexity and long life cycles of many projects, interim milestones become critical. Projects may consist of multiple distinct phases. The framework established at the beginning of the whole project sets the context for later phases. Similarly, the halfway point of the entire project may be the most critical time for evaluating the project's progress and making major changes (Gersick, 1988). The beginning and the midpoint of each phase provide opportunities for intervention and correction, however. Project managers need to be especially aware of the opportunities implicit in a project's life cycle and in the passage of time.

Without the leadership, training, information, and rewards needed to support them, organizations will not have project teams that meet today's business objectives. Reliance on good people and hard work is not sufficient in this competitive environment.

The Future

Organizations will continue to use teams to complete complex, critical projects. What will be new is the way that project teams operate to meet competitive requirements for speed and flexibility. The degree of self-management will expand. Project teams will be expected to resolve major disagreements, without taking the time to use an escalation process. The autonomy given to project teams for developing concepts that fit a general strategic direction will motivate the teams to transcend previous technical limitations. Project teams will fail unless they are composed of members with very high technical skills and conflict-resolution abilities. The capacity to go beyond disciplines and functions and understand the trade-offs required for success in the marketplace will be critical. Organizations will take steps to align their structures and systems to better support integrated project teams. More organizations will begin to hold project team members accountable for overall project success, not just for functional contributions. More work will be project-oriented, with jobs consisting of participation in a series of project teams. Systems for project management will be used to coordinate series of efforts and to track the development of key project competencies. Managers will be responsible for coordinating the flow of people and work (Drucker, 1988; Savage, 1990).

Work Teams

Work teams are responsible for producing products or services. In contrast to parallel team structures and project teams, they perform regular, ongoing work. Although work teams can be traditional groups using external forms of control (for example, assembly-line groups), I will focus on self-managing groups, with the team having the autonomy to make most of the decisions associated with production or service activities. A self-managing team may be responsible for its own support services (such as maintenance, purchasing, and quality control) and may perform certain personnel functions (such as hiring and firing team members and determining bonuses or pay increases). Self-managing teams are sometimes called *autonomous work groups, semiautonomous work groups, self-regulating groups,* and *self-designing groups.*

Self-managing work teams are most frequently found in manufacturing settings, although this team design is applicable to any situation in which people in groups are interdependent and thus can be made collectively responsible for producing a product or providing a service to an external or internal customer. Examples include production teams, assembly teams, administrative support teams, customer sales and service teams, professional support teams, and management teams. An executive team, whose members are collectively responsible for the internal operations of the company and have shared performance goals, is a self-managing team.

Self-managing work teams have been implemented by organizations that use a sociotechnical or a job enrichment approach. Their design is intended to jointly optimize the organization's social and technical systems (Cummings, 1978). They are said to work because this way of organizing work is intrinsically motivating and satisfying and increases the level of effort, knowledge, and appropriateness of strategies for task performance, as applied to the collective task (Hackman, 1987), as well as helping to reduce unnecessary overhead costs. Both sociotechnical approaches and job design theory suggest the same causal mechanisms, and some researchers have argued for a synthesis of the two approaches (Rousseau, 1977; Cummings, 1978; Denison, 1982). High-commitment organizations, interested in maximizing the level of employee involvement, tend to use self-managing work teams (Walton, 1980).

One recent study found that 46 percent of Fortune 1000 companies use self-managing teams (Lawler, Mohrman, and Ledford, 1992). Where they have been implemented, the vast majority of such teams have been limited to involving less than 20 percent of the work force. Most of these applications have been in manufacturing and involve first-level employees; 25 percent of the service companies in the sample (as compared to 36 percent of the manufacturing firms) use self-managing team designs. A study of the Fortune Service 500 and Industrial 500 revealed that 25 percent of these companies used executive-level teams between 1980 and 1984 (Vancil, 1987).

Although the use of self-managing teams appears to be growing, research on their effectiveness has been limited. Many studies lack the controls necessary to draw causal inferences (Wall, Kemp, Jackson, and Clegg, 1986). Nevertheless, some carefully documented individual-firm studies of self-managing teams (Walton, 1972; Goodman, 1979; Wall, Kemp, Jackson, and Clegg, 1986) and several meta-analyses (Macy and others, 1986; Guzzo, Jette, and Katzell, 1985; Roitman and Gottschalk, 1984) have been performed. In a review of these studies, Goodman, Devadas, and Hughson (1988) conclude that self-managing teams have a modest impact on productivity, positively change some specific attitudes of team members, and can improve safety.

The data on absenteeism and turnover are equivocal, and few cost-benefit analyses have been done. Other studies have found that self-managing teams produce a high concern for quality (Cummings and Molloy, 1977).

In a recent study comparing sixty-three matched pairs of self-managing teams to traditionally managed teams that perform the same work in a telephone company, we found that self-managing teams were rated higher in effectiveness (productivity, costs, customer service, quality, and safety) than their matched pairs, both by team members and by upper-level managers. Participants in self-managing groups evaluated them more highly in outcomes related to quality of work life, such as growth satisfaction, social satisfaction, and trust, than the participants in traditionally managed groups rated their own groups (Cohen and Ledford, 1990). No significant differences were found in absenteeism. In general, the findings from this study are consistent with Goodman, Devadas, and Hughson's conclusions (1988).

Given that self-managing teams have positive but modest effects on performance effectiveness and quality of work life, it is important to identify the mechanisms that make them work, and to discover what can be done to make them more effective. At the minimum, a self-managing group needs the authority to determine how to execute its task. Authority can extend to determining performance goals for the team and to being responsible for the design of the team itself (its composition, structure, rewards, and so on). Teams with control over their own design have sometimes been called *self-designing teams* (Hackman, 1987). Management teams and professional support teams are more likely to be self-designing than are production, administrative support, or service teams. It takes additional knowledge, skill, and maturity to be a self-designing team — for example, to determine performance goals appropriately, to hire and fire members, and to determine team rewards. Most organizations are reluctant to make this investment and to transform power relationships so significantly.

The position and role of the team's leader depends on the organization's distribution of authority, its culture, and the maturity of the group. The immediate supervisor is frequently defined as a coach and is given a wider span of control or responsibility for coordinating more than one work team. A supervisor's position may be eliminated, with the team reporting directly to the next-level manager. The members of the team may be responsible for leadership roles, and assignments may be permanent or rotating. The leader of a work team should foster self-management by encouraging the group to set goals, have high expectations, and monitor its performance (Manz and Sims, 1987). The leader should help the team align its efforts with business objectives and help it coordinate its activities with those of other teams and organizational stakeholders. The leader should not perform traditional supervisory functions that can be handled by the team. The most reliable cost savings from self-managing teams are associated with the removal of unnecessary layers of management.

The organization's performance-management and reward systems should be designed to support collective effort. Group performance goals must be defined and measured, with accurate, timely performance feedback shared with the team. The team, with input from its customers and managers, may participate in setting its performance goals. Team members may conduct peer evaluations that assess the degree to which individuals have contributed to team goals.

Performance rewards and recognition should be based on the accomplishment of the team's task. These can include financial incentives or public recognition contingent on group performance. Managers should provide rewards to the group as an intact unit and should not attempt to differentiate individual performance, because competition for valued rewards can result in a divisiveness that undermines collective effort (Hackman, 1987). A mature self-managing group, however, may be able to use a peer evaluation system to differentiate individual rewards on the basis of contributions to the group. In this case, some combination of group rewards and individually based contingent rewards makes sense.

Finally, skill-based pay systems have been used quite successfully with self-managing work teams. Under skill-based pay systems, employees are paid for skills that they can use, rather than for the specific jobs they are performing at a given time. Skill-based pay encourages flexibility and self-management by giving employees an incentive to learn a variety of jobs and increasing knowledge of the production or service process (Ledford and Bergel, 1991). A skill-based pay system can easily be used in conjunction with group-based performance incentives.

The training provided to work teams should ensure that participants have the wherewithal to perform the collective task. Training may include social interaction skills, technical skills, and business knowledge. Like the training provided to parallel teams and project teams, team-building activities and training in problem solving, group interaction skills, and conflict resolution can help members work effectively in groups. Cross-training can provide a work team with flexibility, if its members know a variety of jobs, and may be part of a skill-based pay certification process. Training in quality analysis or statistical process control can help a team monitor and improve its processes. Business and economic education can help a team understand its activities in the context of business goals and financial performance.

Managers of self-managing work teams may need assistance in understanding their new role. Simply telling managers to become coaches or facilitators, rather than bosses, may not be sufficient to support behavioral change (Rosow, 1989). Instead, managers may need help understanding the specific requirements of their new roles, as well as training to improve their participation and delegation skills. If the role of the manager is to encourage self-management, then the manager must have the skills to perform the requisite behaviors, such as encouraging goal setting or self-evaluation (Manz and Sims, 1987). Training can help managers support self-managing work teams more effectively.

Whether training is delivered in the classroom or more informally on the job depends on the requirements of the task, the team's educational needs, and the number of teams in the organization. The content of training should also depend on the team's need for additional expertise. Whatever the content or mechanism used to deliver the training, what matters is enabling self-managing work teams to be excellent performers (Hackman, 1987).

Self-managing work teams also need support from the information systems of the organization. The teams need information about task requirements and constraints, customers' requirements, available resources, and performance standards (Hackman, 1987). In addition, information systems can provide real-time on-line links to customers, suppliers, and those with needed expertise. Information systems should be used to give on-line performance feedback on the team's results and can provide analytical assistance and the capacity to simulate the consequences of different performance strategies. Without appropriate information, a team's decision making will suffer.

Work teams need clear links to their suppliers, customers, and those who provide support. Because a team's work consists of a process of receiving materials or information from suppliers, transforming or adding value to what is received, and delivering output to team customers, coordination with external parties is crucial (Sundstrom, Meuse, and Futrell, 1990).

Self-managing teams are not easy to implement. They require organizational changes and investments of time and resources in order to make them work. Without changes in job design, work may not be organized so that a team is collectively responsible for a product or service. Without changes in management philosophy, a team may not be given the authority to make decisions about how to execute its task. Without additional training, managers may not be able to provide coaching to a self-managing team and may undermine its efforts. The reward, education, and information systems may have to be modified to support effective teamwork. These changes and contextual supports require organizational commitment and investment. Without the willingness to make this investment, an organization is unlikely to sustain the performance and quality benefits that can arise from the implementation of work teams.

Once self-managing teams are implemented and supported by the organization's reward, education, and information systems, they become relatively easy to sustain. They create a momentum of their own. This strength can become a weakness, however, if change has to occur. The mature self-managing team is a relatively self-contained unit with a team identity and modus operandi. Members may be unwilling to transfer to other teams, even if marketplace demands require different assignment of resources. They may be unwilling to apply different methods to team tasks once habitual patterns have been established. This can be managed, to some extent, by providing teams with ongoing performance and customer feedback, by making sure that team representatives participate in forums with representatives of other teams, and by providing rotational opportunities.

Conclusion

This chapter has addressed the use of teams and internal organizational networks. Organizations will probably sustain and increase their interest in teams and networked designs over the next decade. A growing number of organizations will involve an increased percentage of their work forces in networked designs, parallel team structures, project teams, and work teams as a response to competitive forces and the implementation of information technologies.

Teams and networks have to be managed, however. They must be designed to fit the work to be accomplished. They need support from organizational systems and practices, including performance-management and reward systems, education and training, information systems, and management practices.

Self-managing work team designs are not appropriate in situations that do not provide ongoing services or products to internal or external customers. They are not appropriate to tasks that cannot be self-contained, nor are they appropriate to short-term projects. If organizations do not base team design on an analysis of the work to be done but simply imitate the design of the self-managing teams used in manufacturing for service, support, and management functions, then those organizations will have a preponderance of failures.

Because the future will demand empowerment and flexibility, participants in teams and networks must have decision-making authority. Future team and networked designs must be self-managing. Temporary and fluid designs should be used more. Organizations should use work teams where tasks can be self-contained. Project teams and internal networks should be responsible for accomplishing work in the rest of the organization. Organizations must continually initiate, disband, and modify project teams and networked designs. Handling the changing configurations of flexible structures is the greatest challenge that management faces.

References

Ancona, D. G., and Caldwell, D. F. "Beyond Task and Maintenance: Defining External Functions in Groups." *Group and Organization Studies,* 1988, *13,* 468–494.

Ancona, D. G., and Nadler, D. A. "Top Hats and Executive Tales: Designing the Senior Team." *Sloan Management Review,* 1989, *31*(1), 19–28.

Applegate, L. M., Cash, J. I., and Mills, D. Q. "Information Technology and Tomorrow's Manager." *Harvard Business Review,* 1988, *66*(6), 128–136.

Bikson, T. K., and Eveland, J. D. "The Interplay of Work Group Structures and Computer Support." In J. Galagher, R. E. Krauit, and C. Egido (eds.), *Intellectual Teamwork: The Social and Technological Bases of Cooperative Work.* Hillsdale, N.J.: Erlbaum, 1990.

Cohen, S., and Ledford, G. E., Jr. "The Effectiveness of Self-Managing Teams in Service and Support Functions: A Field Experiment." Paper presented at the Academy of Management annual meeting, San Francisco, Aug. 1990.

Cummings, T. G. "Self-Regulating Work Groups: A Socio-Technical Synthesis." *Academy of Management Review,* 1978, *3*(3), 625–634.

Cummings, T. G., and Molloy, E. S. *Improving Productivity and the Quality of Work Life.* New York: Praeger, 1977.

Davidson, W. Comments from presentation at Human Resource Executive Conference, University of Southern California, 1990.

Denison, D. R. "Sociotechnical Design and Self-Managing Work Groups: The Impact of Control." *Journal of Occupational Behavior,* 1982, *3,* 297–314.

Drucker, P. F. "The Coming of the New Organization." *Harvard Business Review,* 1988, *66*(5), 45–53.

Eccles, R. G., and Crane, D. B. "Managing Through Networks in Investment Banking." *California Management Review,* Fall 1987, pp. 176–195.

Eveland, J. D., and Bikson, T. K. *Work Group Structures and Computer Support: A Field Experiment.* Santa Monica, Calif.: Rand Corporation, 1989.

Galagher, J. "Intellectual Teamwork and Information Technology: The Roles of Information Systems in Collaborative Intellectual Work." In J. S. Carroll (ed.), *Applied Social Psychology and Organizational Settings.* Hillsdale, N.J.: Erlbaum, 1990.

Galbraith, J. R. *Designing Complex Organizations.* Reading, Mass.: Addison-Wesley, 1973.

Gersick, C. J. "Time and Transition in Work Teams: Toward a New Model of Group Development." *Academy of Management Journal,* 1988, *31*(1), 9–41.

Gersick, C. J., and Davis-Sacks, M. L. "Summary: Task Forces." In J. R. Hackman (ed.), *Groups That Work (and Those That Don't): Creating Conditions for Effective Teamwork.* San Francisco: Jossey-Bass, 1990.

Goodman, P. S. *Assessing Organizational Change: The Rushton Quality of Work Experiment.* New York: Wiley-Interscience, 1979.

Goodman, P. S., Devadas, R., and Hughson, T. G. "Groups and Productivity: Analyzing the Effectiveness of Self-Managing Teams." In J. P. Campbell, R. J. Campbell, and Associates (eds.), *Productivity in Organizations: New Perspectives from Organizational Psychology.* San Francisco, Calif.: Jossey-Bass, 1988.

Guzzo, R. A., Jette, R. D., and Katzell, R. A. "The Effects of Psychologically Based Intervention Programs on Worker Productivity: A Meta-Analysis." *Personnel Psychology,* 1985, *38,* 275–291.

Hackman, J. R. "The Design of Work Teams." In J. W. Lorsch (ed.), *Handbook of Organizational Behavior.* Englewood Cliffs, N.J.: Prentice-Hall, 1987.

Hackman, J. R. "Conclusion: Creating More Effective Work Groups in Organizations." In J. R. Hackman (ed.), *Groups That Work (and Those That Don't): Creating Conditions for Effective Teamwork.* San Francisco: Jossey-Bass, 1990.

Johansen, R. *Groupware: Computer Support for Business Teams.* New York: Free Press, 1988.

Lawler, E. E., III, Ledford, G. E., Jr., and Mohrman, S. A. *Employee Involvement in America: A Study of Contemporary Practice.* Houston, Tex.: American Productivity and Quality Center, 1989.

Lawler, E. E., III and Mohrman, S. A. "Quality Circles: After the Honeymoon." *Organizational Dynamics,* 1987, *15*(4), 42–55.

Lawler, E. E., III, Mohrman, S. A., and Ledford, G. E., Jr. *Employee Involvement and Total Quality Management: Practices and Results in Fortune 1000 Companies.* San Francisco: Jossey-Bass, 1992.

Ledford, G. E., Jr. and Bergel, G. "Skill-Based Pay Case Number 1: General Mills." *Compensation and Benefits Review,* 1991, *23*(2), 24–38.

Ledford, G. E., Jr., Lawler, E. E., III, and Mohrman, S. A. "The Quality Circle and Its Variations." In J. P. Campbell, R. J. Campbell, and Associates (eds.), *Productivity in Organizations: New Perspectives from Organizational Psychology.* San Francisco: Jossey-Bass, 1988.

Lipnack, J., and Stamps, J. "A Network Model." *The Futurist,* 1987, *21*(4), 23–25.

MacDuffie, J. P. "The Japanese Auto Transplants: Challenges to Conventional Wisdom." *ILR Report,* 1988, *26*, 12–18.

Macy, B. A., and others. "Meta-Analysis of United States Empirical Organizational Change and Work Innovation Field Experiments: Methodology and Preliminary Results." Paper presented at the Academy of Management annual meeting, Chicago, Aug. 1986.

Manz, C. C., and Sims, H. P. "Leading Workers to Lead Themselves: The External Leadership of Self-Managing Work Teams." *Administrative Science Quarterly,* 1987, *32*, 106–128.

Masaki, I. *Kaizen: The Key to Japan's Competitive Success.* New York: Random House, 1986.

Miles, R. E. "Adapting to Technology and Competition: A New Industrial Relations System for the 21st Century." *California Management Review,* 1989, *31*(2), 9–28.

Mohrman, S. A., and Lawler, E. E., III. "Parallel Participation Structures." Working paper, Center for Effective Organizations, University of Southern California, 1988.

Mohrman, S. A., and Ledford, G. E., Jr. "The Design and Use of Effective Employee Participation Groups: Implications for Human Resource Management." *Human Resource Management,* 1985, *24*(4), 413–428.

Naisbitt, J. *Megatrends.* New York: Warner Books, 1982.

Roitman, D., and Gottschalk, R. "Job Enrichment, Socio-Technical Design, and Quality Circles: Effects on Productivity and Quality of Work Life." Unpublished manuscript, Michigan State University, 1984.

Rosow, J. M. *New Roles for Managers: Employee Involvement and the Supervisor's Job.* Scarsdale, N.Y.: Work In America Institute, 1989.

Rousseau, D. M. "Technological Differences in Job Characteristics, Employee Satisfaction and Motivation: A Synthesis of Job Design Research and Socio-Technical Systems Theory." *Organizational Behavior and Human Performance,* 1977, *19,* 18–42.

Savage, C. M. *5th Generation Management: Integrating Enterprises Through Human Networking.* Bedford, Mass.: Digital Press, 1990.

Stein, B. A., and Kanter, R. M. "Building the Parallel Organization: Creating Mechanisms for Permanent Quality of Work Life." *Journal of Applied Behavioral Science,* 1980, *16,* 371–386.

Sundstrom, E., Meuse, K. P., and Futrell, D. "Work Teams: Applications and Effectiveness." *American Psychologist,* 1990, *45*(2), 120–133.

Takuchi, H., and Nonaka, I. "The New New Product Development Game." *Harvard Business Review,* 1986, *64*(1), 137–146.

Thorelli, H. B. "Networks: Between Markets and Hierarchies." *Strategic Management Journal,* 1986, *7,* 37–51.

Tichy, N. M., Tushman, M. L., and Fombrun, C. "Social Network Analysis for Organizations." *Academy of Management Review,* 1979, *4,* 507–519.

Vancil, R. F. *Passing the Baton: Managing the Process of CEO Succession.* Boston: Harvard Business School Press, 1987.

Wall, T. D., Kemp, N. J., Jackson, P. R., and Clegg, C. W. "Outcomes of Autonomous Work Groups: A Long-Term Field Experiment." *Academy of Management Journal,* 1986, *29,* 280–304.

Walton, R. E. "How to Counter Alienation in the Plant." *Harvard Business Review,* 1972, *50*(6), 70–81.

Walton, R. E. "Establishing and Maintaining High-Commitment Work Systems." In J. R. Kimberly, R. H. Miles, and Associates (eds.), *The Organizational Life Cycle: Issues in the Creation, Transformation, and Decline of Organizations.* San Francisco: Jossey-Bass, 1980.

Zuboff, S. *In the Age of the Smart Machine.* New York: Basic Books, 1988.

PART THREE

Developing and Managing Human Resources

Critical to the effective operation of new organizational forms are the capabilities and competencies of the human resources of an organization. In this section, the focus is on how human resource management systems should be designed, to create the right kinds of human resources for tomorrow's organizations. Since leadership will be particularly crucial to the effectiveness of organizations in the future, particular emphasis is placed on how leaders can be developed for complex organizations. The recommended human resource management practices deviate significantly from what has previously been considered good practice. This means that considerable technological development will be needed to support new practices, as will significant internal changes in the ways that organizations structure and manage human resource departments.

Chapter Nine

Human Resource Management: Building a Strategic Partnership

Allan M. Mohrman, Jr.
Edward E. Lawler III

The human resource management function has been evolving in most major corporations for decades. It has been presented with new challenges and knowledge about human resource management and has expanded. Today the situation is no different. Evolutionary change clearly needs to continue because new challenges and opportunities currently face human resource management functions. We begin this chapter with a brief history of human resource roles and follow this with a review of the challenges facing human resources. Then we look at how the human resource management function needs to change and the way it needs to be designed in large organizations.

A Brief History of Human Resource Roles

The history of the human resource department's role in most organizations has been one of gradual evolution and increased sophistication. Early institutional roles were based on the bureaucratic and legal aspects of dealing with employees. Originally, the personnel department ensured that employment records were accurate and that people were paid. The personnel department often reported to an accounting department or to someone in charge of administration. As procedures were developed for making administrative decisions about employees, the personnel function gained some power in its own right, and it began to play a role in making sure that administrative decisions were made appropriately and fairly.

The rise of the union movement in the 1930s and 1940s meant that someone in the organization was needed to counter the union's efforts to organize the company and, when these efforts failed, to deal effectively with the union. The personnel department typically took on these roles, and in many cases the labor-relations people who were responsible for them gained considerable power and prestige within corporations. They positioned themselves as the only ones who could deal effectively with unions and developed special relationships and knowledge with respect to unions and their leaders. Many individuals made (and, indeed, still make) careers out of settling strikes and dealing with union organizing drives and grievances.

A major change in the situation of personnel departments occurred because of the discrimination legislation of the 1960s and 1970s. Because of the large penalties and disruptions that lawsuits could cause for organizations, employment practices became increasingly important in corporations. In some ways, they became important for the wrong reasons (that is, for their potential down side, rather than for their positive contributions to organizational effectiveness). Nevertheless, they became an important and central issue.

Human resource departments have gradually learned to apply behavioral science knowledge to add value to the design of systems and practices. The behavioral sciences have been applied to selection practices, for instance, through the development and use of various assessment instruments and practices based on knowledge of human testing. Similarly, measurement technologies have been applied to performance appraisal. In fact, legal standards often have been based on behavioral science knowledge. Compensation practices have been created on the basis of theories of human motivation. Training practices have utilized expertise in learning theory and instructional technologies.

In addition to applying behavioral science expertise, human resource functions have added value by taking more of a business perspective. This occurred initially in the application of financial and market expertise, primarily in the areas of compensation and benefits. It is here that personnel and human resource functions have been seen as having a direct impact on the bottom line. Human resources has also added value in the areas of recruitment and manpower planning, which are increasingly seen as not just necessary in carrying out business strategies but also important in formulating those strategies.

During the 1980s, the salaries of personnel executives went up significantly, taking them from one of the lowest-paid staff functions to one of the better-paid staff functions. Indeed, for the first time, human resources became a career for some of the more talented people in the organization.

Today, human resource departments can play a major constructive role in making organizations more effective. This, too, offers an opportunity for increasing the power and prominence of the human resource function. For the first time in many corporations, human resource managers are being asked to participate in major business decisions (Ulrich, 1989, Towers Perrin, 1992). They are being asked partly because of their own talent but also partly because human resource issues are increasingly central to how the business is and should be operated.

Current Challenges

In this section, we focus on six major challenges facing human resource management: global competitiveness, the need to manage change, the explosion of new knowledge in human resource management, new information technologies, legal issues, and the new knowledge worker.

Competition

The competitive pressure on modern organizations is probably the strongest force in human resource management. Human resources is being asked to be part of the organization's response to competition. The Introduction explains this challenge in terms of organizations' continual search for competitive advantage (Porter, 1985). As discussed in Chapter Three, this has affected the role of all staff organizations and led to demands that they restructure and refocus themselves. Organizations have focused on productivity, total quality, customer service, and speed of response as potential sources of competitive advantage. Attending to these has made organizations increasingly aware of how important organizational structure and management practices are to their successful accomplishment and to organizational effectiveness. Speed and key organizational competencies are even more dependent on organization. Basic competitive competency and the ability of an organization to learn are shown, in Chapter Four, to be due to the way the company is organized. The more focused an organization is on competition, the more central human resource management becomes to organizational effectiveness. Organizations fundamentally involve people and their management; organizations without people are technologies.

There are two ways in which human resources is being asked to respond to competition: by cutting costs, and by adding value. In many ways, the most immediate challenge for human resource departments is cost pressure. Particularly in corporations facing international competition, all staff departments must justify their cost structures on a competitive basis. Headcount comparisons are made increasingly among corporations, to check the ratio of employees to members of the human resource department. In addition, value-added questions are being asked of the human resource department. As noted in Chapter Three, corporate human resource departments in particular are being asked why they are necessary and what they add to the work being done in local operating units.

Cost pressures are not new in most corporations. They have come and gone over the years, according to the condition of the economy and particular organizations. What is new, however, is the strength of the pressures, the strong emphasis on competitive benchmarking, the strong emphasis on quality, and the role of international competition. Together, these have created a set of cost pressures that are stronger and more difficult to respond to.

Managing Change

Very much related to the issue of cost pressures on the human resource department is the issue of organizing corporations in ways that will make them internationally competitive. Many organizations have decided that they can be competitive in the international area only if they make vast improvements in their performance. If organizations are to be the main source of competitive advantage, this will require more than just using the old practices in a better way. It means a fundamental change in the way organizations operate. Since many change efforts are moving in the direction of new management styles and approaches that try to involve employees more, the human resource department is faced with a major change agenda itself. First and foremost, it must change many of its systems in order to respond to the new management approaches. New training, pay, selection, and appraisal systems are needed.

The opportunity also exists for the human resource department to be a major consultant to the rest of the organization on how it can change the way it does business (Ulrich, 1989). This is particularly true with respect to organizational design, management style, work structures, and change programs. It is also true with respect to strategic planning. Human resource managers are not involved in the strategic planning process in many organizations, at least partly because they are not seen as being partners in the business or as having relevant knowledge. Ironically, many a strategic plan has failed because it has not accounted for the human factor; the plan has either been unrealistic or has failed to change the organization so that it can be implemented. An effective human resource function should be able to contribute to both the planning and the implementation process.

New Knowledge

There has been a knowledge explosion in human resource management. This is partly reflected in the number of professional associations in the field and in the large number of journals and magazines that are currently published. In essence, to be true professionals in many areas of human resource management, individuals virtually have to spend full time in that field and have advanced degrees. Areas like compensation have become incredibly complicated because of their close connections to strategic, legal, financial, and tax matters. In addition, behavioral science knowledge continues to advance, especially in its application to organizations.

New Information Technologies

The record-keeping role of most human resource functions has also changed dramatically with the advent of the new generation of computer technology. The human resource function has always had responsibility for keeping the personnel records of the organization, but minimal records were often satisfactory. Today, managers are used to extensive on-line data bases and see no reason why the same types of information systems should not be in place for the human resource area. Thus the human resource department is increasingly being pressured to have an on-line employee data base that includes not just name, rank, and serial number but also work history, skills, performance history, organizational structural data, and so forth. It is a technical challenge to create this kind of data base, and its creation raises all sorts of issues concerned with the right to privacy, the currentness of the data base, and the obtaining of valid data to enter into the data base.

Legal Issues

The legal issues that the human resource function must deal with also seem to be increasing. Legal issues are not new. For a long time, laws have protected employees in the areas of pay, labor relations, and safety. Nevertheless, there has been a consistent increase in the number of issues that organizations must worry about from a legal perspective, including the costs of failing to behave in a legally defensible manner. Particularly important today are the legal issues concerned with employment at will and discrimination in pay, hiring, firing, and layoffs. In addition, plant-closing issues, drug testing, and the treatment of employees with AIDS and disabilities are increasingly becoming matters for legal scrutiny. Taken together, they mean that the human resource function is faced with an increasing array of legal issues.

The New Worker

The dominant employers in the United States are increasingly the organizations that employ professional and technical employees. In many respects, this means that the key assets of an organization are its employees. The implication is that the recruiting and retention of employees is increasingly important to most organizations and that, indeed, an effective human resource department, not a personnel department, is needed. It is not enough to simply put a want ad in the paper and pay a fair wage to attract and retain outstanding people. Human resource departments must come up with innovative recruiting, training, and development programs and devise appoaches to management that retain and motivate the best and brightest personnel. In order to accomplish this, a human resource department must play an important role in the business, as well as be very good at performing the basics of good personnel management.

Highly skilled technical and professional employees are not readily available in most countries (Johnston, 1991). In the United States, there are fears that the quality of the employment pool will not be high enough to meet the needs of the new organization and its competitive environment. Therefore, the right types of employees, in many cases, may have to be developed within the organization. The employee development tasks facing organizations are compounded by the increasing diversity of the work force (Johnston, 1987). Organizations simply must make sure that the development of highly competent employees takes place in a way that allows and even takes advantage of employees' diversity, rather than being constrained by it.

Overall, it is fair to conclude that the challenge has never been greater. Opportunities for the human resource department to do more and to play an important role in organizations are everywhere. It must respond to an increasing array of pressures, and its effectiveness is increasingly becoming a vital concern of the total organization.

What Should the Human Resource Function Do?

Now that we have looked briefly at the evolution of the human resource function and at the pressures and demands it currently faces, we can consider what it should do and how it should do it. It would be nice to say that it can begin to abandon some of its traditional activities and concentrate on meeting the new demands that it faces. The reality, however, is that there is still a need for it to do all the things that it has done and at the same time to do more. The challenge is to do both the new and the old things and do them well, but at the same time do them in a cost-effective way. Before we discuss how human resource departments can do this, we need to elaborate the new things that the human resource function must do and the new ways it must do old things.

The New Institutional Role

Historically, the record-keeping role was essentially one of keeping a data base of employees and their basic characteristics. This is no longer adequate. What is needed is an information system that covers not only the basics of who works for the organization and their characteristics but also data about the condition of the human organization. In the latter area, information is needed about current satisfaction levels in the organization, turnover, absenteeism, training needs, and schedules for performance appraisal.

This means that the human resource department has to build sophisticated systems and be in a position to update them. Ultimately, such things as paper-and-pencil tests and attitude surveys should disappear. Surveys, for example, can be collected on a real-time basis, with employees sitting down at terminals or networked personal computers and inputting their views on the organization. Networked computers can also create considerable two-way communication in the organization. They can be used to debate human resource management and other organizational policies. New policies and practices can be put on networks and employees can be given the opportunity to comment on and discuss them. The networked computer system in an organization can also be used to train and advise people in such human resource management systems as fringe benefits and pay. Overall, the human resource function must actively commit itself to the revolution now occurring in information systems and use it to improve its data base, lower the cost of delivering its services, and improve the information structures within the organization.

In other words, new information technologies, as well as the normative directions that organizations are taking toward high involvement, teamwork, and other people-oriented values, should give a new look to human resource's traditional record-keeping role. In some large corporations, huge computer-based human resource systems are already a reality, but they are a reality that embodies traditional organizational logic and values. Many of the new approaches to management imply direct accessibility of human resource data bases to all employees. The ability to do this requires the development of a very different systems architecture from the one currently in use.

The increase in team-based organizations and other lateral organizational forms places new demands on various human resource systems. Compensation systems, for instance, will need to be able to reward teams, as well as (or perhaps rather than) individuals, and to pay for skills (Lawler, 1990). The fact that teams and team membership are often in flux and that individuals often belong to multiple teams complicates matters. Nevertheless, these are realities that human resource systems must be able to deal with. To the extent that organizations themselves are continually learning and changing, so must human resource systems. Systems architecture will need to be flexible under changing conditions and will have to be able to be changed in ways that are currently unforeseeable.

Another traditional role for the human resource department has been industrial relations. The changes prophesied in earlier chapters will also have impacts on this role. For instance, the increasing presence of network organizations will likely engender a complete restructuring of the role. Miles (1989) and others (Heckscher, 1988) have commented on the new forms of unionism that are beginning to develop and have extrapolated possible scenarios for the future of industrial relations. Much of the impetus for the new forms of unionism, they feel, will come from the new forms of organization that are emerging to meet the challenges we have enumerated. In an earlier chapter, we discussed a particularly extreme organizational form that is evolving: the network organization. Although not all organizations are going to become networks or parts of networks, there are dimensions of network organizations appearing in many organizations today.

In their purest form, network organizations are coacting groups of small to medium-size organizations that together deliver a product or service. Each organizational member contributes a specialty, a value-added function. One organization might do the designing, another the manufacturing, another the marketing, and so on. One of these or some other acts as the broker of the overall endeavor. Under the reality of networks, there will be constant restructuring of these smaller organizations into different networks. In this setting, companies may find it difficult if not impossible to provide basic-skills training, benefits, and career opportunities for employees. Even the larger organizations today are finding the same difficulties as they become flatter and leaner.

Miles (1989) foresees the advent of a new type of unionism, based on regional unions that provide many of the things not readily available otherwise. These would be based on geographical regions and represent participating employees from the organizations in those regions. These "unions" would provide portable benefits, comparable salary structures, core-skills training, regionwide career opportunities, and job information and would work with organizations to set up mechanisms to protect the basic rights of the represented employees. What is striking about this list of "union" services is the overlap it has with many human resource functions. One way to interpret this is as an example of externalizing the human resource function.

In some networks, the human resource function may be located in one of the nodes of the network. This means that human resource management firms may evolve to house some of the functions now taking place internally. This is already happening, to some extent, with the advent of firms that do the payroll work for subscriber organizations and firms that provide temporary employees of all types to customer organizations.

New Value-Added Roles

Given the increasing complexities of managing human resources in today's environment, the human resource department must provide expert consulting support to the organization. There is simply no substitute for the best possible knowledge in areas like compensation, training, organizational development, and selection. The stakes in these areas are simply too high to operate without the best technical knowledge. The legal exposure involved, as well as the organizational costs of poor decision making, are such that poor practices cannot be tolerated. The human resource department has to have available the best information and the best approaches and practices and be able to provide a "reality check" when line management comes up with ideas for new practices and directions.

We mentioned earlier that an important value-added role that human resource professionals have played is in the area of applied behavioral sciences. As organizations change and are based on different sets of assumptions, the nature of the behavioral science that is applied also requires change. Traditionally, organizations have been managed with the assumption that organizational performance is a function of the predictability and control of employees' behavior, and the behavioral science applied has reflected this assumption; it is the science designed to discover what controls behavior and to predict its effects. Cause-effect relationships, once discovered, are used to inform practitioners about the things that they can do to cause the effects they want. Many of our human resource management practices are based on this approach. For instance, we tend to select individuals who have attributes that, research has shown, will enable them to perform better in their jobs. We try to construct reward systems that pay people for doing what we want them to do, because our behavioral knowledge tells us that setting up such a system will cause people to tend to do what we want.

Many of the organizational forms we have discussed in this book are necessitated by a reality that makes a different set of assumptions more salient. The dynamics set up by network organizations, joint ventures, team-based organizations, flat organizations, customer-focused organizations, and so on, point to behavioral approaches that are largely captured in the chapters on employee involvement. In these new organizational settings, the emphasis is less on prediction and control of the behavior of others and more on self-management and mutual influence of behavior. Consequently, the most useful behavioral knowledge helps practitioners understand and create the social processes through which knowledge, power, and rewards come to be shared, in order to accomplish organizational objectives.

Social science knowledge concerning self-managing and influence will lead to different practices. For instance, selection is not based only on measurement of applicants' aptitudes. In the form of a realistic job-preview approach, it also becomes a social process of sharing information about such things as needs, aptitudes, and job requirements and involves a mutual decision by both the organization and the applicant, so that commitment is maximized. When applied, this type of behavioral science focuses on reward systems that foster commitment to organizational success by sharing the monetary results of performance among employees (as in gain sharing). Similarly, performance appraisal, training and development, career development, and other human resource management practices take on a much different look. The chapters on employee involve-

ment clearly set forth the nature of these new applications. The
legitimacy and usefulness of human resource professionals will
depend on their mastery of the behavioral science of involvement.

Not only should human resource management reflect a
new kind of applied behavioral science, but the value of this
application also must be heightened by increasing integration
of human resource management with the fundamental business
issues of the organization. This is best seen in the trends developing in performance management (Mohrman, Resnick-
West, and Lawler, 1989). Historically, performance appraisal
has evolved as an administrative exercise pushed by and owned
by the human resource function. The purposes of performance
appraisal have included its use in merit pay decisions, developmental plans for the individual, feedback to the individual employee from the supervisor, and documenting the employee's
performance for legal and administrative reasons. All these uses
of performance appraisal are seen as separate from, and superim-
posed on, the "real" work of the employees and the organization. It has generally been considered a necessary piece of administrative work that does not add value to the performance
of the organization and actually risks having more negative than
positive side effects.

In the future, the new performance management must
increasingly be seen as integral to the very core of what the organization is all about. Performance management is coming to
represent much more than performance appraisal and to include
processes for defining what performance should be, processes
for developing resources for accomplishing performance, processes for measuring and reviewing performance, and processes
for sharing in the value of performance. Human resource functions need to play an important part in developing these processes because they should embody the new applied behavioral
science. These processes should not be seen as being owned by
the human resource function, however. They must be seen as
the way the organization does business.

New Normative Roles

The development of more effective organizations requires consistent values by which effectiveness can be judged and values

that provide the direction in which the organization can be improved. Strategic decision making entails, in part, the establishment of shared values and beliefs. Shared mindsets are increasingly being seen as sources of competitive advantage (Ulrich, Brockbank, and Yeung, 1989). A fundamental role that is developing for the human resource function today concerns the development of norms, values, and belief in the organization.

Human resource management has traditionally been associated with a set of people-oriented values, in the form of humanism and the virtues of trust and openness as embodied in organizational development. These values, along with an expanding set of people-oriented values, have now moved to center stage. Employee involvement is at the core of the new management approaches (Lawler, 1992). Teams and teamwork are necessary elements of the various lateral approaches to organizing.

Recognition of the central strategic importance of employees and their involvement in the organization elevates the importance and centrality of human resource management. Organizational change is not just a matter of changing technologies, structures, and tasks. More fundamentally, it entails a change in the values and beliefs that employees hold, and so the human resource function must become a central player in organizational change.

Corporate strategy is the area where the greatest change in human resources involvement is needed. The human resource function must change to become a partner in developing the business strategy of the organization (Towers Perrin, 1992). The human resources of an organization are a key determinant of what strategies are practical and implementable. Human resource managers must understand the business well enough to react to and help develop business strategies.

Numerous reports have emphasized the problems that organizations have with implementing strategies. One common reason is that the human resource function does not change its practices to encourage strategy implementation. In many cases, this is so because the human resource department is not involved in developing the strategy. It is simply asked to implement it. Clearly, this needs to change. Human resource managers need to be involved in the formation of strategy, so that they can be full partners in its implementation.

The human resource function needs to integrate its different subsystems so that they reinforce a single strategic direction. All too often, the different technical specialties within a human resource department go their own way, without concern for integration. This is not acceptable, since the interdependence of the pieces of the human resource system requires their integration. In short, the pay system has to fit with the training system, the performance-management system, the selection system, and so forth. If the systems are designed well and in tune with the business strategy, as well as with each other, then an organization can be built that supports the business direction.

More than any other staff group, the human resource function tends to play a major role in influencing the culture and probably should be held particularly accountable for its evolution and maintenance. It is not, however, simply a matter of the human resource function's maintaining the historical culture of the organization; it needs to continually help shape the culture to fit the organization's current business direction. While there is no one right culture for an organization, the one chosen needs to fit the current business direction and strategy of the organization. Organizational cultures cannot be allowed to serve only the immediate needs of the organization, however, because there are the larger and more fundamental areas of ethics and social responsibility that need to be incorporated. It is always right for an organization to value these and behave appropriately (O'Toole, 1991). Ultimately, an organization must conform to the basic values of the larger society, which come to be expressed in its laws and sanctions.

Throughout the history of the human resource function, it has been the conscience of the organization, more than any other function. Undoubtedly, this is because of its responsibility for the human side of the organization. In any case, the result is that human resource managers have often been expected to raise issues of what is right, fair, and just with respect to employees and with respect to the community at large. This role is rarely formally assigned to the human resource function, but it is nevertheless expected. Indeed, it has sometimes led other managers to refer to human resource personnel as "do-gooders" and "employee advocates." With the growing legal protection that employees have, this role has changed substantially. In many cases, the things that human resource managers argued for are now required by law. Nevertheless, the need continues for the human resource function to be a steward of the human resources of the organization and, at times, an advocate for what is ethical and just in dealing with employees and communities.

In a highly competitive environment, with rapidly developing and shifting sources of competitive advantage, the ultimate source of competitive advantage lies in the ability of the organization to learn new ways of functioning. This moves the processes of organizational learning to the foreground. Organizational learning is fundamentally a social process and may be the most difficult and most important role of the human resource function. At one level, this role can take the form of helping the organization understand how to organize, manage, and reward efforts aimed at achieving innovation, whether in the products or the processes of the organization. At another level, this role may involve supporting organizational improvement processes, such as those that are initiated in total quality management programs. Human resource support for these continuous improvement processes is still underdeveloped in companies with these efforts (Bowen and Lawler, 1992). The highest level of contributions to organizational learning will involve institutionalizing the learning process itself as the central business process, rather than as something to be invoked on an as-needed basis.

Strategies for Effective
New Human Resource Management

So far, we have argued that the new human resource department has to meet a number of new demands, as well as keep fulfilling its traditional responsibilities well. A question remains: How can all this be accomplished? In this section, we will answer that question in terms of the substantive context of this department's work, the structure of the human resource function, and the processes it uses.

The New Substance of Human Resources

The new human resource management will have to support teams and other lateral forms of organization. It will have to support employee involvement. It will need to foster the leadership necessary in the organization of the future. Like all staff functions of the future, it will have to support the strategy-setting processes and provide services for the line organization, rather than controlling it. Finally, human resource management will have to orchestrate organizational change and facilitate processes of continued organizational learning.

Supporting Teams and Lateral Organizational Forms. As the team increases in importance and takes its place alongside the individual as a fundamental performing entity in the organization, it becomes imperative that systems and practices for managing human resources be developed to recognize this fact. A whole array of human resource systems for teams that parallel those for individuals will have to be put in place. For instance, managing the performance of teams will require practices for setting goals and defining and planning work, practices that develop the team's capabilities (such as team problem-solving techniques, practices for appraising the team's performance, and practices for rewarding the team). Furthermore, these team performance-management practices will have to be integrated with individual performance-management practices, so that the two levels of performance management work in concert.

Supporting Employee Involvement. All the human resource management practices that exist in an organization (performance management, career planning and development, succession planning, training, selection, and rewards) can be designed to maximize the involvement of the employees who are affected. For instance, as mentioned earlier, selection can become a mutual process based on complete knowledge and understanding on the part of all parties to be affected, especially the potential selectee. (Chapter Seven, on employee involvement, spends some time indicating the nature of these new management practices.)

Perhaps the most important aspect of employee involvement is the necessity that it be implemented in an authentic way. If it is to work, employee involvement must truly make a difference. Otherwise, involvement practices become manipulative tools to achieve employees' compliance. This will backfire in the long run. Real involvement allows for the possibility that the results will reflect company, work-group, and individual needs and, to that extent, will achieve results not predictable at the beginning of an involvement exercise. Carrying out employee involvement is an important way for the human resource function to ensure that it is playing the role of advocate for the individual employee. Employee involvement is a way for the employee to be his or her own advocate.

Fostering Leadership. If ever there were an organizational variable that dealt entirely with people, it would be leadership. Therefore, the fostering of leadership is squarely in the domain of human resource management. As McCall states in Chapter Ten, we do not need a new kind of leader; we need leaders with the skills that we know are necessary. We have not yet made the effort to develop them, and the human resource department has to ensure this effort is made. Not coincidentally, many of the things that the human resource function can do to foster leadership are compatible with other things that it needs to do to contribute to organizational effectiveness. The basic characteristics of leadership (see Chapter Ten) are not innate; they are skills that can be developed in people, and some people will be better than others at learning them. These are also skills that will be in general demand throughout the new organization. Therefore, the new organization will provide fertile ground for these skills to grow and for leaders with the most ability to surface (see Weick and Berlinger, 1989).

The proper role for the human resource function is to provide opportunities for leadership to surface and to offer real-time training about leadership needs to all teams and groups as they organize for their tasks. Human resources has to be alert for leadership to emerge from any quarter. It is not the human resource function's role to identify, in some all-knowing fashion, those who are leadership material and then to provide them with the appropriate training and experiences. Rather, its role is to provide everyone with leadership opportunities and to take note of which people step up to the role, provide them with further training and opportunities, and continue the process in an iterative way that accentuates constant learning and adaptation. This approach makes individuals full partners in the development of leadership and allows them to progress in a way that fits their natural stages of development (Weick and Berlinger, 1989).

Providing Strategic Support: Expertise and Service. Employee involvement, leadership, and team/lateral organization are all examples of cultural and organizational strategies that organizations are desirous of implementing in order to meet competitive challenges. The human resource function needs to supply expertise in these areas and to provide service in support of them. Such service is no longer embodied in a control-oriented role. In fact, the term *service* can be misleading in that it implies a subservient status to the line in these areas. Competitive pressures are such that only those human resource management roles that are value-added will remain. Since these roles strategically add value, they are an increasingly important part of the mainstream of organizational functioning. As this occurs, there is a growing realization that these roles should therefore be part of the line management. The only way for human resource management to be of service to these important emerging line functions is for the human resource department to become a partner with line management in these areas.

Full partnership demands that human resource managers develop the necessary business knowledge. In the future, human resource managers not only will be involved in the implementation of strategic initiatives, such as employee involvement and teams, but will also need to be full partners in the strategizing process. Human resource management's expertise is useful at two levels in the strategy process: it is an important input to substantive deliberations about strategy, its implementation, and its consequences, and it is an important input to the strategy process itself. Strategizing is a social process involving people, and the human resource function should be a source of expertise about how to organize and conduct it.

Orchestrating Change and Organizational Learning. Organizational strategies change, either to keep up with the changing nature of competitive advantage or to establish new sources of competitive advantage. Evolving strategic directions will demand evolving organizational forms — with people, of course, as the most important components. Change creates the necessity of learning how to cope in the new order, and learning creates the basis for change. Chapter Four points out that change and learning are part of the self-design processes. Human resource managers need to become experts in a self-design process and to help implement it by teaching it to others as they work through the process together.

The New Structure of the Human Resource Function

In order to play its substantive roles, the human resource function will have to respond with new structural approaches, as mentioned in the discussion in Chapter Three on staff organizations. The human resource function needs to be decentralized and close to the "customer." In many situations, a front-end/back-end organization will be appropriate to the human resource function; in others, a type of network organization will be appropriate. Both of these can lead to the human resource function's becoming a part of the management team of the organization. It needs to operate under a much leaner structure, with some and perhaps many of its traditional roles contracted out to external entities or performed by "back office" teams that are organized around customers and processes (such as benefits administration).

Decentralization. Every emerging role of the human resource function demands close contact between itself and the line. This is necessary for partnership. It is the connection by which human resource managers can come to understand the business.

It is the connection by which the line organization can become fully involved in the design and execution of the organization's human resource management practices and systems. Organizationally, therefore, the function needs to be decentralized to the extent necessary for it to play this role. Since it is a partner in the business, it must report to the head of the business, with a dotted-line connection to the corporate-level human resource department. In some local units, the separate function may disappear entirely and be incorporated into the general management processes.

Front-End/Back-End. The traditional record-keeping role requires large data bases and information technologies. The maintenance and some of the development of these systems can be most efficiently handled by functional organizations. The use and much of the development of these systems will demand close connection to and participation by the end user. This situation can be dealt with by using a front-end/back-end model of organization. The most difficult aspect of this approach is the link between the front and the back. The trend in the near term will be toward a tighter and tighter link between the two, so that the systems will have an increasingly customized nature. The need to provide a virtually customized system to different users while retaining needed links among systems will drive the development of new architectures. The development of these new systems will be a major endeavor of most corporate and divisional human resource functions and will require a strong link between the front and the back.

Becoming Part of the Management Team. At each business level, the human resource function needs to be part of the management team and report to the line general manager at that level. This is already happening in companies like Kodak. There are degrees to which the management staff of an organizational business unit really acts as a team. Human resource management will become truly integrated with the line to the extent that there is such a team. It should be through management's team process that senior human resource executives come to truly know the

business and make an impact on it. The more the team approach
applies, the more other members of the management team will
come to understand and value the human resource function.
In the extreme, much of the human resource function may be
absorbed into the line structure. For instance, at Dana Corporation the function has become part of the responsibility of one
of the line managers of the top management team.

Contracting Out. As human resource managers become more
generally involved in the runnning of the business, and as line
managers assume more human resource management responsibilities, two things will tend to happen. First, there will be fewer
human resource managers and, second, there will be a tendency
toward human resource generalism and generalists. Specialized
expertise will become more scarce, thus increasing the need for
contracting out these specialized areas to consulting firms and
others.

   One form of contracting out is connected with the rise
of the network organization. Under this scenario, entire ongoing human resource management responsibilities, such as payroll, training, selection, and the like, are done by outside contractors. This would not be practical for those areas with unique
requirements but should definitely be considered in situations
where needs are ongoing and relatively stable. In some ways,
this might amount to moving the back-end activities out of the
organization.

   Both kinds of contracting out, to consultants or to service-
providing organizations, create relationships that have to be
managed. Management of these relationships will require both
time and skills. Human resource management professionals need
to acquire such skills and, in many cases, broker and facilitate
direct links between the contractor and the line organization.

Customer-Based Teams. Just as organizations are increasingly
using multifunctional teams to completely serve external customers, the human resource function can mount similar teams
to serve the line organization. In many cases, these teams can
be co-located with the client organization. Since human resource

management will be more integrally involved in the management of the business, and vice versa, many of these customer-based teams should include customers. These could evolve into human resource teams, made up of human resource management professionals and line personnel, that assume human resource leadership in the business unit. When contracting out is used, it will be necessary for representatives of the external contractors also to be members of these teams. Unions and regional industrial-relations organizations might also be represented on these teams.

Cross-Functional Careers. Cross-functional teams can enhance integration between the human resource function and the line, but the team members still need to stay true to their disciplines. To that extent, there will still be differences in world views that prevent complete understanding. Human resource people can acquire a line perspective only by being completely thrown into that role, and vice versa. For this reason, we expect the practice of building organizational careers by lateral moves between the human resource function, the line, and other functions to increase. It is not enough to begin this at the upper management levels. Individuals can begin to cycle through these lateral career moves very early in their tenure.

Blurred Boundaries. The ultimate result of all the structural approaches just discussed is a blurring of the lines between human resource managers and others. In fact, the direction is toward fully integrating human resource roles into the functioning of the organization. The extreme of this trend will lead human resource management to be considered part of every manager's role.

The New Human Resource Process. The processes used by the new human resource function will have to be service-oriented. Contracts for these services should be negotiated. Human resource management systems and practices must be jointly developed and jointly owned with the line organization. Organizational change and learning should be facilitated by the use of a self-design process.

Service Orientation. Traditionally, human resource departments have tended to be production-oriented. They have worried about the number of people trained, recruited, and interviewed (Bowen and Greiner, 1986). In many cases, they have even handled most of the activities associated with hiring, firing, and paying people. In short, they have not been just human resource or personnel departments; they have done the personnel management for the organization. The line manager has often left personnel management up to the human resource function and personally had only a minor role in the major personnel activities. This, clearly, is not a cost-effective means of managing personnel, nor is it a strategically effective approach.

One key to the development of a successful human resource function is to become less production oriented. In a service model, the human resource function needs to listen to the individuals it serves and respond to their needs and requests, but it cannot be a blind servant to the desires of customers in the line organization, for two reasons. First, the line organization may ask for things that are unethical, unwise, and too short term in their orientation. Second, the line organization may want too much service and may ask the personnel organization to do too much of the work for the line rather than to enable line employees to do human resource management for themselves.

The challenge for the human resource department is to create an environment where individuals enjoy serving themselves. Consider automated bank tellers. Such automation has effectively transferred much of the service function to the customer, and in many cases the customers prefer it to dealing with human tellers. The challenge for the human resource function is to work with the rest of the organization in ways that lead managers to want to deliver and conduct their own selection interviews, performance management, and pay reviews. In short, human resources has to create a situation where line managers own the delivery systems and, as a result, are happy to deliver the services or activities associated with them.

Joint Development. To own the delivery systems, the line organization will have to play an active role in developing them.

Setting up continuous learning processes is fundamental to carrying out the new organization. This requires the ability, at any level of the organization, to assess how human resource management systems are operating and to "bootstrap" a new way of doing things, as conditions warrant. The human resource function cannot play the all-knowing expert and tell the line organization what it needs to do in major areas. It needs to work with the line organization to develop systems that are owned by line managers and, in most cases, are implemented by the line managers. The human resource function will play a consulting role and will therefore need a particular set of skills, some of them different from the traditional skills of the human resource function. Process skills will be particularly needed, so that human resource managers can facilitate involvement activities that lead to the line organization's developing new systems and technical skills.

Contract Negotiation. Just as joint development with the line organization is necessary, it should also be part and parcel of the involvement of any outside contractor. The contracting process itself is likely to be problematic because of the many uncertainties involved. Much of the relationship with contractors will have to rest on trust and sharing. Strict management of the relationship solely through a written contract will be impossible. Therefore, the contracting process is more important because it has to establish the trust and understanding necessary to carry a contract out. The contract will include not only financial arrangements but also, and perhaps more important, role negotiation, team building, process planning, and design.

Conclusion

The new roles, structures, and processes of human resource functions are already working. Their embryonic manifestations are seen in many settings, and we are learning from them. The revolution will come when they reach a critical self-reinforcing mass that forever transforms the human resource function.

The new approaches have been developing in a somewhat hostile administrative environment. Critical mass is not very far off, however, and human resource functions had best be ready. One way to prepare is to begin experimenting with and learning from the approaches discussed in this chapter.

References

Bowen, D. E., and Greiner, L. E. "Moving from Production to Service in Human Resources Management." *Organizational Dynamics,* 1986, *15*(1), 35–53.

Bowen, D. E., and Lawler, E. E., III, "Total Quality–Oriented Human Resources Management." *Organization Dynamics,* 1992, *20*(4) 29–41.

Heckscher, C. *The New Unionism: Employee Involvement in the Changing Corporation.* New York: Basic Books, 1988.

Johnston, W. B. *Workforce 2000.* Indianapolis: Hudson Institute, 1987.

Johnston, W. B. "Global Workforce 2000: The New World Labor Market." *Harvard Business Review,* 1991, *69*(2), 115–127.

Lawler, E. E., III. *Strategic Pay: Aligning Organizational Strategies and Pay Systems.* San Francisco: Jossey-Bass, 1990.

Lawler, E. E., III. *The Ultimate Advantage: Creating the High-Involvement Organization.* San Francisco: Jossey-Bass, 1992.

Miles, R. E. "Adapting to Technology and Competition: A New Industrial Relations System for the 21st Century." *California Management Review,* 1989, *31,* 9–28.

Mohrman, A. M., Jr., Resnick-West, S. M., and Lawler, E. E., III. *Designing Performance Appraisal Systems: Aligning Appraisals and Organizational Realities.* San Francisco: Jossey-Bass, 1989.

O'Toole, J. "Do Good, Do Well: The Business Enterprise Trust Awards." *California Management Review,* 1991, *33*(3), 9–24.

Porter, M. E. *Competitive Advantage: Creating and Sustaining Superior Performance.* New York: Free Press, 1985.

Towers Perrin. *Priorities for Competitive Advantage.* New York: Towers Perrin, 1992.

Ulrich, D. "Tie the Corporate Knot: Gaining Complete Customer Commitment." *Sloan Management Review,* 1989, *30*(4), 19–27.

Ulrich, D., Brockbank, W., and Yeung, A. "Human Resource Competencies in the 1990s." *Personnel Administrator,* Nov. 1989, pp. 91–93.

Weick, K. E., and Berlinger, L. R. "Career Improvisation in Self-Designing Organizations." In M. B. Arthur, D. T. Hall, and B. S. Lawrence (eds.), *Handbook of Career Theory.* New York: Cambridge University Press, 1989.

Chapter Ten

Developing Leadership

Morgan W. McCall, Jr.

The Greek philosopher Heraclitus "the Obscure" observed in 500 B.C. that there is nothing permanent except change. He was called "the Obscure" because his philosophy was hard to understand, but his observations about change are both timeless and timely. Few question that the future holds more change—at a rapid rate, and in a roller-coaster ride of unexpected twists and turns. Examples of sweeping, often stunning, change have come so fast that they are outdated and overshadowed before they can be used. While the ongoing revolution in Eastern Europe is change at its most dramatic, fundamental changes are occurring in even the tiniest nooks and crannies of our lives. For example, the world of model railroading is a relatively quiet pool, but even here the drama of the changing world economy and global competition is playing out. In a recent issue of *Model Railroader,* a commentator reports, "Here we were in Hong Kong

Note: The author wishes to thank his colleagues at the Center for Effective Organizations, especially Edward Lawler and Gerald Ledford, for their helpful comments and suggestions on earlier drafts of this chapter.

256

watching as parts for American and British-prototype [minia-ture] trains were manufactured by workers in China and Hong Kong using raw materials and components from the United States and elsewhere and [made with] equipment bought from Germany, Switzerland, and Japan" (Christianson, 1989, p. 104). To see the manufacturing of such all-American products as Cabbage Patch Dolls, *Star Wars* and *Ghostbusters* figures, or My Little Pony requires travel to places like Kowloon Bay, Shekou, or Donguen. Commenting on the changing global economy, Carlzon (1987, p. 4) notes, "Today cows are slaughtered in Texas and the hides are sent to Argentina for tanning and then on to Korea to be made into baseball gloves. Finally, the gloves come full circle and are shipped back to Texas where they are sold to local sporting goods shops."

Pieces of the Berlin Wall are sold as souvenirs in U.S. department stores. Russia struggles toward a free-market economy, and U.S. executives, recently preoccupied by the Western European alliance of 1992, are now wondering how to do business in Poland, Czechoslovakia, and Romania. There is change from all directions. Within thirty years, one in six of us will be over sixty-five. Along with increasing numbers of women, large numbers of immigrants from Asia, Mexico, Latin America, and the Caribbean will change the complexion of the work force. These and other demographic shifts will fundamentally alter the work force of the next decades, ending the domination of the white male (Krupfer, 1988).

The familiar list of expected future changes goes on and on. We stand poised on the edge of awesome technological break-throughs, which may lead to social changes every bit as dramatic as those created by the automobile, the airplane, and the television set. Environmental crises — oil shortages, ozone depletion, deterioration of air and water quality — will sorely test our will and resourcefulness. Competition from more places in more industries will continue to heat up the global economy. The bottom line is that organizations will be forced to adapt quickly and dramatically or be swept mercilessly aside. There will be no place to hide.

Faced with a turbulent future, scholars and stockholders

have been asking tough questions about the kind of leadership that will be required to survive, and perhaps thrive, in the years ahead. Kotter (1988) has argued persuasively that leadership is now, and will continue to be, more important than ever. He contends that the historical sources of the U. S. competitive advantage, such as abundant manufacturing capacity in capital-intensive industries and control over sources of key raw materials, are less helpful today because they "can be easily purchased (e.g., capacity or patents) or destroyed (e.g., regulation) by aggressive and rich competitors" (p. 132). Kotter concludes that the "leadership factor" will be *the* major competitive advantage in the future.

Leadership was moved to center stage in the 1980s, but it is not clear that all the attention provided a lot of answers. A nonstop parade of books by and about leaders generated a new lexicon of leadership, marked by terms like *transformational, charismatic, inspirational, visionary,* and *empowering.* The 1970s asked, "Where have all the leaders gone?" The 1980s answered that they were running Disney, Chrysler, Federal Express, Herman Miller, SAS, and baseball. As we move through the 1990s, many pundits suggest that a new kind of leader will be needed to take us into the future.

This emphasis on new kinds of leaders implies that the selection and development of leaders was adequate in the past, but that changing times have made those skills selected for in the past inappropriate for the future. There is another possibility: perhaps the past was simply more forgiving of poor leadership. Some have argued that leadership did not matter much during the boom years following World War II (Kotter, 1988); no matter what we did, it turned to gold. As times got tougher, however, competition increased, and the marketplace became global; ineffectiveness in key leadership roles crippled industry after industry. Habituated and sometimes complacent leaders watched from their corner offices as the changing world almost swallowed up the U. S. steel, automobile, energy, electronics, textiles, and other basic industries. Repeated crises inspired a "search for excellence" and a Darwinesque emergence of gifted leaders who, in spite of (or perhaps because of) turmoil, led their organizations to success.

Perhaps the crisis of leadership occurred, not because we did not know what effective leadership was, or because we did not have people who could lead, but because we did not act on what we knew. Since it was not necessary to select and develop the kind of leadership that was truly effective, organizations found themselves unprepared for change. There has been a sudden rediscovery of things known for a long time to enhance leadership effectiveness. For example, clear goals, involving people in decision making, motivating people through challenge and ownership, and other leadership practices identified decades ago (Campbell, Dunnette, Lawler, and Weick, 1970) have resurfaced under such contemporary labels as *empowering others.*

As technical solutions generated by formal planning, forecasting, control systems, and other professional managerial approaches failed to meet the challenges of change, distinctions between leadership and management became increasingly frequent (Bennis and Nanus, 1985; Kotter, 1990). However accurate an explanation this distinction may be for the miserable performance of organizations, effective leadership was described as early as 1966 as incremental influence over and above mechanical compliance (Katz and Kahn, 1966). The point is that the searching for "new" or "different" leadership is a red herring to some degree. If current leaders are inadequate, it is less because the qualities of effective leadership have changed than because our standards have slipped. Leadership roles were filled with people who were mediocre, or too narrow, or incapable of inspiring anyone else. Too little energy went into identifying and developing leadership talent because a forgiving environment allowed it. As Andy Pearson, former chairman of Pepsi, wrote recently, "Everyone knows how important it is to attract talented managers, develop them quickly, and keep them challenged and effectively deployed. Yet not everyone does what is required to achieve this. In fact, very few companies do. Lack of management talent ranks right behind low standards as a cause of poor performance" (1989, p. 98). The environment will no longer tolerate mediocre leadership. The good news is that a lot is known about what it takes to be an effective leader (it is not a mystery, or something we must discover totally anew), and a great deal is known about how to develop these attributes (they are not all congenital). The bad news is that it takes a lot of effort, and many organizations have not been willing to do what it takes.

This chapter is a storm warning for the decade ahead. For leaders to improve their ability to handle the coming challenges, the destructive practices of the past must be stopped, and a new commitment must be made to effective development strategies for the future. In this chapter, I will begin by diagnosing the common errors that have led to many of the leadership inadequacies seen today. I will go on to suggest a consensus in the research about senior leaders on certain basic attributes that *effective* leaders must *develop;* the kinds of changes predicted put a premium on these attributes. This chapter closes with specific strategies for developing the kinds of leadership talent that will be crucial to the future.

The Origins of Sloth

There seems to be a fundamental belief among senior executives that the cream rises to the top. Those who survive the various trials by fire and ascend the hierarchy are not just tougher but also somehow better leaders. The performance of many U.S. corporations over the last two decades might cause us to question the adequacy of this kind of selection process, but this implicit belief — that good leadership will emerge on its own — lies at the root of the current situation. If one assumes a natural-selection model of leadership, then it is neither critical nor even necessary to invest in sustained selection or development efforts. Added to that is a common belief that, should the fittest not emerge from inside, it can always be bought on the outside. Between them, Charles Darwin and Adam Smith provided the rationale for corporate neglect of the leadership resource. This neglect, in turn, is reflected in five fundamental sins that lead to inadequate senior leadership: accepting mediocrity, ignoring fatal flaws, acting as if tomorrow will never come, waiting for heroes, and compounding earlier mistakes.

Accepting Mediocrity

The path to senior management often begins with entry into the corporation, either as a nonmanagerial employee or as a first-level manager. It is from this pool that most later managerial selections will be made. It is not surprising, then, that poor early decisions reduce the overall quality of the leadership talent pool later on. Yet companies that would not tolerate hiring mediocre engineers or administrators sometimes pay no attention to the leadership potential of their recruits. Worse yet, they tolerate putting people in managerial jobs who are "just okay" or "no worse than anybody else" or "better than nothing." This is especially true during rapid growth, when there are many managerial jobs to be filled quickly. It is also true when things are running well, that "adequate" people are promoted with little consideration for what might happen when things get tough and a higher order of skill is needed. When talent pools are ineffectively managed, promotion-from-within policies perpetuate and exacerbate leadership problems.

The first sin, then, is to open wide the gates at entry, with no or low standards when it comes to managerial potential. By sheer probabilities, the less talent in the initial pool, the less there will be to choose from later on. This is perhaps why Kotter (1988) has found that the companies with the best reputations for quality management put a lot of time and effort into recruiting.

Ignoring Fatal Flaws

This sin is committed when people are put in managerial roles and then promoted on the basis of an outstanding strength (getting results, being the best at a technical specialty), even though those promoting them know they have weaknesses that one day will cripple them (McCall and Lombardo, 1983). Weaknesses are often overlooked or forgiven when a person gets results or is valuable to the current operation. In the worst possible case, managers are chosen whose strengths (for instance, technical achievement) have little to do with effective leadership and whose major flaws (for instance, inability to deal effectively with people) are crucial to it.

These kinds of selection mistakes are common at the lower and middle managerial levels, where success can be driven by a few strengths, or where outcomes are determined by a relatively narrow range of skills. Research indicates, however, that the situation changes as managers ascend the hierarchy, and that flaws that are forgiven early on can become fatal at later stages (McCall and Lombardo, 1983). Further, flaws can develop over time, especially in people who have a long history of success after success (Kotter, 1982).

Overall, then, this sin consists of promoting people on the basis of their strengths while ignoring the significance of their demonstrated weaknesses in new situations. There may be some pertinent lessons to be drawn from what happened to the dinosaurs as their environment changed around them.

Acting As If Tomorrow Will Never Come

U.S. corporations have been accused of taking a short-term orientation, focusing on annual or even quarterly performance rather than on long-term payoffs. Whether or not it is true for strategy, such an accusation is often true of managerial placement decisions. People can get promoted on the basis of the short-term demands of today, and the people who promote them forget that removing ineffective people later on can be more difficult than promoting them in the first place. If a division is in trouble, the company might choose a "tough guy" who will slash and burn, only to discover later that he cannot make anything grow in the wasteland he has created. One company in desperate financial trouble brought in an outside chief financial officer with a reputation for ruthlessness. He did turn the situation around, but his approach and actions were totally out of character for the company. As a result, the "saved" corporation lost its culture (a values- and quality-driven heritage of many years), lost many of its best senior managers (who resigned rather than carry out some of the decisions), and was stuck with a senior executive who not only had alienated everyone he had to work with but also knew nothing about running this kind of business.

This sin is committed each time someone is promoted on the basis of a short-term need, with little or no thought given to what comes next. In times of change, the accumulation of sins like this one can be quite rapid. The higher the level of the misadventure, the more difficult it can be to undo later on.

Depending on Heroes

Instead of investing the time and energy it takes to cultivate leadership talent, corporations sometimes cruise along on the faith that, when they are needed, John Wayne and the Lone Ranger will emerge to save the day. This fantasy is bolstered by the belief that if they cannot be found, they can be hired. There has been just enough success in doing that for people to believe in it, even though the evidence on the success of outside hires at the top is not encouraging (Gabarro, 1987; Kotter, 1982; Shetty and Perry, 1976).

Another dangerous aspect of this sin is the implied belief that a single leader can "save" a corporation. The Lee Iacocca and Michael Eisner myths aside, effective corporate leadership is something that must permeate an organization, not something that resides in one or two superstars at the top. Depending on a single hero is at best a risky strategy, lest something happen to the person, or lest the situation move away from that person's strengths; by definition, it cannot last indefinitely. Even when superstars serve for an extended period, their influence may not reach to all parts of a large organization.

Compounding Earlier Mistakes

Because these sins can be committed independently of one another, several can be committed at once. Over time, the accumulated errors, like compound interest, grow rapidly. The ultimate result is that the key decision makers — the only ones who can fix the mistakes or change the practices of the past —

are the same people put in power by the very mistakes they are now expected to fix.

This multitude of sins can be summarized as Five Commandments for not mismanaging executive resources:

1. Thou shalt not ignore leadership potential in recruiting and early promotion decisions.
2. Thou shalt not allow great strengths to camouflage fatal flaws.
3. Thou shalt not make decisions based on today's emergencies, without considering the long-term consequences of those decisions.
4. Thou shalt not fail to do what needs to be done under the illusion that the needed talent will emerge coincidentally at the right moment ("just in time" leadership).
5. Thou shalt not allow previous mistakes to accumulate or be perpetuated; at some point, someone must bite the bullet.

Because these sins are subtle, easy to commit, easy to rationalize, and pervasive, the task of doing things right can be daunting. What is more significant, simply refraining from sin does not ensure virtue. Unless one is satisfied with the outcome of natural selection, sound and strategic decisions about executive resources require knowledge of what to look for and how to develop it. Knowledge in these areas is not perfect or complete, but there is a growing consensus about the qualities required for effective leadership.

Leadership Is Not Magic

Some people cling to the view that leadership is an individual trait: either you have it or you do not. This makes a great excuse for doing nothing to develop leadership talent, but it has very little basis in fact. Innumerable studies of people in leadership roles have failed to generate much evidence for a single set of stable traits consistently and strongly associated with leadership effectiveness (Bass, 1981; Yukl, 1989). On the contrary, there is a growing consensus that effective leaders have identifiable attributes dominated by _learned skills_ and _developed attitudes_ and values, rather than by a handful of stable personality traits. Traits may help some people learn the necessary skills, but even though some people may have more potential than others, the skills of leadership are nonetheless learned and polished over time. Whatever their personalities and natural gifts, effective leaders must learn to set the direction, align people with that direction, act consistently within a set of fundamental values, cope effectively with the demands and stresses of a managerial job, understand themselves, and learn from experience (McCall, Lombardo, and Morrison, 1988). Obviously, these skills are at the heart of adapting to the many changes that will face us in the decade ahead, and we simply do not have enough slack to accept leaders who do not have these skills.

Setting the Direction

A consensus in the research on the abilities crucial to setting the direction can be found in Bennis and Nanus's concept of "management of attention" (1985), Kotter's description of "setting agendas" (1982) and "setting direction" (1990), and McCall, Lombardo, and Morrison's "setting and implementing agendas" (1988).

It is in vogue these days to say that all leaders must have a "vision," but vision is not something that comes from eating certain kinds of mushrooms. Leaders who can see the possibilities know their business, know how to assess markets and environments, can mobilize their people to generate ideas and plans, know their customers, and are able to do a lot of things to make something happen. In short, they work very hard at it. A term like "setting the direction" connotes the many complex skills involved in dreaming what might be, gauging its feasibility, and figuring out what has to be done to pull it off.

There are two half-truths commonly associated with "visionary" leadership that make it seem beyond the reach of mere mortals. One is the notion that visions are always profound (even "transformational"). The other is the idea that a leader must be inspirational or charismatic to carry out a vision. Both of these can be true, but there are other ways to achieve the same ends.

For example, consider L.L. Bean, a premier catalogue-sales company with an outstanding reputation for customer service and quality merchandise. L.L. Bean was a runner-up for the 1988 Baldrige quality award for service companies (there was no winner) and was chosen by IBM as a quality comparison point for its distribution system (Main, 1990, p. 112), yet the "vision" driving that performance is as simple as the catalogue is plain: "Sell good merchandise at a reasonable profit, treat your customers like human beings and they'll always come back for more" (from an advertisement in *Newsweek*, Sept. 4, 1989, p. 9). What is profound is not the thought or even the expression of the thought; what is profound is doing what is necessary to achieve it—bringing that vision into reality and sustaining it over time. What does it mean to treat customers well? How does one translate that principle into answering telephones, responding to complaints, handling orders and returns, or performing customer service? What does it mean to sell good merchandise? How is quality assessed and enforced with myriad suppliers? The details are what set the direction. Leadership means using knowledge of the business (its products, its customers, its suppliers), its technologies (computers, telecommunications, packaging, delivery), the organizational structure (consistent with the chosen direction, which may require something other than a traditional hierarchy), the reward systems (structuring pay and other rewards to reinforce behavior consistent with the direction), the information flow (getting information and authority to the people in the best positions to make decisions) in designing jobs and work flow. Creating change—setting a direction—can begin with any of these facets (many have been described in detail in earlier chapters of this book). It does not require charismatic leadership, although that will be helpful. More important is that, over time, each of the major elements is consistent with the overall values, direction, and strategy. That is the responsibility of leadership, and that is a lot more demanding than eloquence.

That eloquence does not hurt, however, is demonstrated

by Jan Carlzon, chief executive of SAS. He articulates the direction he has set for SAS to become the preferred airline of the business traveller: "Last year, each of our 10 million customers came in contact with approximately five SAS employees, and this contact lasted an average of 15 seconds each time. Thus, SAS is 'created' 50 million times a year, 15 seconds at a time. These 50 million 'moments of truth' are the moments that ultimately determine whether SAS will succeed or fail as a company. They are the moments when we must prove to our customers that SAS is their best alternative" (1987, p. 3). As far as it goes, this is an inspiring statement, but if SAS stopped with eloquence and a slogan, nothing much would happen. Leadership is not just seeing a niche and understanding what it will take to grab it; it is *doing* whatever it takes. It is arranging people, structure, rewards, information flow, and job design so that what emerges is an organization headed in the direction chosen. Carlzon goes on to say, "We cannot rely on rule books and instructions from distant corporate offices. We have to place responsibility for ideas, decisions, and actions with the people who *are* SAS during those 15 seconds: ticket agents, flight attendants, baggage handlers, and all the other frontline employees" (p. 3). Getting this much of the act together is what setting the direction means in a leadership context.

Alignment

A consensus on alignment as the use of interpersonal skills to achieve strategic goals can be found in Bennis and Nanus's "management of meaning" (1985), Kotter's use of "network" (1982), "aligning people," and "motivating and inspiring" (1990), and McCall, Lombardo, and Morrison's "handling relationships" (1988). The theme of interpersonal competence as a crucial factor in leadership is, of course, as old as thought about the concept.

Dealing with personnel, information, systems, and structure is only part of the battle. Leaders must also have the skills to align the relevant parties behind the chosen direction. Critical relationships may include those with superiors, directors, customers, suppliers, unions, stockholders, subordinates, bankers, partners, and anyone else whose cooperation is essential to success or whose opposition would represent a serious obstacle. Dealing with these people — especially people who may have no reason on earth to cooperate but may have considerable impact on outcomes — is something effective leaders must learn to do.

The broad rubric used to describe this complex array of skills is _interpersonal competence_ (a term brought into popular usage by Argyris, 1962), but the singularity of the term masks the diversity of abilities required. Handling an angry customer does not require the same finesse as working effectively with a difficult boss. Motivating a group of incompetent subordinates requires different skills from those used in negotiating with a joint-venture partner. Handling such eyeball-to-eyeball individual relationships effectively is not synonymous with aligning diverse groups so that they work (knowingly or not) toward the chosen direction.

The idea of having a variety of sophisticated skills for dealing with people and constituencies is not new, but two kinds of changes make a paucity of such skills a serious barrier to effectiveness. First, alternative means of attaining compliance (such as punishment and sanctions) are not particularly effective in motivating people to go "the extra mile." New high-involvement and "delayered" organizational forms that require people to accept greater responsibility make greater interpersonal skill mandatory because the basis of influence is shifted from narrowly defined hierarchical authority to persuasion across large lateral spans, functions, and traditional boundaries. Second, the increasing shortage of skilled labor and professionals makes attracting and retaining them more important than ever, and reliance on compliance-based motivational strategies may not be sufficient to keep, much less inspire, the needed human resources (Hall and Richter, 1990).

Add to these pressures the new organizational forms that are built on coalitions, joint ventures, and special relationships among suppliers; the requirement of doing business in an international marketplace; and the increasing diversity within the U.S. labor pool. It becomes clear why leaders in this decade cannot get by with minimal alignment skills. Success is increasingly dependent on learning the complex and broad array of skills required to effectively align key relationships.

Values

If leadership were viewed as value-neutral, skill in setting the direction and aligning constituencies could be applied as easily to ill as to good ends. Organizations can be designed and built to efficiently accomplish evil ends as well as just ones, and people and groups can be aligned through deception, fear, and greed as well as through inspiration, commitment, and pride. From a moral point of view, however, most of us would like to see any definition of leadership include some essential statement of values. Burns (1979, p. 430) describes in great detail the concept of modal values which guide the conduct and style of leadership: "Fairness, civility, tolerance, openness, and respect for the dignity of others undergird and legitimate the elaborate system of due process that characterizes decent relations among human beings." Behavior that falls within widely accepted principles of how people should be treated is not merely desirable; according to at least one study of successful senior executives, it is related to sustained effectiveness as a leader (McCall, Lombardo, and Morrison, 1988). The long-term ability of a leader to influence others hinges on credibility, integrity, and trust (see also Bennis and Nanus, 1985). Short-term compliance can be extracted by threats, fear, and coercion, but these sources of influence are too narrow and evanescent to support the situational variation in modern leadership. Instead, partners, suppliers, subordinates, customers — name the group — look for people who do what they say they will do when they say they will do it, and who let others know when for some reason they will not. They look, too, for people who treat other people with dignity and respect, even when those other people are different from themselves.

Times of change put an even higher premium on leaders who can use their other skills with integrity, respect for others, and compassion. Because the environment changes so rapidly and unpredictably, it is crucial that a leader be trustworthy. In a fickle environment, the word of the leader may be the only glue holding things together. Integrity is more than desirable or admirable; it is the foundation of action. In an ironic twist, the emerging organizations of the twenty-first century are partly

throwbacks to an earlier, simpler time, when one's word and
a handshake were the basis of business relationships. In this fast-
changing, complex, and sophisticated era of network organization, global alliances, and instantaneous information sharing,
organizations depend once again on individual integrity. There
simply is no time to wait for decisions to be trundled through
the bureaucracy, to draw up and sign contracts, or to check and
double-check and verify every transaction. For example, in the
new Saturn plant at General Motors, "as each finished car exits
the plant, Saturn's computers will automatically authorize payment to suppliers. . . . It does away with the invoices and mounds
of paperwork involved in parts purchasing" (Treece, 1990, p. 61).

Integrity goes a long way in leadership, but by itself it
may not be enough for dealing effectively with the increasingly
diverse work force of the decade ahead. These changes are here
now and will intensify in the years to come, making increasingly crucial the ability of managers to learn to work effectively
with different groups of people. *Fortune* reports that "over 80 percent of the additions to the work force in the 1990s will be blacks,
Hispanics, recent immigrants, and women" (Richman, 1990,
p. 74). The implications of this change for white males, who
dominate the management ranks, are obvious, but dealing with
a wide range of people will be required of whoever holds a leadership position. Effectiveness will depend on the trust and credibility established with people of different backgrounds, motives,
and values, and ultimately it will depend on genuine respect
for others.

Temperament

Consensus on a single set of executive attributes is hard to docu-
ment, although extensive research has been conducted on various traits, motivational inclinations, attitudes, personal characteristics, and related topics. Bass (1981) and Yukl (1989)
review these studies. McCall, Lombardo, and Morrison's (1988)
study identifies a variety of learned reactions to characteristic
demands of managerial jobs (such as ambiguity) and labels them
"executive temperament." In a sense, the research consensus is

that managerial work is characterized by a common set of demands (see, for example, McCall, Morrison, and Hannan, 1978; Mintzberg, 1973) and, by inference, that effective leaders develop the temperament to function comfortably in that environment.

A person who is thrown by ambiguity, folds up in the face of criticism, goes down with setbacks, or loses confidence in tight spots will have a tough time as a leader in the stress and change of the coming years. Of course, leaders have always faced unpredictability, opposition, and risk, and substantial research evidence suggests that effective leaders are helped by self-confidence, emotional stability, and stress tolerance (Yukl, 1989). There is clearly a cluster of qualities that make up a temperament for leadership—a manner of thinking, behaving, and reacting that helps an individual operate with relative comfort in a job characterized by making decisions and taking chances under uncertainty, being at the mercy of uncontrollable and capricious forces, and being responsible for large numbers of people, dollars, and resources. While some of these qualities sound like enduring traits formed in early childhood, there is evidence that executive temperament can be learned (Howard and Bray, 1988). Wherever they come from, such personal characteristics will be even more crucial for leaders because the future will be even more personally demanding than the past has been.

Self-Awareness

A recent *Newsweek* poll discovered that 77 percent of those polled believed there is a heaven, and 76 percent thought they had a good chance of getting there; 58 percent believed there is a hell, and 6 percent thought they had a good chance of ending up there ("Visions of Eternity," 1989). This distortion in appraising potential outcomes is not unlike the self-delusion that appears in appraising work performance. One study (cited by Von Glinow, 1988, p. 117) found that 80 percent of the employees surveyed believed they were in the top 30 percent of performers. The study surveyed engineers, finding that 100 percent of them believed they were "above average." Looking specifically at leadership, the researchers report that 70 percent of the employees rated themselves in the top 25 percent on leadership skills (and only 2 percent rated themselves "below average"). Graduates of the Harvard Advanced Management Program have also demonstrated this perceptual bias. Asked how they would rate themselves by comparison with other executives in the program, 86 percent rated themselves in the top 50 percent (Hollenbeck, 1989).

The consistency of these findings indicates that self-awareness — the realistic assessment of one's strengths and weaknesses — is neither automatic nor easy, yet it is crucial to effective leadership, especially as situations increasingly require leaders to develop great skill at doing things like understanding other people's perspectives, empowering others, and taking risks and absorbing failures. Bennis documents self-knowledge as one of the critical characteristics of the successful leaders he studied. He concludes, "Nothing is truly yours until you understand it — not even yourself. Our feelings are raw, unadulterated truth, but until we understand why we are happy or angry or anxious, the truth is useless to us" (1989, p. 61).

The idea that we must first understand ourselves to be effective with others is, of course, not new. Self-examination and the importance of understanding one's own behavior were central to Socrates' philosophy as early as 400 B.C. More recently, a study of John F. Kennedy's Harvard class documented that the most successful among them were the best adjusted overall — the most in tune with who they were and what they wanted, and the most likely to have effective relationships in the various spheres of their lives (Vaillant, 1977). It is no surprise, then, that leadership, so centrally concerned with influencing others through one's own actions, also hinges on self-awareness. For leaders, self-awareness is crucial to knowing their own limits, knowing what they really want to do and what they are willing to sacrifice to get it, taking responsibility for their own careers and growth, and being ready to seize opportunities when they appear (Howard and Bray, 1988).

Constant Learning

Because leadership is complex and because demands on leaders are constantly changing, leaders, too, must constantly learn, grow, and change. The requirement for constant learning and development is documented by Bennis and Nanus (1985), Howard and Bray (1988), and McCall, Lombardo, and Morrison (1988), among others. Bennis cites Mark Twain to capture the current situation for leaders: "Two things seemed pretty apparent to me. One was, that in order to be a [Mississippi River] pilot a man had got to learn more than any one man ought to be allowed to know; and the other was, that he must learn it all over again in a different way every 24 hours" (Bennis, 1989, p. 101). Heraclitus, the Greek philosopher with whom we started this chapter, anticipated Twain's insight, observing that a person cannot step into the same river twice.

If they have done nothing else, the enormous changes in the competitive arena have upped the ante for continual growth and change on the part of leaders. It may have been in vogue only a few years ago to focus on matching leaders to situations (Fiedler, Chemers, and Maher, 1976), but the rapid changes in recent history point up the futility of such an approach. With the rate of environmental change, matching leaders to situations would amount to a never-ending game of musical chairs. The disruption involved in frequent and massive movement of managers was a painful lesson at Douglas Aircraft when McDonnell Douglas headquarters dismissed five thousand managers from their jobs and had them reapply (Vartabedian, 1989). When situations are moving targets, the leaders who fit a specific situation today will be misfits tomorrow unless they can adapt and change as rapidly as their context. Continual growth is no longer a luxury for leaders; it is a fundamental requirement for them and their organizations (see Chapter Three). Therefore, leaders need the attributes that allow them to adapt rapidly and effectively — in short, to continually learn and grow.

In summary, leadership is not magic — or at least it is not *all* magic. Six basic characteristics of effective leadership have emerged across a number of studies, and they provide a reasonable platform for talking about the leadership requirements of the coming decade:

- An ability to translate direction and mission into reality
- An ability to align people with the chosen direction
- Integrity and the ability to develop trust

- Comfort with uncertainty
- Strong self-awareness
- Constant learning and adaptation

These characteristics do not represent a new kind of leader — effective leaders have always needed these abilities, and a few of the very best have had them — yet the situations that leaders are facing today and into the twenty-first century will both demand more leaders with more of these skills and be less forgiving of leaders who are seriously deficient in any of them. The business world of even the recent past had plenty of room for mediocre leaders and for managers who could operate bureaucracies. The 1980s may be remembered as the decade of "lean and mean," during which the Fortune 500 shed 3.2 million jobs (Henkoff, 1990), many of them managerial. Not only was much of the slack removed, but the delayered firms also found themselves more dependent than ever on fewer key leadership roles and on the assumption of leadership responsibilities by lower-level managers and nonmanagerial employees. Given the ever-increasing complexity of the world economy and global competition, as well as the loss of sources of competitive advantage that offset the lack of leadership ability, there is simply less room for inept or even marginal leadership. We can no longer afford the price of sloppiness in how leaders are selected and developed. The naïve belief that the cream will rise, more or less, and that adequate leadership will emerge of its own accord, leaves success in this turbulent world purely to chance. "More or less" and "adequate" will not be sufficient in a world where leadership is a significant competitive advantage. More highly skilled leaders are needed, and significantly more of them are needed in the fewer managerial jobs. Significantly more people in nonmanagerial roles as well must develop and exercise leadership skills. Fortunately, we have more knowledge about selecting and developing leadership talent than we have put to use.

Nurturing Greatness

Not everyone is cut out to be a leader, much less a leader in the turbulent corporate environment of the years ahead. Not everyone is cut out to be a great pianist or an Olympic runner either, but there is a significant lesson in the difference. When we think about developing pianists or runners, we do not think of throwing them into the toughest situations we can find, to see if they survive. When great talents are found in these spheres, they are trained and nurtured. To be sure, they enter challenging competitions relative to their current level of development, but each such trial is viewed as a learning event, to be critiqued and learned from. Typical corporate practice stands in stark contrast: take promising talent, throw it into tough assignments, stand back, and watch what happens. Survivors, it is assumed, must have "the right stuff" or must have learned by virtue of having the experience. But no great pianist or runner, no matter how naturally gifted, has achieved greatness without years of practice, learning, dedication, and sacrifice (Bloom, 1985). Similar hard work is at the core of developing leadership attributes (McCall, Lombardo, and Morrison, 1988). It is not survival of the fittest that counts; it is *development* of the fittest.

Organizations, then, face two substantial challenges if they hope to have effective leaders: they must identify those who have the potential to acquire the abilities described earlier, and they must nurture them as tenaciously and carefully as they would nurture any other precious resource critical to success.

The six attributes are dearly bought, however. They take a long time to develop (Gabarro, 1987; Kotter, 1982, 1988), the investment required is substantial (Kotter, 1988), and the return on investment is not guaranteed. Further, the goal is a moving target, meaning that an effective leader is not a set of static attributes, put in once and for all, but must be a flexible, adapting person who constantly learns. Facing situations that require substantial adaptation is *the* driving force for executive learning (McCall, Lombardo, and Morrison, 1988), and inability to adapt is *the* derailing force for executives who have been successful in the past (McCall and Lombardo, 1983).

The ways in which the six executive abilities can be learned have been described in detail elsewhere (Lindsey, Homes, and McCall, 1987; Kotter, 1988; McCall, 1988; McCall, Lombardo, and Morrison, 1988; McCall, Hutchison, and Homes, 1989; McCauley, 1986). My purpose here is not to repeat what has already been said, but rather to conjecture on what this decade and those to come may mean for leadership development strategies. If, as I have argued, the attributes required of effective leaders are not changing so much as becoming more critical, then the basic strategies for developing them also remain the same. Challenging job assignments, exposure to exceptional people, emerging from hardships, and certain educational experiences remain important for developing leadership attributes (see Table 10.1). But while the ways in which leadership abilities are developed may not change, some of the content may be quite different. Job experiences may have to reflect changing business challenges and the increasingly international playing field. Cross-boundary movement, a developing strategy that used to mean assignments in different parts of the business or in different functional areas, may now mean crossing international boundaries, working in strategically allied businesses or in partners' organizations, or managing areas with a diverse work force. Organizational delayering and adoption of high-involvement strategies may mean that exposure to developmental opportunities has to begin much earlier and penetrate much deeper in the hierarchy than it has in the past. Many people who are not managers may need to develop some managerial skills or take on leadership responsibilities.

Exposure to exceptional role models is another potent developmental event. This can be accomplished by the kinds of activities just described — frequent cross-boundary movement, widespread use of task forces, special projects and staff assignments, and other mechanisms that create changes in working relationships. By paying attention to the structure of assignments, organizations can exercise some control over exposure to a diverse set of possible role models (McCall, Lombardo, and Morrison, 1988). Some organizations have tried to manipulate this process directly, through formal mentoring programs. Recent work in this area confirms how difficult it is to effectively force mentoring (Kram and Bragar, 1992). Indeed, organizations that create a culture for development and engage in a variety of different developmental activities are more likely to glean the benefits of mentoring as it occurs naturally.

Table 10.1. Sixteen Developmental Experiences.

Assignments	Hardships
Starting from scratch: Building something from nothing	Business failures and mistakes: Ideas that fail, deals that fall apart
Fix it/turn it around: Fixing/ stabilizing a failing operation	Demotions/missed promotions/poor jobs: Not getting a coveted job, or being exiled
Project/task force: Discrete projects and temporary assignments done alone or as part of a team	Subordinate-performance problem: Confronting a subordinate with serious performance problems
Scope: Increases in numbers of people, dollars, and functions to manage	Breaking a rut: Taking on a new career in response to discontent with the current job
Line to staff switch: Moving from line operations to corporate staff roles	Personal trauma: Crisis or trauma, such as divorce, illness, or death
Other People	*Other Events*
Role models: Superiors with exceptional (good or bad) attributes	Coursework: Formal courses
	Early work experiences: Early nonmanagerial jobs
Values playing out: "Snapshots" of chain-of-command behavior that demonstrate individual or corporate values	First supervision: First-time managing of people
	Purely personal: Experiences outside work

Source: McCall, 1988, p. 3. Copyright © 1988, the Human Resource Planning Society. Used with permission.

Preparation for the future may mean that more of these models have to come from other cultures and diverse ethnic backgrounds and be drawn from people who have mastered new contexts (consider the network organization). Courses and formal training programs may have to deal more explicitly with differences among cultures and with the implications of the international marketplace. They may become an even more crucial part of development as the necessary technical and business knowledge increases rapidly. Some specific suggestions follow for making better use of experience in the decade of change.

On-Line Leadership

Start-ups (bringing something new into existence), turnarounds (fixing businesses in trouble), and big-scope assignments (running large operations that are doing well) will still be crucial developmental experiences for a host of executive skills, but in the future more emphasis may be placed on certain aspects of these kinds of assignments. Foremost may be carrying out these leadership roles in other countries, where success will *require* learning to deal effectively with a different culture and its people. Some of these assignments (particularly start-ups) lend themselves to developing new skills by virtue of working with a partner, working on teams, or working with a diverse work force. In an era when many companies are flatter and promotions are fewer and slower, the use of challenging on-line assignments will be increasingly important for retention (not just development) of executive talent. Challenges and rewards (other than promotion) may make lateral moves across geographical regions and types of leadership opportunities (for example, start-ups and turnarounds) even more important.

Leading by Persuasion

Assignments to projects and task forces and certain staff jobs can be potent teachers of the use of persuasion and influence. As organizations form new kinds of alliances with larger numbers of other organizations across the world, executive skills based on influence, rather than on authority, will become even more important. Good, short-term developmental experiences may involve project teams and task forces working on international issues of significance, composed of people with diverse backgrounds or of representatives of allied organizations.

Projects, task forces, and staff assignments (see Chapter Five) are potentially valuable learning events for two more reasons. First, because they are relatively short in duration, they make efficient vehicles for exposing high-potential people to a variety of things. For example, product planning, market analysis, financial analysis, and the like have been traditional topics in developmental staff jobs. They are a particularly flexible form of developmental experience in terms of content, and they lend themselves to including international exposure, dealing with new organizational forms, involving different technologies, and trying out new ideas. Second, these kinds of assignments are suitable for younger managers and nonmanagers and can be used as temporary assignments for people who would otherwise not be exposed to this kind of developmental experience. These features make projects, task forces, and staff jobs helpful for moving developmental opportunities lower down in the organization, making them available to more people, and providing development when there are not many promotions around.

Role Models

High-potential managers can learn a great deal from their exposure to exceptional bosses. As already suggested, it is increasingly important that these role models reflect *diversity* in the work force and in the varying cultures of the international business scene. If people are staying in jobs longer, it is still important to keep their exposure to talented people high, whether through temporary assignments and rotations or simply changes of bosses.

On a slightly different note, the behavior of remarkable bosses is the primary means by which the values of the organization are transmitted (McCall, Lombardo, and Morrison, 1988). Organizations attempting to change must make every effort to see to it that visible managers model the values that they are seeking to inculcate.

Setbacks

Career setbacks, mistakes, and other hardships play a crucial role in development (Bennis, 1989; McCall, Lombardo, and Morrison, 1988), and the future probably holds even more of them as corporations withdraw employment-for-life guarantees, employees increasingly view careers in nontraditional ways, and the changing world leaves no choice but to brave the unknown and take risks. Because learning occurs from trying something and seeing the results, corporations will have to pay more attention to how they handle risk and error. Mistakes are both inevitable and expensive developmental experiences, and so it is a terrible waste to lose a high-potential manager who has just learned from a mistake. Corporations will have to find creative ways to handle mistakes—for example, by developing temporary punishments (like ice hockey's penalty box) that allow people to recover, or even by rewarding people who make good tries. As Carlzon points out, "the right to make mistakes is not equivalent to the right to be incompetent" (1987, p. 83), but the opportunity to make *competent* mistakes is essential to the development of higher-order executive skills.

Coursework

Formal courses may become more crucial to leadership development than they have been in the past. The classroom has always played a pivotal role in transmitting knowledge, and the next decade promises more, not less, new knowledge. At the managerial level, organizations with exceptional reputations for the quality of their management typically invest heavily in formal training programs (Kotter, 1988). The emphasis on the classroom has shifted recently to its use as a vehicle for introducing change, carrying out culture shifts, and solving crucial business problems (Bolt, 1989; Kotter, 1988). Various strategies exist for achieving these ends. It is increasingly common for organizations to design formal education programs for their senior managers that directly address crucial business issues. Motorola began an annual event in 1985 to address topics of critical concern to the chief executive officer (Wiggenhorn, 1990), and through its Motorola University it has taken the ultimate step in dealing with the educational deficits of the work force.

Some organizations are using the classroom as a crucial forum for the implementation of strategic change. General Electric has used its famous Crotonville facility in this way for many years (Tichy, 1989). In this setting, key managers and executives are exposed to the corporate strategy by senior executives, and they work on projects central to the achievement of strategic objectives.

In the future, the classroom may become even more important in preparing people for international assignments, in creating project teams and helping them learn to work together effectively, and in learning crucial leadership skills through simulation and feedback.

Conclusion

Our collective sin has been that we have not done a very good job of developing leaders at all, much less for an uncertain future. Fine-tuning makes little sense where leadership development has not existed or has been haphazard. For the vast majority of organizations, the lesson for the 1990s is not that we need a new kind of leadership, but that we can no longer afford the mediocre leadership produced by our past neglect. We should be grateful indeed that a few leaders have emerged despite our practices, and we should hope that we can be carried by the natural talent around us long enough to develop leaders for the future. The leaders for the 1990s are already with us. The leaders for the turn of the century are already on the job. Unless we start doing what we know how to do, we will continue to get the leadership we now deserve.

References

Argyris, C. *Interpersonal Competence and Organizational Effectiveness.* Homewood, Ill.: Irwin, 1962.

Bass, B. M. *Stogdill's Handbook of Leadership.* New York: Free Press, 1981.

Bennis, W. *On Becoming a Leader.* Reading, Mass.: Addison-Wesley, 1989.

Bennis, W., and Nanus, B. *Leaders: The Strategies for Taking Charge.* New York: HarperCollins, 1985.

Bloom, B. S. *Developing Talent in Young People.* New York: Ballantine, 1985.

Bolt, J. F. *Executive Development: A Strategy for Corporate Competitiveness.* New York: HarperCollins, 1989.

Burns, J. M. *Leadership.* New York: HarperCollins, 1979.

Campbell, R., Dunnette, M., Lawler, E., and Weick, K. *Managerial Behavior, Performance and Effectiveness.* New York: McGraw-Hill, 1970.

Carlzon, J. *Moments of Truth.* New York: Harper Business, 1987.

Christianson, D. "MR Visits a Train Manufacturer in China." *Model Railroader,* 1989, *56*(10), 104–111.

Fiedler, F. E., Chemers, M. M., and Maher, L. *Improving Leadership Effectiveness: The Leader Match Concept.* New York: Wiley, 1976.

Gabarro, J. J. "The Dynamics of Taking Charge." Boston: Harvard Business School Press, 1987.

Hall, D. T., and Richter, J. "Career Gridlock: Baby Boomers Hit the Wall." *Academy of Management Executive,* 1990, *4*(3), 7–22.

Henkoff, R. "Cost Cutting: How to Do It Right." *Fortune,* Apr. 9, 1990, pp. 40–49.

Hollenbeck, G. *What Did You Learn in School? Studies of the Advanced Management Program.* Boston: Harvard Business School Press, 1989.

Howard, A., and Bray, D. W. *Managerial Lives in Transition: Advancing Age and Changing Times.* New York: Guilford Press, 1988.

Katz, D., and Kahn, R. L. *The Social Psychology of Organizations.* New York: Wiley, 1966.

Kotter, J. P. *The General Managers.* New York: Free Press, 1982.

Kotter, J. P. *The Leadership Factor.* New York: Free Press, 1988.

Kotter, J. P. *A Force for Change.* New York: Free Press, 1990.

Kram, K. E., and Bragar, M. C. "Development Through Mentoring: A Strategic Approach for the 1990s." In D. Montross and C. Shinkman (eds.), *Career Development Theory and Practice.* Springfield, Ill.: Thomas, 1992.

Krupfer, A. "Managing Now for the 1990s." *Fortune,* Sept. 26, 1988, pp. 44–47.

Lindsey, E. H., Homes, V., and McCall, M. W., Jr. *Key Events in Executives' Lives.* Greensboro, N.C.: Center for Creative Leadership, 1987.

McCall, M. W., Jr. "Developing Executives Through Work Experiences." *Human Resource Planning,* 1988, *2*(1), 1–12.

McCall, M. W., Jr., Hutchison, E. T., and Homes, V. "Using Experience to Develop Managerial Talent." Working paper, Center for Effective Organizations, University of Southern California, 1989.

McCall, M. W., Jr., and Lombardo, M. M. *Off the Track: Why and How Successful Executives Get Derailed.* Technical report no. 21. Greensboro, N.C.: Center for Creative Leadership, 1983.

McCall, M. W., Jr., Lombardo, M. M., and Morrison, A. M. *The Lessons of Experience.* Lexington, Mass.: Lexington Books, 1988.

McCall, M. W., Jr., Morrison, A. M., and Hannan, R. L. *Studies of Managerial Work: Results and Methods.* Technical report no. 9. Greensboro, N.C.: Center for Creative Leadership, 1978.

McCauley, C. D. *Developmental Experiences in Managerial Work: A Literature Review.* Technical report no. 26. Greensboro, N.C.: Center for Creative Leadership, 1986.

Main, J. "How to Win the Baldrige Award." *Fortune,* Apr. 23, 1990, pp. 101–116.

Mintzberg, H. *The Nature of Managerial Work.* New York: HarperCollins, 1973.

Pearson, A. E. "Six Basics for General Managers." *Harvard Business Review,* 1989, *89*(4), 94–101.

Richman, L. S. "The Coming World Labor Shortage." *Fortune,* Apr. 9, 1990, pp. 70–77.

Shetty, Y. K., and Perry, N. S., Jr. "Are Top Executives Transferable Across Companies?" *Business Horizons,* June 1976, pp. 23–28.

Tichy, N. M. "GE's Crotonville: A Staging Ground for Corporate Revolution." *Academy of Management Executive, 3*(2), 1989, 99–106.

Treece, J. B. "Here Comes GM's Saturn." *Business Week,* Apr. 9, 1990, pp. 56–62.

Vaillant, G. E. *Adaptation to Life.* Boston: Little, Brown, 1977.

Vartabedian, R. "The Remaking of Douglas by McDonnell."
   Los Angeles Times, Oct. 15, 1989, p. D1.
"Visions of Eternity." *Newsweek,* March 27, 1989, p. 53.
Von Glinow, M. A. *The New Professionals.* New York: Harper
   Business, 1988.
Wiggenhorn, W. "Motorola U: When Training Becomes an
   Education." *Harvard Business Review,* 1990, *90*(4), 71–83.
Yukl, G. *Leadership in Organizations.* (2nd ed.) Englewood Cliffs,
   N.J.: Prentice-Hall, 1989.

Conclusion

Effective Organizations: Using the New Logic of Organizing

Jay R. Galbraith

Edward E. Lawler III

In this, the concluding chapter, we would like to examine the major themes that run through the earlier chapters. A set of clear issues is discussed repeatedly. Together, they point to what organizations need to do to be effective in the future. Taken as a whole, they represent a new logic of organizing.

Decentralization

Decentralization of decision making is a theme that runs throughout the book, and numerous reasons argue for it. Competitive pressures, total quality management, the trend toward knowledge work, and time-based competition are all business forces that create a need for decision making and staff support to be closer to customers and products.

In the corporation, companies moving toward value-adding structures, decisions, and people need to move from corporate headquarters to business units or to clusters of business units. Businesses have to move from single profit centers to multiple profit-measurable units. In business units, general management decisions have to move to teams with direct product, project, or customer contact. As decision power moves to teams, the teams need additional knowledge, information, and rewards that are tied to the businesses they manage. Finally, in work units, employee involvement must move decisions to work teams. In all cases, faster decision making, control of quality at the point of origin, and delivery of service at the point of customer contact require that decisions be moved to lower levels, which in turn leads to a focus on new, more distributed organizational structures, smaller organizations, and the decline of hierarchy.

The Distributed Organization

Any student of organization knows that there are two sides to any discussion of decentralization (or, for that matter, to any organizational design decision). There is good news and bad news associated with all alternatives. In addition to faster decision making, decentralization can also lead to fragmentation, duplication, and lack of coordination. The arguments made earlier suggest, however, that the benefits of speed exceed its associated problems. Therefore, in most cases, organizations must choose to decentralize. Some business forces also lead toward integration of activities and away from decentralization and unit autonomy. The compromise that more and more organizations are choosing is the distributed organization.

The distributed organization gets its name by analogy with distributed computing. Originally, most corporate computing was centralized on big mainframe computers. Later, the alternative came along of distributing computer power around the organization by using personal computers, workstations, and minicomputers. More recently, networks have allowed people access to the computing power of the whole distributed network.

Similarly, such activities as management training were originally centralized and performed at corporate headquarters. The distributed model takes these corporationwide activities and distributes them to the best locations for their execution. The best locations are not corporate headquarters, but rather the divisions with the best training capability. The purchasing of semiconductors goes to the division that purchases the largest number; another division, which has the most experience with computer-aided design and manufacturing (CAD/CAM) systems, now negotiates for all divisions in the corporation. In this manner, activities are distributed around the corporation. The locations are referred to as *centers of excellence* or of *lead division responsibility.*

The distributed organization decentralizes an activity by moving it out of corporate headquarters and into a division or business unit. The activity is therefore performed close to the action, and a sense of urgency develops that is not usually found at corporate headquarters. The distributed organization centralizes or consolidates the activity so that it is still performed in only one or a few places. This arrangement allows for high levels of excellence and reduces the likelihood of duplication. The distributed organization is a compromise that responds to requirements involving speed, coordination, and cost. It appears to be the organization of choice for corporations that are trying to add value to businesses through shared capabilities and key competencies.

The distributed model also fits international organizations. Stategies that require global integration require business units to make certain decisions. To get the scale, volume, and consistency needed for a global strategy, the corporation may need to have a business that is centralized and performed in one place. Traditionally, that place was corporate headquarters or the country of ownership. Today, more activities are moving out of the country of ownership and into the best locations in the world for those activities to be performed. Several forces are causing the distribution of value-adding activities around the world.

Value-adding activities are moving out of the country of ownership in order to get market access. Some governments insist on adding design or manufacturing value to products sold in the host countries. To prevent fragmentation and duplication, the company in turn places worldwide responsibility in the country, to satisfy the government and to fulfill that responsibility in one place. For example, Hewlett-Packard has its worldwide headquarters for the personal computer business in Grenoble, France.

In some cases, there are better places for a worldwide responsibility than the country of ownership. Some countries have unique skills. India is a powerhouse for software, and northern Italy is a world leader in design skills. Companies move value-adding activities to countries that have superior skills. Other responsibilities are moved to markets where state-of-the-art competition is taking place. Worldwide responsibility goes to the country where the company finds its most demanding customers and its toughest competitors. Today's contest in the marketplace is tomorrow's contest in the country of ownership and in other parts of the world. To be prepared, a company must strategize in the leading market. For many industries, the use of the distributed organization results in an arrangement whereby, for example, the Japanese subsidiary is responsible for the low end, the North Americans are responsible for the high end, and Europe is responsible for the middle range. This distribution satisfies the governments, locates responsibilities in the best places, and reduces duplication by locating in one place.

In practice, distributed organizations are proving difficult to operate. Distribution was not used before, because it was feared that a local unit would give priority to its own needs and its own market first, and to others second; corporate headquarters was neutral. Several actions are required to implement the model. The distributed activity must be measured and rewarded on corporate criteria. These criteria need to be derived from a plan prepared by the unit and approved by other units and reviewed by headquarters. Very often, it should receive corporate funding. Evaluations can be conducted by other divisions that are customers. The managers of the activity need to think globally and corporationwide. They should also have experience in the other divisions and countries. Units that have corporationwide responsibility should also have corporationwide staffing. Typically, half the employees in a center of responsibility are division employees; the other half come from other participating divisions and are on rotating assignments. All participating units are linked electronically, for constant communication through electronic mail, computer conferencing, and video conferencing.

Changes in the corporation's staff, planning, measuring, rewarding, and informing systems are necessary, but the keys to success are reciprocity and balance. Combined, these two features create mutual dependence and the sense of a shared fate.

Reciprocity means distributing responsibilities so that each organizational subunit has one; as a result, each subunit is dependent on the others. For example, SKF, the Swedish bearing manufacturer, focuses its factories by giving each country subsidiary a pan-European responsibility for a product line. As a result, the U.K. subsidiary is dependent on the French subsidiary for a product line needed by SKF's U.K. customers, but the French are dependent on the British for supplying another product line to French customers. Each is dependent on the other, and there is mutuality of interest. Mutuality creates an incentive to give equal priority to each subsidiary's interests.

Mutuality will work, however, only when there is balance among dependent units. Each unit must be balanced in terms of size and competence. If one unit is very much larger than the others, the smaller units may fear dependence on the unit that is less dependent on them. Moreover, if quality levels are different, a subsidiary will be reluctant to sell lower-quality products to its customers. Mutuality falls apart under these circumstances; the payoffs to the participants become asymmetrical, and dependence is resisted. Mutual dependence works best among peers, where the dependence truly is mutual and where payoffs are symmetrical. The hierarchical centralized model uses simplified, one-to-one communication channels, since most decisions are made at the corporate level. It is a parent-child relationship. Under the distributed model, many decisions are moved from corporate headquarters to subsidiaries. Communication is among peers and is much more complex. Each unit communicates with all other units. The distributed model creates a very communication-intensive organization, and it must be facilitated by modern information technology. All units have to be connected with the others through electronic mail networks and the like. Nevertheless, connection leads to communication only if people share a common language. The distributed model does create complexity, which is feasible today because of information technology and language skills.

The last issue is one of leadership skills. The corporate leader in a hierarchical organization can manage the organization through a series of one-to-one encounters. The leader in the distributed model has to manage by using a team. The leader requires team management, problem solving, and conflict resolution. The leaders of the subsidiaries have to be team players, as do the managers of the units.

In summary, the distributed organization provides solutions to a number of current and future organizational issues. It is becoming the organization of choice for many companies. To implement the model successfully, certain changes in the organization's systems and processes are needed. This is a very complex organization, requiring new staffing, reward systems, information systems, measurements, planning, and so on. The key is to subtly create mutual dependence through reciprocity and balance. The resulting mutual dependence is managed through modern communication networks and team-based management styles.

Organizational Size

The decentralization of decisions to teams and units that have direct product and customer contact raises the question of whether large size is necessary or desirable. It is possible that large organizations are becoming obsolete: IBM and General Motors may simply be too large to be managed and much too large to be changed to play under the new rules of organizational effectiveness.

The micro-organizers have a strong case (Gilder, 1989; Mills, 1991). In many areas, economies of scale are declining. Enormous amounts of memory and computing power can be purchased for next to nothing. Smart products are being miniaturized. Markets are being fragmented into niches. These markets are best reached through cable TV and target marketing, rather than through the mass media. Mass production and mass media are being replaced by mass customization and flexible manufacturing. The wave of the future is small, fast-moving entrepreneurial business units that are best at serving the fragmented markets. The strength of small businesses to generate jobs adds to this argument.

In addition to being faster and delivering more personal service to customers, small companies can achieve higher levels of motivation and involvement. Smallness means that employees can identify with their company, see the results of their work, understand the whole company, know everyone's name, see how their work is linked to company success, and feel responsible for the company's success or failure. Decades of research have shown that small units have greater trust, cohesiveness, and involvement. Combined with ownership and equity interest in the company, smallness can unleash enormous energy directed toward company goals.

Another group believes that only giants will be able to compete with Japan (Ferguson, 1990). This group does not believe that IBM is large enough: according to this view, IBM must combine its efforts with those of Siemens of Germany to produce the next few generations of semiconductor chips. The investment in research and development and in fabrication facilities will run to billions of dollars. Niche companies all over Europe are consolidating to compete in the new market. Jaguar and Saab have merged into larger companies because they could not afford the costs associated with the new technologies. It still takes sales of a few million to justify an engine plant. While economies of scale are still alive and well in some industries, the niche companies are an endangered species.

In recent speeches and articles, Peter Drucker has taken the middle ground. He suggests that the future belongs to the medium-sized companies. They are not too large to be quick and responsive; they are not too small to afford the investments needed for tomorrow's technologies. Drucker suggests that the medium-sized companies are the real strength of German industry.

Who is right in this debate? Our position is that everyone is partially right. There is no question that "small is beautiful" when it comes to unleashing energy, speed, and focus. In buying and selling, however, the market power of size is an advantage.

The challenge in these businesses is to be simultaneously big and small, so that the organizations can be big when that is an advantage and small when that is an advantage. IBM is a case in point. IBM is simultaneously getting larger and smaller. In addition to working with Siemens, IBM and Motorola are working together on semiconductor memories. IBM participates in the European and American consortia for developing semiconductors and has formed a joint venture with Apple, as well as taking a minority-share interest in Bull. The purpose is to produce more computers using IBM's RISC technology. Volume and scale are needed to get the world's software developers to write programs that run on IBM technology. It is software that sells computers. In this way, IBM is getting larger. IBM is also breaking apart and getting smaller, however. Units making storage disks and peripheral equipment have been spun off as semiseparate businesses. The unit for office products was spun off as a separate company, but IBM maintains a minority share. More will happen—or has to happen—if IBM is to adapt. It is forming its own network organization, a loosely coupled network with IBM as the integrator. The network gives IBM the ability to act cohesively and be large in circumstances where size is an advantage, and offers the ability to be small when smallness is an advantage. Application software is often best created through the talents of an outstanding software/hardware architect, two superprogrammers, and ten "worker bees" who follow through. They own their company and profit from it. IBM takes a minority stake, certifies the program, and markets it through the IBM distribution system. IBM is both large and small in this instance.

There will probably be more large-and-small organizations. Companies will partially break apart and decentralize and differentiate. If legal harassment and litigation by shareholders can be minimized, equity and ownership will be spread. Otherwise, simulations of buyouts will occur. At the same time, companies will extend themselves and expand through joint ventures, alliances, minority stakes, and consortia. The creation of an organizational capability to negotiate and manage relationships worldwide will become the determinant of success.

Nonhierarchical or Less Hierarchical Structures?

We have repeatedly stressed the need for reduction in hierarchy. Throughout this book substitutes for hierarchy have been suggested. The first section of this chapter has described how mutual dependence, rather than authority emanating from headquarters, coordinates subsidiaries. Does this mean that hierarchy will disappear? There are two responses. One is "That depends on what you mean by *hierarchy.*" The other is "Not yet, and most likely never."

There are different types of hierarchies. The term *hierarchy* is often used to designate rank and stature in a social order. It is also used to describe decision processes in which increasingly difficult issues are raised to higher "courts of appeal." In Anglo-Saxon cultures, the first type of hierarchy is disappearing. In others, such as the Asian cultures, hierarchy is seen as a virtue; one is defined by who is above and below one in the social order. Such designations of rank and status are impediments and barriers in some kinds of organizations. They prevent the flow of information, cooperation, decision making, and learning. Therefore, status, rank, and positional authority must disappear in tomorrow's fast-moving, learning organizations; Perquisites and other trappings of status must disappear with them.

What about hierarchical decision processes? They should disappear only when the appropriate software and social technologies appear. Hierarchical decision processes are used because of human limits in processing information and reaching collective agreements (Galbraith, 1977). For example, assume that an organization makes ten products. It uses ten fifteen-person teams to produce them. Each team is self-managing and self-contained except for two resources: one large, expensive piece of test equipment is used to accredit each product before it is sold, and five software specialists troubleshoot across all ten teams. How do the teams decide on priorities for allocating the shared resources? It is difficult to conceive of a nonhierarchical decision process whereby all the people on all ten teams interact to reach a decision in a reasonable time. There would be too many interfaces and discussions. One alternative would be to have each group select a representative. These ten people would then discuss the priorities and decide. The interfaces would be manageable, but there might be difficulty in getting agreement and consensus. It could take a great deal of time, particularly if decisions needed to be changed regularly. Instead, one person could be selected to play Solomon. This person would represent the unit to the outside and would be accountable for its performance. Thus we would have a hierarchy of three levels. Its purpose would be to reduce communication overload by reducing interfaces and reaching outcomes within a reasonable time. In an era of speed, timely decisions are necessary.

We could develop social technologies and problem-solving skills that would allow each group of ten to discuss an issue and reach a consensus in a reasonable amount of time. Then there would be less need for a tie breaker, but we would still have a hierarchy. It would be a two-level hierarchy of teams, but it would be a hierarchical decision process nevertheless. There might be breakthroughs in creating software (referred to as *groupware*) that would permit hundreds of people to interact for real-time decisions (Johansen, 1989). Even with "groupware," however, subgroups would probably be selected to resolve issues.

In summary, hierarchy is decreasing. Fewer levels, smaller staffs, distributed organizations, and decentralization are reducing the power of headquarters. Reductions in perquisites and rank are reducing the social distance and the barriers between the groups that must cooperate, but we still need to employ hierarchical decision-making processes to reduce interfaces and resolve conflicts. These processes are a useful component of hierarchy; status and rank are increasingly dysfunctional components.

Fluid and Transitory Design

The world of organizational design has been dominated by charts, boxes, and hierarchical reporting relationships. Most of the changes that organizations have made to improve performance have been changes in reporting relationships. These have not challenged fundamental, underlying assumptions about how organizations should function. Such changes tend to be marked by a switchover point at which new organizational and reporting relationships go into effect. This hierarchical, planned approach to organizational change fits the realities of decades when changes in the environment (and, therefore, the need for change on the part of the organization) were often incremental and predictable.

The new reality is that many important features of the environment are rapidly and continuously changing. The implication for organizational design is that it, too, must be fluid and, in many respects, transitory, just as it needs to be more lateral and less vertical. The ongoing changes may not be (and may not have to be) captured in new lines and new boxes on organizational charts. Indeed, the changes may be embedded in relatively subtle and informal relationships built up within teams or even between teams. These relationships are what have been called the *informal organization.*

In a flatter, more responsive, constantly changing organization, the informal organization may have to become dominant. The more formal organization certainly still needs to reflect the macro-level design decisions that the organization has made about such issues as which groups and teams are responsible for particular customers, services, products, processes, and particular geographies, but it need not reflect the day-to-day interactions and activities of the individuals and teams necessary to getting the work done and responding quickly to customers' needs and environmental changes. Overall, the new organizational chart may seem to depict aggregations of individuals with collective responsibility for particular processes, customers, and products.

The new approaches to organizing represent a move away from jobs (as the term is traditionally defined and used). Indeed, the traditional concept of a job, as a fixed thing that can be captured in a job description, is inconsistent with most of the points that have been made in this book. Chapter after chapter has emphasized the importance of focusing on the skills of individuals and on the skills that teams can bring to bear on serving particular customers or building and developing particular products. This fact suggests an emphasis on the competencies of individuals and teams and the abandonment of the historical focus on jobs and job requirements.

The movement away from jobs and job requirements is consistent with the movement toward a focus on customers' requirements and needs. Total quality management programs and the research on employee involvement suggest that it is important for teams and individuals to be focused on customers and their satisfaction. Again, this is a change from the traditional pattern of holding individuals accountable for meeting certain job requirements and performing certain job functions. The traditional pattern, of course, has had the advantage of defining accountability, but it has also led individuals to look on many things as being outside their job descriptions. When a more dynamic and responsive approach to organizing is taken, the issue becomes what the customer requires and whether the customer is satisfied, rather than what is in an individual's job description.

When organizations are constantly evolving according to a self-design, fluid model, it may mean that different pieces of the organization, at any time, are organized quite differently. This is a natural result of allowing parts of organizations to adapt to the diversity that is inevitable in the environment and of allowing local options for responding to the demands of the environment. It is a sharp departure from the old mechanical or engineering model, which looks for the optimum solution that can be applied in every situation (Mohrman and Cummings, 1989). A self-design approach seems more appropriate. In this approach, organizations assess and redesign themselves to fit the particular issues they face and to suit their own abilities.

The Information-Rich Organization

Central to the evolution of flatter, customer-focused, dynamic organizations is the availability of information within the organization. The traditional movement of information within an organization was based on models derived from a strong hierarchical orientation and from cost constraints that made it very expensive to move information throughout the organization. The availability of information technology and information "highways" now makes it feasible to move information relatively cheaply in multiple directions throughout an organization. Speed is not a problem, because individuals can be constantly and instantly linked with computer networks and television networks.

Flexible, dynamic organizations require information to move freely throughout. Lateral organizations require much greater horizontal movement of information, with little reliance on hierarchical control over the information flow. Similarly, high-involvement organizations also require horizontal information flows, and they require lower-level employees to have access to a great deal of information that traditionally was available only at the highest levels of the organization. Indeed, if new information flows cannot be created in a cost-effective and expeditious manner, it is hard to imagine how most of the new organizational design models discussed here will ever be used.

The challenge in developing multidirectional, rich information movement is in creating the technology and in developing the individuals who know how to access and use the information. In essence, people may need to be made capable of being information-rich and information-safe. They need to understand the importance of information and how to get it. In many cases, they also need to understand the importance of keeping particular kinds of information confidential to preserve a competitive advantage.

Overall, new organizational forms represent a potential competitive advantage only to organizations that are able to manage the new world of information complexity and richness. This ability requires a whole new paradigm of thinking with respect to information and its movement throughout an organization, a paradigm whose core is abundance and availability of information.

The New Logic of Organizing

A number of themes have emerged, which capture our thinking about how organizations should be managed in order to be effective in a demanding, rapidly changing, complex environment. The following lists contain adjectives that describe the new versus the old style of organization:

New	*Old*
Dynamic, learning	Stable
Information-rich	Information-scarce
Global	Local
Small-and-large	Large
Product/customer-oriented	Functional
Skills-oriented	Job-oriented
Team-oriented	Individual-oriented
Involvement-oriented	Command/control oriented
Lateral/networked	Hierarchical
Customer-oriented	Job requirements–oriented

In many important features, organizations will have to think quite differently about how they coordinate and organize the work of individuals. In essence, there is a whole new logic of organizing, which demands that new practices be associated with all the management systems of an organization. The overall direction of the changes represents a significant movement away from the traditional, hierarchical command-and-control model of organizing that has been so dominant since the beginning of the industrial revolution. Change of this magnitude is frightening, but what is the alternative? In many respects, the alternative is even more frightening. The evidence grows every day that traditional organizational approaches do not allow organizations to perform effectively in the environments that now dominate.

Applying the New Logic of Organizing

We opened this book by pointing out that no one organizational structure is right for all organizations. We now return to that point. We have been emphasizing major themes that organizations need to adopt if they want to be effective in a dynamic, competitive environment. There is little question in our minds that, at a relatively high level of abstraction, these are good themes for most organizations to pursue. How they are pursued, however, and how they ultimately work themselves out in terms of particular structures and practices in organizations, must be thought about in terms of contingency and self-design. The organization must examine its own situation and decide how these themes apply to it. Organizations must also adapt a learning or self-design approach to the implementation of particular practices and structures. The process of trying, experimenting, assessing, and perfecting is clearly the right one to use. In many cases, new practices and structures entail new technologies, or at least new evolutions of existing technologies. As such, it is unrealistic to expect them to be perfect from the moment they are installed; the opposite is likely. They need to be piloted, studied, and improved. Indeed, one of the great abilities that organizations increasingly need to develop is the ability to assess and continuously develop themselves. This theme is very strong in the total quality management literature, as well as in the literature on organizational effectiveness. The future is likely to belong to those organizations that never stop asking, "How can we better organize and manage ourselves?"

References

Ferguson, C. H. "Computers and the Coming of the U.S. Keiretsu." *Harvard Business Review,* 1990, *68*(4), 55–70.

Galbraith, J. R. *Organization Design.* Reading, Mass.: Addison-Wesley, 1977.

Gilder, G. *Microcosm.* New York: Simon & Schuster, 1989.

Johansen, R. *Groupware.* New York: Free Press, 1988.

Mills, D. Q. *Rebirth of the Corporation.* New York: Wiley, 1991.

Mohrman, S. A., and Cummings, T. G. *Self-Designing Organizations: Learning How to Create High Performance.* Reading, Mass.: Addison-Wesley, 1989.

INDEX

301